BOMBS, CITIES, AND CIVILIANS

MODERN WAR STUDIES

Theodore A. Wilson
General Editor

Raymond A. Callahan
J. Garry Clifford
Jacob W. Kipp
Jay Luvaas
Allan R. Millett
Series Editors

BOMBS, CITIES, AND CIVILIANS

AMERICAN AIRPOWER STRATEGY IN WORLD WAR II

CONRAD C. CRANE

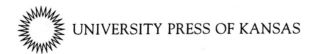
UNIVERSITY PRESS OF KANSAS

Photographs are from the USAF Photographic Collection, National Air and Space Museum, Smithsonian Institution, unless otherwise noted.

The views expressed herein are those of the author and do not purport to reflect the positions of the United States Military Academy, Department of the Army, or Department of Defense.

Published by the University Press of Kansas (Lawrence, Kansas 66049), which was organized by the Kansas Board of Regents and is operated and funded by Emporia State University, Fort Hays State University, Kansas State University, Pittsburg State University, the University of Kansas, and Wichita State University

Library of Congress Cataloging-in-Publication Data

Crane, Conrad C.
   Bombs, cities, and civilians : American airpower strategy in World
War II / Conrad C. Crane.
      p.   cm.
   Includes bibliographical references and index.
   ISBN 0-7006-0574-6 (alk. paper)
   1. World War, 1939–1945—Aerial operations, American.   2. Bombing,
Aerial.   3. World War, 1939–1945—Moral and ethical aspects.
I. Title.   II. Title : American airpower strategy in World War II.
D790.C69   1993
940.54'4973—dc20   92–28141

British Library Cataloguing in Publication Data is available.

Printed in the United States of America

10 9 8 7 6 5 4 3 2

Produced digitally by Lightning Source Inc.

CONTENTS

ILLUSTRATIONS

ACRONYMS

AAF   Army Air Forces

ACTS   Air Corps Tactical School

AEAF   Allied Expeditionary Air Force

AEF   American Expeditionary Forces

AFB   Air Force Base

AWPD   Air War Plans Division

BC   Bomber Command

CBO   Combined Bomber Offensive

CCS   Combined Chiefs of Staff

CGSS   Command and General Staff School

CSI   Combat Studies Institute

CWS   Chemical Warfare Service

FEAF   Far Eastern Air Forces

HE   high explosives

JCS   Joint Chiefs of Staff

MAAF   Mediterranean Allied Air Forces

MEWS   Microwave Early Warning Stations

ORSA   operations research & systems analysis

OSRD   Office of Scientific Research & Development

ROTC   Reserve Officer Training Corps

SHAEF   Supreme Headquarters, Allied Expeditionary Forces

USASTAF   U.S. Army Strategic Air Forces

USMA   U.S. Military Academy

USSBS   U.S. Strategic Bombing Survey

USSTAF   U.S. Strategic Air Forces

WPD   War Plans Division

PREFACE

The inspiration for this book came from two questions. The first, asked by a professor during a graduate seminar at Stanford, focused on the precedents leading to the decision to drop the atomic bomb on Hiroshima and on why discussions about the new weapon's employment dealt with how to use it, not whether to do so. The second, posed by a West Point cadet trying to understand the ethical restrictions on his actions in war, asked to what extent moral considerations and other limitations on combat can really be effective in a high-stakes, high-intensity conflict in a heavily populated area like Western Europe. In response to the first question, I believe that I have presented in this book many of the lures that drew American leaders and airmen down the path to total war in World War II. At the same time, I have also described how some leaders, for a variety of reasons, did slow the rush to unlimited aerial warfare. I hope that the material in this volume will provide future civilian and military leaders with some motivations and ideas about how to limit the slide toward total war in future conflicts.

As with any project that takes as long as this one, there are many people to acknowledge for their help and support. Three deserve my special thanks. Without the patience and guidance of Dr. Barton Bernstein at Stanford University, this work would have never been started or completed. Lt. Col. Charles F. Brower IV at the United States Military Academy provided me with leadership and inspiration to do research and continue work. And in a demanding assignment at Fort Bliss, Texas, I was guided by Lt. Col. Michael Putnam, who showed me how to manage my time more efficiently and encouraged me to finish this project; he also furnished me with insightful critiques of my work.

Numerous others deserve mention. Col. Robert Doughty and the soldier-scholars of the History Department at USMA provided a rich supply of ideas during discussions and seminars. Dr. Kenneth Werrell and Dr. Jesse Stiller gave me the benefit of their criticism in analyzing my early work, as did Col. Paul Miles. Dr. Werrell also contributed significantly to the final manuscript. Dr. Ronald Schaffer deserves special mention; not only did we have some valuable discussions at historical conferences, but he generously provided me with much important source material from his own research. I received help with photographs from Larry Dodd of the Northwest and Whitman College Archival Collections, Alan Aimone from Special Collections Division of the U.S. Military Academy Library, and Melissa Kaiser, Tim Cronen, and Nick Parrella of the Smithsonian. Michael Briggs, Susan McRory, and Claire Sutton at the University Press of Kansas were invaluable in sharpening my prose and ideas and transforming them into this book. My parents also gave me support and encouragement during this long and arduous effort. Finally, I express gratitude to my wife, Sung Im, and my sons, C. J. and William. With demands of my military occupation, most of the time necessary to complete this book was taken away from my time with them. I hope I can make it up to them in the future.

1. INTRODUCTION

There is no doubt in my mind that the RAF want very much to have the U.S. Air
Forces tarred with the morale bombing aftermath which we feel will be terrific.
—*Gen. Carl Spaatz*[1]

Allied strategic bombing during World War II has generated considerable
controversy among historians, regarding both results and motivations. Perhaps the most heated debate has focused on the intentional bombardment of
civilians to break their morale, a practice called "morale bombing" or "terror
bombing." Basil Liddell Hart, the noted British military historian, called the
practice of indiscriminate Allied area bombing of cities "the most uncivilized
method of warfare the world has known since the Mongol devastations." An
American counterpart, Walter Millis, termed such tactics "unbridled savage-
ry."[2] Many American historians have perceived a difference between the
practices of the Royal Air Force (RAF) and the United States Army Air
Forces (AAF), however, especially in the European theater. While the British
enthusiastically embraced a policy of indiscriminate night area bombing, the
Americans pursued daylight aerial offensives against well-selected military
and industrial targets that were justified by both "strategic judgment and
morality."[3]

During World War II, the United States Army Air Forces did enunciate a
policy of pinpoint assaults on key industrial or military targets, avoiding indiscriminate attacks on population centers. This seems to differentiate U.S. policy from those of Germany, Great Britain, and Japan, all of which resorted to
intentional terror attacks on enemy cities during the war.[4] Scholars who have
cited the official AAF history emphasize the intention of American leaders to
resist bombing noncombatants in Europe for both military and ethical reasons.[5] Many of these writers contend that U.S. airmen regarded civilian casu-

1

Two contrasting views of Allied strategic bombing of Germany in World War II, a section of Munich razed primarily by British night raids (above) and a destroyed oil refinery at Harburg hit by American daylight bombers (opposite). Note the many craters from near misses in the fields around the oil plant. (Northwest and Whitman College Archival Collections, Penrose Memorial Library, Whitman College, Walla Walla, Wash.)

alties as an unintentional and regrettable side effect of bombs dropped on military or industrial objectives; in contrast, the Royal Air Force campaign to destroy the cities themselves and kill or dislocate their inhabitants was a deliberate strategy.[6]

A few British writers, such as Max Hastings, have for some time criticized the claimed ethical superiority of AAF strategic bombing as "moral hairsplitting."[7] Most recently, however, the tar of morale bombing that Spaatz feared has been applied by American historians such as Ronald Schaffer and

Michael Sherry. In a groundbreaking 1980 article, Schaffer analyzed the statements of AAF leaders as well as numerous wartime bombing documents in
Europe and concluded that ethical codes "did little to discourage air attacks
on German civilians." In fact, "official policy against indiscriminate bombing
was so broadly interpreted and so frequently breached as to become almost
meaningless." He argued that both the policy against terror bombing and
ethical support for that policy among AAF leaders were "myths." In his most
recent work, *Wings of Judgment*, which also discusses strategic bombing in the
Pacific, Schaffer examines the issue in more detail. He has softened his harsh
judgment somewhat, but he still concludes that although "virtually every
major figure concerned with American bombing expressed some views about

the moral issue . . . moral constraints almost invariably bowed to what people described as military necessity," another disputed concept.[8]

Sherry's award-winning book focuses on the development of American airpower, which ultimately led to the use of the atomic bomb. He concentrates on the bombing campaign against Japan and contends that strategists adopted the policy of indiscriminate firebombing of cities after precision bombing against military and industrial targets proved only marginally effective in 1944. Though racism made such tactics easier to adopt against Japan, firebombing was the inadvertent but inevitable product of an anonymous "technological fanaticism" of Allied bombing and airpower. The assumption that using everything available would lead to eventual victory was key in the decisions to firebomb and eventually to use the atomic bomb. The American press and public at the time accepted such measures as retribution for war crimes or as preparation for invasion. Since 1945 concerned Americans have focused on the decision to use the atomic bomb as "the moment of supreme moral choice"; Sherry argues that the whole bombing campaign was the product of "a slow accretion of large fears, thoughtless assumptions, and incremental decisions."[9]

DOCTRINE, COMMAND AND CONTROL, AND OPERATIONS

Certainly AAF leaders had varying motivations and opinions about terror bombing. But a sophisticated understanding of military processes, particularly of doctrinal development, command and control, and operational execution, is needed to evaluate American strategic bombing. Both Schaffer and Sherry contend that the AAf failed to live up to the letter and spirit of precision-bombing doctrine. Sherry is especially critical because doctrine was not inspired and shaped to a greater degree by technology. Because of the limitations of the bombers of the 1930s, when precision bombing was developed, he argues, wartime technology was "more demonstrably than usual . . . the offspring, not the parent, of doctrine," leading to vague and unrealistic assumptions about the potential of pinpoint strategic bombardment and diminishing utility and support of the doctrine as the war went on.[10]

Doctrine, however, is supposed to be developed to meet national goals, perform battlefield missions, or counter a perceived threat, and technology is then designed to implement the doctrine. Technological developments may force modifications in doctrine; ideally they should not drive it. Otherwise, the result is something like the Army's rejected Sergeant York Air Defense

Gun, an expensive piece of sophisticated equipment whose capabilities were shaped more by technological possibilities than by an accurate appraisal of the evolving threat of enemy aircraft.[11] The entire family of U.S. armor and antiarmor weapons in World War II illustrates the problem of allowing current technology to define tactical doctrine. Developed by technical experts to be light and mobile, American tanks and tank destroyers were employed to maximize mobility. But they could not support the army's overall strategy and doctrine of firepower and direct assault, which was required by the conditions of European combat. This flaw affected U.S. ground operations throughout the war.[12]

Allowing current technology to define doctrine can also limit the scope of doctrine without providing guidance or flexibility for later developments. A study of the evolution of military doctrine in the three decades after World War II by the U.S. Army's Combat Studies Institute (CSI) concludes that "the great value of doctrine is less the final answers it provides than the impetus it creates toward developing innovative and creative solutions" for future problems.[13] Air Forces Chief of Staff Gen. Henry "Hap" Arnold understood this process. In his final report to the secretary of war in 1945 he emphasized, "National safety would be endangered by an Air Force whose doctrines and techniques are tied solely to the equipment and processes of the moment." The Air Force must keep "its doctrines ahead of its equipment, and its vision far into the future."[14]

It can be argued that the technology for precision bombing really did not exist until the "smart bombs" of the Vietnam War. The destruction of the French Embassy during the 1986 air strike on Libya, however, as well as the few televised misses with guided munitions and admitted poor accuracy with unguided weapons during DESERT STORM, demonstrates that the ideal of perfect pinpoint accuracy under all combat conditions has still not been reached.[15] Yet the pursuit of accurate bombing remained a primary goal throughout World War II, influencing American tactics and technology during that conflict and setting precedents for later wars, including DESERT STORM, in which the U.S. Air Force gave an impressive demonstration of advances in precision methods and munitions. And when examined in comparison with the bombing results of other air forces in World War II, the intent, if not always the effect, of American air attacks, was consistently to achieve the most precise and effective bombardment possible. Wartime improvements in bombing accuracy demonstrate that such a goal was realistic, not a dream always to be abandoned in favor of military expediency. Changing conditions influencing combat effectiveness in the European and Pacific theaters did lead to the Army Air Forces' acceptance of greater risks for enemy civilians by 1945, but in Europe at least the operational record shows that the avoidance of noncombatant casualties in accordance with precision doctrine remained a component of American bombing.

Military doctrine is simply a condensed expression of an accepted approach to campaigns, major operations, and battles. The general purposes of doctrine during and after World War II remained basically the same: "to provide guides for action or to suggest methods that would probably work best" and to facilitate communication between different elements by defining terms and providing concepts.[16] Historically, American field commanders have felt free to interpret doctrinal guidance generally as they pleased. Indeed the Soviets taught that "one of the serious problems in planning against American doctrine is that the Americans do not read their manuals nor do they feel any obligation to follow their doctrines."[17] This is certainly an exaggeration, but field commanders have rightly assumed that doctrine is basically a set of guidelines that permits much situational leeway. And traditionally these same field commanders have been given considerable freedom from strict command and control, far in the rear. Even the official AAF history of World War II admits that "air force commanders actually enjoyed great latitude in waging the air war and sometimes paid scant attention" to directives from higher up.[18]

This means that the attitudes of leaders in Washington do not always determine operations in far-flung theaters of war. As Schaffer and Sherry have pointed out, the leader in Washington most concerned about moral issues, Secretary of War Henry L. Stimson, was either ineffective or isolated. His position was basically administrative, and unlike the president or the chiefs of staff, he was not deeply involved in making strategy. And whatever their public pronouncements to the contrary, neither Roosevelt nor Arnold had any aversion to terror bombing when it suited their purposes. But the extent of their control over commanders in the field should not be overstated. At times Arnold's shifts in commanders had considerable influence on bombing policies, such as when he replaced Lt. Gen. Ira Eaker with Maj. Gen. Jimmy Doolittle and Brig. Gen. Haywood Hansell, Jr., with Maj. Gen. Curtis LeMay. In addition, Arnold's consuming desire to justify an independent air service put pressure on AAF combat leaders to produce decisive bombing results. Yet whether because of distance, heart trouble, or the complexity of the war, Arnold rarely wielded a great deal of direct influence, especially in key operations late in the conflict. Sherry's contention that he consistently exercised particularly strong direction of American strategic-bombing operations and units is not supported by the operational record.[19]

This loose doctrinal and command direction resulted in a bombing policy that was shaped by the operational and tactical commanders who actually dropped the bombs. To understand fully American strategic bombing, we must look at day-to-day planning and operations in the field, not just policy papers in the Pentagon. In his exemplary study of the escalating air war between Germany and Great Britain in 1940, F. M. Sallagar notes that "changes crept in as solutions to operational problems rather than as the consequences of considered policy decisions. In fact, they occurred almost independently of the formal decision making process."[20] In that case, the operational solutions always led toward terror bombing; the same is not true for the AAF. An examination of the actual execution of operations in Europe, such as CLARION, THUNDERCLAP, and the War-Weary Bomber project, reveals that American air commanders there consciously tried to avoid terror bombing even when superiors were encouraging it. Some, like Carl Spaatz, seemed to have genuine moral concerns about such bombing; others, like Ira Eaker, were apparently more concerned with public opinion against such tactics or believed they were ineffective or inefficient. AAF operations in Europe contrast starkly with the American strategic bombing of Japan, where the destruction of cities by firebombing was adopted. Yet this decision also was made by the commander on the scene, Curtis LeMay, without real direction from Washington. Bombing policy in each theater was shaped by the "military necessity" of combat, but it was also affected by the individual personality of each commander, who defined that necessity. Air campaigns were also influenced by command relationships. In Europe, U.S. Strategic Air Forces (USSTAF) Commander Spaatz worked closely with the theater commander, General Eisenhower, to synchronize air and ground operations. The Pacific theater had no such unified command, nor such a unified strategy.

Certainly air operations in the European and Pacific theaters had come to accept more risks for noncombatants by 1945. In both cases, this evolution came about as planners and commanders in the field interpreted doctrine and searched for optimum bombing strategies. In Europe, the change resulted from an increasing resort to attacks on transportation targets as higher-priority industrial objectives were destroyed. Such operations assisted ground advances by restricting the movement of reinforcements and supplies, by putting extra burdens on a transport system already strained by the destruction of oil targets, and by facilitating widespread attacks that used the increased air assets present in the theater. Large transportation objectives could also be discerned by radar used for nonvisual bombing through overcast, a technique that allowed American bombers to increase their missions significantly during German winter weather but that also contributed to an acceptance of less accurate bombing results. Precision doctrine recognized the validity of trans-portation targets as a means to weaken the enemy's economy, but attacks on marshaling yards in cities were bound to increase the number of noncomba-tant casualties from errant bombs. In the Pacific, the evolution toward total war went much further. The strategic air campaign targeted factories and military facilities, but normal precision tactics did not seem to work. In order to destroy these objectives, LeMay resorted to incendiary attacks on urban areas that were bound to kill thousands of civilians. If European air com-manders were showing less concern for noncombatant casualties in 1945, Pacific air leaders were demonstrating none at all. Proponents of precision bombing had long argued that it was both the most efficient and humane way to fight a war. But once LeMay became convinced that pinpoint tactics were no longer effective, morality alone was not enough to prevent the firebomb-ing of Tokyo.

OTHER INFLUENCES ON COMMANDERS

It is usually difficult to pinpoint moral considerations in the decision making of key U.S. commanders in World War II. Their primary objective was to win the war in the shortest time with the most efficient use of resources and the fewest possible American casualties. Mission requirements usually prevented any sense of morality from being "an overriding criterion" on aerial opera-tions, although one planner stated that his group "took some comfort that our proposals would be much less costly in terms of the lives of civilians."[21] The need for Allied cooperation also tended to mute ethical arguments because the British so strongly supported attacks on civilian morale and the Ameri-cans did not want to cause a rift or aid German propaganda. Although it is hard to determine moral positions from official records and correspondence, it is probably true that ethical restraints were not the most important limita-tions on terror bombing by United States Strategic Air Forces. Such consid-erations, however, cannot be completely discounted.

At the same time, it must be noted that psychological effects have always been an important part of air warfare. Like the bayonet or the tank, the air-plane has a shock effect that is intended to unnerve an enemy and break the will to resist. Unlike those other weapons, however, the long range of the airplane encompasses vast regions of the enemy's rear area, inhabited mainly by civilians. Once factories became acceptable bombing targets as part of the enemy's capacity for making war, factory workers could no longer be seen as noncombatants. Once the trend to recognize some civilians as belligerents began, it was only a matter of time until the justification would be made, as in Japan, that everyone supported the war effort in some way. And the temptation to exploit and magnify the psychological effects of bombing civilians would also be hard to resist. American airmen, even those most devoted to precision doctrine or morally opposed to bombing any civilians, expected that the destruction of economic and industrial targets would have a significant effect on enemy civilian morale. Yet at least in the European theater AAF leaders were not willing to achieve the same goal by intentionally killing women and children or burning down their homes. Even LeMay's first fire raids had the destruction of industrial targets as the primary objective. But once a campaign of psychological warfare was launched to terrorize the rest of Japan with the threat of more conflagrations, there was no longer any major difference between this American air campaign and RAF Bomber Command's area raids on German cities or the Luftwaffe's Blitz against London.

Other influences on air commanders also affected their decisions. Pressures from various levels of command and perceptions of public opinion helped shape planning and operations. Any mission includes implied tasks to fight, win, and return with honor intact, but these elements have different weight, depending on where the soldiers are on the battlefield. Although Arnold hoped to achieve an independent air force with "Victory through Airpower," B-17 crewmen were more concerned with doing the best job they could and surviving. Operational and tactical commanders were caught in the middle; they had to be loyal to the goals of their organization and to the welfare of their men.[22] A quick and overwhelming victory served both purposes and was also in keeping with the "Airpower Ethic" by preventing long and bloody land combat. The lure of achieving the Allies' stated aim of winning the war "as decisively and speedily as possible" through technological solutions or by a single operation to produce a deathblow became especially strong after the success of Operation OVERLORD in Europe and as the invasion of Japan approached.[23] With the exception of some officers like LeMay, devotion to precision-bombing doctrine remained strong in the field, especially with those officers who had helped develop it, though its applications changed as the military situation evolved. Contrary to many American doctrines in our military history, this one was uniformly known, understood, and believed by most of the soldiers who were supposed to follow it. Indeed it often seems that precision bombing was better understood in the field than in Washington. In his recent book, *Wartime*, Paul Fussell claims that "precision bombing became a comical oxymoron relished by bomber crews with a sense of black humor" although he provides no real evidence to back up this statement about American strategic bombing.[24] In reality, aircrews and their leaders were convinced of the effectiveness and appropriateness of their pinpoint tactics and missions and were quick to express dissatisfaction with any perceived deviations from proven and accepted methods and operations.

This continuity in doctrine is not really evident unless one focuses on day-to-day operations. Though archival sources such as the papers of Spaatz or Arnold provide invaluable topical information, letters or documents are grouped by subject more than by time period, and even unit histories can be narrow in focus. The best source for a full understanding of the milieu of air operations is the daily operational diaries of Frederick L. Anderson, U.S. Strategic Air Forces deputy commander for operations. Each daily file contains bound packets of correspondence that passed in and out of USSTAF headquarters, including letters from Arnold and Spaatz, press releases, and battle reports from the field. This concentrated operational and tactical level documentation describes the course of the air war in great detail and shows the continuity and persistence of precision-bombing doctrine even while temptations to use terror bombing increased.[25]

Yet in the Pacific theater, a unique combination of military problems and an innovative commander less committed to prescribed doctrine produced a far different response to these temptations. This contrast makes the European record even more remarkable, especially when one considers the need to cooperate with an ally dedicated to terror bombing. Though adverse weather, technological limitations, or enemy countermeasures such as flak or smoke-screens often made it difficult to achieve the standards of precision-bombing doctrine, most AAF airmen did live up to the spirit of it. Moreover, in the Pacific theater, Brig. Gen. Haywood Hansell, LeMay's predecessor, was replaced because he would not swerve from the tenets he had helped develop.

Most critics of precision bombing have been asking the wrong question since it is impossible to determine accurately the specific ethical motivations for strategic bombing from the documentation available. On the narrower issue of the application of precision-bombing practices in the field, an impartial observer must conclude that in general most American airmen did the best they could to win the war with consistent application of a doctrine that favored military and industrial targeting over terror bombing. Their intent was to spare noncombatants, and they succeeded better than many historians are willing to concede.

Perhaps the survivors of strategic bombing attacks understood this better than the historians. As one German who lived through the American bombing and the RAF-induced firestorms in Hamburg commented, "The Americans were regarded by us as *soldiers*. Their attacks were during the daytime and were nearly always directed on military targets, even if the civilian population sometimes suffered heavy casualties because of them. They flew in good visibility and risked the aimed fire of our Flak. Hence [we had] a certain respect for the 'Amis' as we called them."[26]

Yet it is undeniable that for a number of reasons strategic-bombing principles and precedents from Europe contributed to "the slide to total war" in the bombing of Japan. Military conditions were different in the Pacific theater, as were perceptions of the enemy; command and control was much looser also. According to the official history of the Joint Chiefs of Staff, "The division of the Pacific Theater between two major commands [Nimitz and MacArthur] complicated the problems of war and undoubtedly reduced the efficiency with which the war was fought."[27] And as the Army and Navy pursued competing strategies, the AAF also mounted an essentially independent campaign. Perhaps the most important difference from the European theater was that in the Pacific, the air commander who instituted the firebombing campaign had not been involved in the development of strategic-bombing doctrine, had learned "not much" when he attended the Air Corps Tactical School (ACTS), and "was always more practical than theoretical."[28] Once LeMay decided on the burning of Japanese cities as the solution to his operational problems and the practice became accepted by leaders in Washington and in the field, the next step in the escalation to total war, dropping the atomic bomb on Hiroshima, was indeed, to use Sherry's words, only an "incremental decision."

An ironic legacy of strategic bombing in World War II, evident in more limited conflicts such as the war in Vietnam and in the recent campaign against Iraq, is that even though public opinion tends to focus on the image of the mushroom cloud destroying cities or on B-52s carpet bombing enemy populations, the American military ideal in both doctrine and wars has remained the pursuit of precision bombing. The military ethics and accuracy espoused in doctrinal literature on air operations today and demonstrated so convincingly during Operation DESERT STORM have evolved directly from the effort and intent of the experience in World War II.

2. DEVELOPING DOCTRINE

The consensus of world opinion is not only opposed to the employment of air power in direct attacks against civilian personnel, but such attacks cannot be justified on the basis of efficiency.

—*Draft, 1935 Air Corps Tactical School text.*[1]

During June 1918 the director of military aeronautics in the United States prepared a study on strategic bombardment for the chief of staff, Gen. P. C. March proposing the development of a "long distance independent bombing force" intended "to operate on a bombing campaign against German industrial centers."[2] Despite this growing interest in an official doctrine for strategic bombing, aircraft production could not support it. The July 1918 "202 Squadron Program" for the American Expeditionary Forces (AEF) Air Service allocated 60 pursuit squadrons, 101 for observation planes and only 41 for bombers. This decision, based on industrial capacity rather than doctrine, had significant repercussions. The American air arm had no operational organizations to determine the course of engineering development or doctrine, and AEF end-of-war reports were generally written by ground-oriented staff officers in the field with little understanding of air warfare or its potential. As a result of the limitations on production that plagued the air service's structure and performance, postwar U.S. Army staff schools taught that "strategical bombing is . . . a luxury."[3]

Nevertheless, some studies would influence the development of future doctrine. These were compiled for Maj. Gen. Mason M. Patrick, chief of Air Service, AEF, and would eventually be deposited at the Air Corps Tactical School (ACTS) at Maxwell Field in Alabama. In December 1918 he directed his assistant chief of staff, Col. Edgar S. Gorrell, to prepare a history and final report on U.S. air activities in Europe during the war. The choice of Gorrell ensured that strategic bombing would not be ignored; he had been made head of Strategic Aviation for the AEF because of his work as chief of the Air Service Technical Section, a position that had required him to antic- ipate production and supply the essentials for bombing operations. From his investigations he developed a bombardment plan in November 1917 charac- terized later as the "earliest, clearest, and least known statement of the Amer- ican conception of the employment of air power." His work so impressed Brig. Gen. Benjamin Foulois, chief of Air Service, AEF, that the general recom- mended the plan to Pershing in December.[4]

Gorrell collected all available materials, including his own 1917 plan, "a truly striking forerunner of the doctrine which matured years later at the Air Corps Tactical School." Some of that later doctrine even used the same word- ing and metaphors of Gorrell's document.[5] His plan aimed to "wreck Germa- ny's manufacturing centers" with a round-the-clock campaign of day and night bombing. Targeting chemical plants would cut artillery shell output, and bombing aircraft engine plants would limit airplane production. He stated: "The object of strategical bombing is to drop aerial bombs upon the commercial centers and the lines of communications" in order to "cut off the necessary supplies without which the armies in the field cannot exist." Also cognizant of the psychological effects of air raids, he proposed concentrated attacks by all available aircraft on single cities, expecting to shatter "the mo- rale of the workmen" as well as the factories. Some towns' morale seemed especially vulnerable, and he surmised from press reports that bombing Co- logne "would create such trouble that the German Government might be forced to suggest terms." Gorrell also projected that fire protection in under- manned German villages would break down under a lengthy bombardment, "and therefore the results would be out of proportion to the immediate effect of the bombs." The advantage of this new aerial warfare would be to break the stalemate on the ground and thus save lives and material.[6]

Gorrell's collection also included a short paper, "Area vs. Precision Bomb- ing," from the organization responsible for providing bombsights for the Air Service. French and British bombardiers favored area-bombing techniques using outboard sights that allowed them to stay at their guns, but the Amer- icans developed a formation technique in which a chosen bombardier pro- tected by other planes climbed inside the fuselage, used his better sight, and picked the bombing point for the whole formation. This practice of using a lead bombardier and the perception of superior American bombsights and technique would appear again in World War II.[7]

As Gorrell accumulated material for General Patrick, the colonel realized that he needed a more systematic analysis of the effects of aerial bombing on the enemy. Air Service officers under the supervision of the Air Intelligence Section of General Headquarters, AEF, were sent out to survey bombed towns and to interview inhabitants. Teams were to determine whether day or night bombing was more effective in damaging both material and morale. In general, the information was scanty and incomplete, but the report's summary provided many ideas for future consideration. Though bomb damage as a whole was relatively slight, bombing did affect the morale of fighting forces as well as the civilian population. In addition, government employees could not perform their work because of bombing, transportation of troops and supplies was hindered, and the manufacture of war material was hampered to some degree. The Germans were also forced to spend much time and effort defending their homeland. The effects on civilian morale described dealt mainly with loss of sleep and lowered worker performance; the idea of a Hamburg or a Tokyo firestorm was far in the future.[8]

Yet the bombing survey did provide a disturbing preview of attitudes that would help create those holocausts. It mentioned that the casualty figures of 641 killed and 1,242 wounded in twenty-two German cities "may not be considered very important, inasmuch as most of these were civilians," but it further explained that helping the wounded and the dependents of those killed could entail considerable additional expenses to the government.[9] Many of the Allied raids that produced these casualties were motivated by similar German attacks, especially on England, where attacks by dirigibles and bombers had killed 1,414 people and wounded 3,416. The British were incensed at what they perceived as "wilful murder," but a captured Zeppelin commander denied the accusations in terms that could have been echoed by American airmen in World War II. "You must not suppose that we set out to kill women and children," he tried to explain. "We have higher military aims. You would not find one officer in the German Army and Navy who would go to war to kill women and children. Such things happen accidentally in war."[10]

The conclusions and criticisms in the bombing survey could be seen as a portent for the precision-bombing theory to come. The British and French were criticized for inaccurate bombing as well as for "the unintelligent choice of targets," in particular "the bombing of a town rather than some definite objective of military value in the town." Arguments against the bombing of cities were based on practical considerations, not ethics. Directly targeting civilian morale "is not a productive means of bombing. The effect is legitimate and just as considerable when attained indirectly through the bombing of a factory." Instead, the three most important objectives for bombing were war industries, railroad lines, and troops in the field. The survey concluded that the industrial bombing attack should be concentrated night and day on the enemy's most important and vulnerable economic sector and that communications lines were best hit immediately preceding and during major operations.[11]

THE INFLUENCE OF THEORISTS

Gorrell's exhaustive work eventually ended up at the library of the Air Corps Tactical School, where it undoubtedly influenced the officers who developed precision-bombing doctrine between the wars. A progression of theorists also made their mark on American air doctrine during that period. Perhaps most important was British Maj. Gen. Hugh Trenchard, commander of the Royal Flying Corps and a power in the highest military and political circles, who believed in an independent air force pursuing a radical strategic-bombing offensive. He exerted a powerful influence on American officers serving in France during World War I, including Brig. Gen. William "Billy" Mitchell, the most outspoken American airpower advocate in the postwar period.[12]

Mitchell was first exposed to airpower theory as the assistant to Maj. George O. Squier, commandant of the Signal School at Fort Leavenworth during 1905 and 1906. In 1908 Squier wrote a position paper that anticipated many of the future tactical and strategic roles for American aviation. Since dirigibles outperformed airplanes at that time, he envisioned strategic airships bombing enemy factories and capitals. Like many future air theorists, he predicted that strong air forces would make war less likely since enemy leaders would be in personal danger once war began. Squier was an attaché in London when World War I began, and he kept his American colleagues well informed on developing theory and the conduct of the air war.[13]

Service with Squier and exposure to Trenchard were not the only theoretical influences on Americans such as Mitchell. As the Germans bombed London with Zeppelins and Gothas in 1917, Field Marshal Jan Smuts predicted that in the future "aerial operations, with their devastation of enemy lands and destruction of industrial and populous centers on a vast scale, may become the principal operations of war."[14] French and British airmen exposed their allies to a European outlook on airpower that was perhaps most clearly expressed by the Italian Giulio Douhet, sometimes called the "Father of Airpower Doctrine."[15] Mitchell may have met Douhet on a trip to Italy in 1922,

Brig. Gen. William "Billy" Mitchell displaying his decorations from World War I. This photo was taken in 1924, a year before a court-martial convicted him of "conduct prejudicial to good order and military discipline" for accusing the War and Navy Departments of incompetence and negligence in their air policies. He then resigned from the service and continued his airpower crusade as a civilian.

though the American never attributed any special influence on his thinking to the Italian.[16]

The outspoken Douhet had been imprisoned by his government for a year during World War I for criticizing staff policies. His court-martial conviction was repudiated and expunged after the war, and he became a general and head of his nation's aviation programs. Douhet's book *Command of the Air* was published in 1921, but he had been voicing his position since 1910. Although the bulk of his volume dealt with the technical problems of establishing and organizing a large independent air force to be used en masse, he also graphically portrayed a total war with "no distinction any longer between soldiers and civilians." He further expanded these views in a number of revisions and articles until his death in 1930.[17]

Douhet foresaw that attacks of high-explosives, gas, and incendiaries on cities would produce effects on morale exceeding material damage. Like intense artillery bombardments, air raids would subject the people in the target area to significant shock and stress. German and British airmen during World

War I had noticed the decreases in factory production and the increases in public discontent that had resulted from their primitive attempts to strike targets in urban areas. Trenchard estimated that the psychological "yield" of his air attacks on Rhine towns was twenty times greater than the damage from actual physical destruction.[18] Other recent precedents existed for attacking civilian morale with distant bombardment. In 1870 the Prussians had decided that the quickest and ultimately the most humane way to reduce French fortresses was to shell the civil population so that they would force the garrison to surrender. Douhet expanded on that idea to predict the collapse of whole nations. People would panic at the mere sight of airplanes and demand an end to the war, "driven by the instinct of self preservation." He argued that such wars could not last long, "since the decisive blows will be directed at civilians, that element of countries at war least able to sustain them." Douhet also espoused the principle that some writers have called the "Airpower Ethic": Such future wars would be more humane because "they may in the long run shed less blood." Never strong on hard data to back up his claims, Douhet seems to have based his conclusions on incidents such as the one at Brescia during the war, where mourners at a funeral for bombing victims panicked when a bird was mistaken for an airplane. He was also supposedly impressed by the reported effects of German bombing on the population of London.[19]

Douhet's effect on the development of American bombing doctrine has been hotly debated, with critics contending that the Italian's writings had a particularly strong influence on AAF teachings and practices. Billy Mitchell may have incorporated some of Douhet's ideas, but he tailored his concepts to the American situation. By 1930 Mitchell did consider cities as attractive targets, but only for disruption, not destruction. "It will be sufficient," he wrote, "to have the civilian population driven out so they cannot carry on their usual vocations. A few gas bombs will do that."[20] When for publicity he advocated Douhet's views in 1933, Mitchell was no longer a major influence on those individuals developing AAF doctrine. Whether because of his earlier military experience in the ruthless guerrilla war in the Philippines or from his incessant desire for publicity, Mitchell tended as time went on to become more extreme in support of terror bombing and more out of touch with mainstream views.[21]

By 1923 Army Air Corps schools had access to Douhet's writings, but his theories on mass-area bombings of civilians did not gain any wide acceptance. The Italian expanded his theories with publications in 1926, 1928, 1929, and 1930, and the comprehensiveness of his ideas "has made it a too convenient reference for anyone who would ascribe the origins of American ideas on strategic bombing to a single, overriding influence." At best, "Douhet must rank as no more than one of the multiple influences on Mitchell, his colleagues, and their successors, as they slowly evolved a strategic bombardment doctrine that was sensitive to the American political and military tradition."[22]

Douhet did have significant influence on the strategic level, however. Before his writings appeared, the dominant strategic schools of thought were the Continental School, following the landpower theories of Clausewitz that focused on destroying enemy armies, and the Maritime School, based on Mahan's seapower teachings with the goal of dominating critical sea lanes and choke points. Douhet is given credit for founding the Aerospace School, emphasizing that airpower alone can be decisive and that by controlling the air and destroying the enemy's war-making potential it can make protracted wars obsolete. Probably a more accurate epithet for Douhet is the "Father of Airpower Strategy." Though it is hard to find the sources for the ideas American airmen generated between the wars, the Army Air Corps did pursue an aerospace strategy as it developed its own precision-bombing doctrine.[23]

In the years preceding World War II, Douhet's ideas had a more significant impact on some European air forces. In England, influential writers such as J. F. C. Fuller and Basil Liddell Hart echoed Douhet's opinion that civilians could not withstand aerial bombardment. Assisted by a hopeful governmental policy that the British could avoid becoming engaged with land forces in another Continental war, the independent Royal Air Force pursued plans to win any future conflict through controlling the air. By the end of 1941 the RAF was the only means available for the British to strike back at Germany, but daylight raids were proving too costly and night bombing too inaccurate for pinpoint targets. Faced with the need to take some offensive action to meet public demands for retaliation and to justify the large resources invested in an independent air service, Sir Arthur "Bomber" Harris's Bomber Command adopted a Douhetian strategy for mass night raids on German cities to break civilian morale.[24] In contrast, the RAF's American allies developed a different aerial strategy based on daylight precision bombing of key economic and military objectives.

THE CREATION OF PRECISION-BOMBING DOCTRINE

While Mitchell's doctrinal ideas moved closer to Douhet's in the 1930s and the contrasting official Army position remained that airpower was only an auxiliary force to assist ground troops, a small group of officers at the Air

Corps Tactical School were creating their own strategic-bombing doctrine—precision attack on critical points of specified industrial target systems.[25] This development would soon have added impact because these same airmen would plan America's air war in World War II and also figure prominently in executing it.

There are two prerequisites for creating new military doctrine. First, higher authorities must realize the need for change and support new ideas. Second, a small and creative group of thinkers must work together to synthesize a body of thought expressing a new approach to war. Organizational doctrine arises from an evolutionary process influenced by interpretations of military history, environmental factors like geography and technology, and the fundamental beliefs of a society.[26] In the 1920s and 1930s the Air Corps' leaders sought a coherent doctrine that would be acceptable to the American people and to politicians and that at the same time would be offensive in nature, thus necessitating an independent air service. While congressional and War Department boards continued to relegate the air arm to auxiliary status, the faculty at ACTS pursued their new doctrine. The theory of precision bombing had begun to take shape in the early 1930s, when Col. John F. Curry was commandant of the school; he performed the essential function of shielding his faculty from Washington while providing much freedom of thought and expression.[27] Rising Air Corps leaders such as Carl Spaatz and Frank Andrews supported and contributed to the new ideas being created as did ACTS instructors (and future generals) Laurence Kuter, George Kenney, Kenneth Walker, and Haywood Hansell. But the officers most responsible for solidifying precision-bombing doctrine into a coherent form were Harold George, Donald Wilson, and Robert Webster.[28]

George, Wilson, Webster, and other ACTS instructors did not work in a vacuum; they had many lessons from the 1920s to draw on. Everyone acknowledged that the public opposed terror bombing of civilians, and this led to military corollaries. "No nation will use its air forces to bomb cities, just for the purpose of destroying the morale of the people by instilling them with fear," an infantry lieutenant colonel wrote in 1928. "Such action could only bring on the nation the active resentment of the rest of the civilized world, a thing that no nation can afford." Army and Navy officers as well as congressmen continually attacked the practice of strategic bombardment as a violation of international law.[29] Precision-bombing doctrine, attacking factories instead of women and children, offered a way for the Air Corps to be decisive in war without appearing immoral. Moreover, improvements in technology made the doctrine feasible. Air Corps maneuvers in 1929 impressed observers with the "invincibility of the bomber." Accurate daylight bombardment began to receive increased emphasis during the next decade, with the development of the Norden and Sperry bombsights and the B-17 airplane. Precision bombing also called upon a traditional American respect for marksmanship that dated back to frontier days. Moral, legal, cultural, technical, strategic, and tactical reasons combined to shape the theory of precision bombing of industrial targets by the 1930s.[30]

Perhaps the most important rationale for the new doctrine was the belief that aerial bombardment of specific industrial objectives constituted the most effective and economical way to wage war, a conclusion drawn from the work of George, Wilson, and Webster. Without their efforts, precision-bombing theory might not have been so coherent, and it definitely would not have been such a powerful influence on the AAF in World War II.

One writer has called the precision-bombing concept "one of those rare creative ideas that generate in several minds at about the same time."[31] It seems to have begun with instructor Donald Wilson, chief of the Air Force section, when he observed in 1933 that the operation of a whole railroad system could be stopped by the lack of one lubricating ingredient. He then applied his observation on a larger scale and looked for specific structures in industrial nations that supported their capability to wage war. Since the War Department, in accordance with public opinion, prohibited any study of offensive actions against other nations, ACTS had no strategic air intelligence. Wilson therefore looked at the American industrial and social fabric for vulnerabilities, assuming that they would pertain to other industrialized nations. The study could also be used to shape U.S. defenses and thus be within War Department guidelines.[32]

When Wilson left ACTS in 1934, his inquiry was expanded by two captains in the Department of Air Tactics and Strategy, Harold George and Bob Webster. In a detailed analysis of American transportation networks, power systems, and factories they found that the number of critical targets was relatively small and vulnerable to accurate bombardment. They then turned to cities, "the most politically and morally sensitive target system of all." After studying New York, they estimated that the destruction of only seventeen targets within its transportation, water, and electrical systems would render the city uninhabitable. They also concluded that "with very precise bombing, this could be done without vast destruction or mass casualties."[33]

The changes in Air Corps thinking were reflected in ACTS texts. In 1926 the position that an air force was auxiliary to ground forces was abandoned in favor of an independent, offensive strategy in the manual *Employment of Combined Air Forces.* The document declared that the enemy's population and vital points were the true objectives in war. Expressing ideas similar to Douhet's, it argued that air attack was "a method of imposing will by terrorizing the whole population" and preferable to costly land combat; but, as Gorrell had argued, it maintained that large-scale killing was not necessarily required to affect morale. Though this document has been used as evidence of Douhet's influence at ACTS, with its concentration on "complete destruction of vital parts of the enemy's sources of supply," the manual is much more in keeping with Gorrell's work.[34]

A 1931 text claimed that "with the exception of operations against an enemy force, a large proportion of the operations of an air force will be against strategical objectives . . . the enemy's system of supply, reinforcement and evacuation." It did not neglect cities, but it called them "political objectives," whose population can be attacked directly with gas or explosives or "indirectly" through their water, food, or power supplies. Air forces should not be employed against political objectives "except as the result of a careful estimate of the results to be accomplished, when weighed against the suffering of women and children, and the effect of public opinion in neutral countries." The text emphasized that "some foreign authorities will advocate the direct attack of the enemy civil population to bring about a decision in war," but it did not support such a position.[35]

In 1933 for political effect ACTS was distributing translations of a Douhet article, "La guerre de l'air," to the House Committee on Military Affairs even as instructors were moving further away from his theories on bombing civilians. The 1934 text for the Air Force course described in detail attacking the "social sphere" and stated that "large urban populations and high standards of living broaden the possible range of dislocation and add length to the lever that an air force can apply against morale." Cities were vulnerable and hard to defend. Although it was "an undeniable fact that the consensus of world opinion is opposed to such employment of air power," it was also "common knowledge" that "nearly all of the leading powers" were making plans and training civilians in order to minimize the effects of attacks on cities. Despite the "wrath of world opinion" such attacks would incur, the threat of such action "will certainly exist in modern war" and might actually prove more persuasive than the results from an actual attack. But, the text continued, "fortunately a more desirable and more effective approach is available to an Air Force, . . . [which] entails the careful selection of certain material targets . . . upon which the social life of the nation depends," such as food and power supplies. This text reflected a move toward precision bombing, but it still envisioned attacks against the social sphere.[36]

The influence of Wilson, George, and Webster was more apparent in the next year's text. Stating that "loss of morale in the civil population . . . is decisive," it also recognized that direct attacks on civilian personnel are inefficient as well as opposed by world opinion. Whether a strategic air attack aims "to deny the enemy the means that are essential for the prosecution of the war" or to so dislocate normal life that people are willing to surrender to regain it, "transportation facilities and sources of energy and raw materials are the vital elements in a nation upon which both the welfare of the population and the ability to wage war depend." By 1939 ACTS lesson plans bluntly stated: "Direct attack of the civil populace . . . is rejected as an air objective due to humanitarian considerations." The text concentrated on precision-target systems although terror attacks were considered "as a possible means of retaliation."[37]

PRECISION DOCTRINE BECOMES OFFICIAL POLICY

The teachings at ACTS had a strong impact on the Air Corps. Though the lessons did seem informally to influence higher military educational institutions such as the Command and General Staff School (CGSS) at Fort Leavenworth, airmen coming to ACTS had rarely been exposed to any coherent air doctrine taught by another military school.[38] The primary flying school at Randolph Field and the advanced school at nearby Kelly Field were designed to give practical flying skills to newly commissioned airmen. There was not a true basic-training program for officers, and specialized training of Air Corps officers in the 1930s was largely limited to Army extension courses. It was hoped that West Point, which produced a large proportion of the new aviators, would provide its graduates with some sort of theoretical base.[39]

Air Service and Air Corps officers were continually frustrated by the ground-oriented nature of the instruction at West Point. Even as late as 1939, the observation mission dominated practical instruction conducted at Mitchell Field on Long Island.[40] In classes on military theory, cadets discussed Clausewitz, Saxe, Jomini, Frederick, Marlborough, Gustavus, and Schlieffen but not Douhet or Mitchell.[41] Aerial warfare in the 1930s could not be ignored, however, and the bombing lessons from conflicts in China and Spain received much attention in class.

Generally, such discussions focused on the tactical ground support role of air operations, which was in keeping with official Army policy and probably reflected a lack of Air Corps instructors as well. Lessons from the Sino-Japanese War showed that aircraft were "very effective in pursuit, useful in artillery spotting, helpful but not decisive in driving infantry from defensive positions." The best target was troop concentrations. The bombing of cities was dealt with in great detail, however, and conclusions supported the new doctrine evolving at ACTS. "The mistaken Japanese policy of indiscriminate airplane bombing" aroused people in Shanghai and brought them together against Japan; a handout for students stated that "frightfulness united them as no peacetime propaganda could have." The chief result of the bombing of Canton "was to change indifference of the South China masses to intense hatred of the Japanese." A primary lesson of the war taught that "Japanese air bombing of crowded cities destroyed millions of dollars worth of property and took an enormous toll of civilian lives, but gained little or no military advantage thereby. In most cases the reaction was exactly the opposite of the desired and anticipated effect of breaking the nation's will to fight and undermining support of the Nationalist Government." A similar handout on the Spanish Civil War concluded that though bombing was quite effective in destroying the morale of untrained troops, "far from demoralizing the populace it seemed to stiffen their determination to resist and to bring home to their leaders the necessity for cooperation to repel the attackers."[42]

Studying terror bombing such as that used in China, Spain, and Ethiopia led to similar conclusions from other military strategists, who also noted that such raids often led to reprisals and destruction of the attackers' cities.[43] Writers in publications such as The Infantry Journal condemned "aeromaniacs" who ignored the lessons of history and continued to believe that "the determination of a people to carry on war can be broken by mere punishment."[44] Attacks on Shanghai and Madrid evoked the expected public outcry, expressed by newspaper editors who claimed that the "laws of war are becoming scraps of paper." The League of Nations and the U.S. government condemned the attacks as "contrary to principles of law and humanity."[45]

By 1939 higher-level military schools such as the Army War College were teaching America's senior leaders that despite European acceptance of wanton air attacks on defenseless civilians as inevitable, such tactics were considered "butchery in the eyes of a trained soldier" and signs of "a state of moral chaos among nations." Moreover, bombing cities required too many air resources, and even if these were available, results were uncertain. Communications (transportation and signal facilities) and industrial installations were the best targets for strategic airpower. A 1940 staff study at the War College on the "Desirability of Cities, Towns, and Villages as Bombardment Objectives" concluded, "There is no historical evidence that aerial bombardment of cities, towns, and villages has ever been productive." It recommended that such targets should be bombed only "where they contain definite objectives, military or political, the destruction of which will be productive of decisive military results."[46]

After Mitchell's death in 1936, émigré aircraft designer Alexander P. de Seversky became the best-known American air theorist. A keen observer of the lessons of modern warfare in early World War II, he was also a former Russian naval officer who had been strongly influenced by the seapower theories of Mahan. Civilian morale was not a direct objective but would be affected by the results of an aerial blockade of the enemy homeland that precision bombing made possible. He mentioned industrial targets, but he focused more on destroying social structures without the indiscriminate slaughter of civilians, going beyond George's and Webster's work to meld Douhet's theories with precision techniques. "The will to resist can be broken in a people," he argued, "only by destroying the essentials of their lives—the supply of food, shelter, light, water, sanitation, and the rest." He even saw some uses for terror bombing, either to lure an enemy air force into a tactical engagement defending cities or to embarrass an enemy through propaganda if it could not defend its populace from air attack. Seversky did not advocate such tactics, but he did feel that the public should be prepared for them. His ideas circulated widely among Air Force officers and in numerous journals.[47] Walt Disney even made Seversky's influential book, *Victory through Airpower*, into a movie and thus exposed the American and British public to his views on strategic-bombing doctrine.[48]

But Seversky's ideas did not accurately reflect the mature precision-bombing doctrine that ACTS was teaching and that would guide the Army Air Forces into and through World War II, a philosophy that focused on destroying "carefully selected targets in the industrial and service systems on which the enemy people, their industries, and the armed forces are dependent."[49] The clearest and most important enunciation of that doctrine came in an August 1941 document known as AWPD/1.

Army Regulation 95-5 of June 1941, creating the Army Air Forces, gave the new organization limited autonomy, but despite a growing appreciation for airpower in official circles, the actual role of strategic bombing was unclear.[50] The AAF's opportunity to establish its role in winning the war came in July 1941 when President Roosevelt sent a letter to the secretaries of War

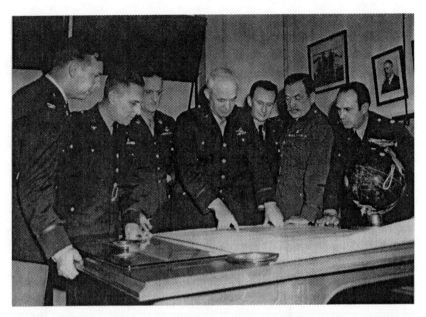

Maj. Gen. H. H. "Hap" Arnold and his staff, in 1941, many of whom were instrumental in developing precision doctrine and AWPD/1. From left to right, Lt. Col. Edgar Sorenson, Lt. Col. Harold George, Brig. Gen. Carl Spaatz, Maj. Gen. Arnold, Maj. Haywood Hansell, Jr., Brig. Gen. Martin Scanlon, and Lt. Col. Arthur Vanaman.

and Navy "requesting the preparation of the Over-All Production requirements required to defeat our potential enemies." Since the services could not agree on a joint strategy, they each estimated their own requirements. The Army's report was the responsibility of the War Plans Division (WPD) of the General Staff. Lt. Col. Clayton Bissell, an Air Corps officer in the WPD, persuaded his bosses to ask Lt. Gen. H. H. Arnold, commanding general, U.S. Army Air Corps, to detail some Air Corps officers to produce an aviation annex. With the cooperation of Brig. Gen. Carl Spaatz and the strong support of Lt. Col. Harold George, the mission was given to the newly established Air War Plans Division (AWPD) of the equally new Air Staff, Army Air Forces.[51]

By 1941 the development of theories for employing airpower had shifted somewhat from ACTS with the reassignment of many key instructors to staff positions in Washington. Lieutenant Colonel George assembled a task force of himself, Lt. Col. Kenneth Walker, Maj. Laurence Kuter, and Maj. Haywood Hansell, Jr., all of whom had contributed to developing precision-bombing doctrine at ACTS. They received their assignment about a week before it was due on August 11. Meanwhile, Arnold had been called away for the Atlantic Conference in Placentia Bay, Newfoundland. Lacking clear guidance or objectives and pressed for time, the group had to lay out a plan that would determine the future of the Army Air Forces, but as one of the planners wrote, "If the task was staggering, so too was the opportunity." They selected an overall strategic concept and air objective and prepared an air plan to achieve that goal. The result was "straight American air power doctrine" as developed at ACTS, with the provision to support an invasion in order to make the plan more acceptable to Army planners who had not yet accepted the AAF's independent strategic role. Using their broad latitude to their advantage, the task force went beyond setting out production requirements and devised a plan for an all-out strategic air offensive. It was an amazing effort. As one writer has described it, "A plan that should have been assembled by dozens of experts in a period of months was written by four young men in nine days while their boss was out of town."[52]

The final document, officially titled "Munitions Requirements of the AAF for the Defeat of our Potential Enemies," accepted the "Germany First" policy of overall strategic direction. AWPD/1 planned to apply airpower "for the breakdown of the industrial and economic structure of Germany" by destroying "a system of objectives vital to the German war effort": primarily power, transportation, and oil industries. Though the plan recognized the drawbacks of bombing cities, it did envision that area bombing of civilian concentrations might commence as a final blow when German morale began to crack. AWPD/1 did not define whether such a move would entail a single assault or a series of attacks, but it did state that "the entire bombing effort might be applied toward this purpose when it becomes apparent that the proper psychological conditions exist." This one-time exception to general policy was sanctioned only as a way to end the war quickly, but late in the war this concept of an aerial *Todestoss* (deathblow) would prove a potent lure for American leaders, helping to sanction the use of the atomic bomb.[53]

After review by Spaatz and Arnold and discussions with Gen. George C. Marshall, Army chief of staff, and Secretary of War Henry L. Stimson, AWPD/1 was accepted as part of the overall reply to the president's assignment. Its ready acceptance may have been due to the pressure of time to meet the commander-in-chief's request, for the plan did not conform completely to War Department views. "Tacitly, though not legally, the AAF staff had assumed on this occasion a position of equality with those of the older arms." All future air planning would build on the foundation of AWPD/1. Though the Pacific theater was not addressed, a strategic air offensive based on precision-bombing doctrine was written into official policy. Like Gorrell's initial work, this plan had also been developed in response to a need to predict production requirements, not to create strategy. Yet with the impetus of AWPD/1, the air assault on enemy war industries and transportation lines that Gorrell's study had envisioned over two decades earlier would soon become reality.[54]

3. ATTITUDES OF LEADERS
AND THE PUBLIC

Last month my son Ted won his wings at Randolph Field. He is now going through a bombardment school, and in a short time expects to go to the front.

Will you tell me—has he become what our enemies call him, "A Hooligan of the Air?" Is he expected to scatter death on men, women, children—to wreck churches and shrines—to be a slaughterer, not a fighting man?

I remember so well when you and Frank Lahm, and Tommy Milling won your wings. We all thought it was a new day in chivalry, bravery, manhood. What do Air Force wings mean today? In winning his wings, has Ted lost his spurs? Please tell me.[1]

This letter from a concerned mother in Massachusetts to the Army Air Forces chief of staff raised some of the same questions being debated by modern historians. When it was written in May 1943, American daylight bombers had been in action over Europe for nine months; they had already been involved in controversy over civilian casualties in occupied countries and had become the subject of much German propaganda.[2] AAF leaders were especially sensitive to public opinion since the airmen believed they needed all the support they could get to achieve independent status. Between the wars, Army aviators had exploited American dreams that the airplane could revolutionize daily life and transform the world for good, and at the core of precision-bombing doctrine was the belief that the American public would not stand for the indiscriminate aerial bombardment of civilians.[3] AAF leaders interpreted the few letters from concerned correspondents as representative of public opinion, and this viewpoint acted as a restraint upon some airmen who might otherwise have been inclined to imitate Air Vice Marshal Arthur "Bomber" Harris, commander of the RAF Bomber Command and architect of the RAF night-bombing campaign against German cities. Stopped one night for speeding by a policeman who warned, "You might have killed someone, sir," Harris allegedly retorted, "Young man, I kill thousands of people every night."[4] American leaders probably could never have been that callous, but actual wartime public opinion was not as intolerant of civilian casualties as the AAF perceived.

Pearl Harbor transformed American public opinion about terror attacks on civilians. A poll on 10 December 1941 revealed that 67 percent of the population favored unqualified and indiscriminate bombing of Japanese cities, and only 10 percent responded with an outright no.[5] The same justification of tit for tat that motivated earlier Luftwaffe and RAF raids on London and Berlin seemed to be evident here.[6] Subsequent surveys produced similar results. A majority of Americans favored urban bombing even if it brought Axis retaliation against U.S. cities, implying either a deep commitment or a resignation to total warfare and reflecting the intense anxiety about a war that appeared to be going so disastrously. For religious reasons, most Americans expressed resistance to bombing Rome, but by early 1944 three-quarters of those polled approved bombing historic religious buildings and shrines if military leaders believed such attacks were necessary.[7]

The only significant flurry of U.S. protest against strategic bombing came in response to a pamphlet "Massacre by Bombing," written by a British citizen, Vera Brittain, and published in America by the Fellowship of Reconciliation, a small pacifist group. She contended that mass bombing just sped up the slaughter and destruction normally occurring only on fighting fronts, produced a downward spiral of moral values, did not induce revolt or break morale, and caused destruction that would cripple postwar Europe and sow the psychological seeds of a third world war. She also noted that the British in bombed areas were less likely to support RAF attacks on enemy cities than their compatriots who had been spared.[8] Her work did not attract significant attention, however, until March 1944 when the New York Times reprinted excerpts along with an introductory petition signed by twenty-eight prominent educators, professionals, and clergy (mostly the last). The article, "Obliteration Raids on German Cities Protested in U.S.," caused intense public reaction, and over 200 articles were written condemning Brittain.[9] The paper received "unusually heavy mail" about the piece and estimated that letters of protest concerning Brittain's views were running "50–1 against."[10] Most responses agreed with author MacKinley Kantor, who deplored the "softheartedness" of those people who worry about "socking the rapacious German nation with every pound of high explosives available." A rabbi declared that "the Germans must reap the fruits of their own wicked deeds." Other clergy echoed his sentiments, citing Nazi precedents as the final justification for

American bombing. Editorial comment in general disclaimed moral questions and recognized the raids as a "revolting necessity."[11]

Though relatively few commentaries addressed the ethical issues Brittain had raised, articles discussing the morality of obliteration bombing did appear in *Fellowship*, *Saturday Review of Literature*, *Christian Century*, the *Nation*, *Newsweek*, *Politics*, *Spectator*, *Commonweal*, *America*, the *London Tablet*, and the *Labor Leader*.[12] The issue was even debated on the radio during "America's Town Meeting" on the evening of 30 March. Norman Cousins, editor of the *Saturday Review of Literature*, and military analyst Maj. George Fielding Eliot were for bombing cities; C. C. Paulding, literary editor of *Commonweal*, and Socialist party leader Norman Thomas attacked the practice.[13] But the furor caused by Brittain's article soon abated, with no effect on bombing policy.

Other writers had protested aerial bombing. Oswald Garrison Villard penned critical articles in *Christian Century* beginning in 1943, R. Alfred Hassler wrote "Slaughter of the Innocent" in *Fellowship* in February 1944, and German-American Gerhart Segar was condemned for his editorials in *Neue Volkszeitung* and for his commentary on "Town Meeting of the Air," when he stated that American pilots were exhibiting "totalitarian thinking" by "finding satisfaction in blowing up women and children." The national religious press, especially Catholic journals, were also often critical of indiscriminate bombing.[14]

In one of the most penetrating critiques, Father John C. Ford argued that even in industrial cities in wartime, at least two-thirds of the civil population would be immoral targets: "most women, almost all children under 14 years, almost all men over seventy, and a very large number of men who are engaged neither in war manufactures, transport, communications, nor in other doubtful categories." He correctly predicted that the bombing of cities would weaken ethical constraints and take us "a long step in the direction of immoral total war." By using explosives and incendiaries "to a hitherto unheard of degree," the practice left "only one more step to go to the use of poison gas or bacteriological war" (or the atomic bomb).[15] Yet no clear consensus was reached among American church leaders on the immorality of city bombing. In 1944 the theologians of the Federal Council of Churches Commission on the Relation of the Church to the War in the Light of the Christian Faith agreed that "the massacre of civilian populations" was immoral but stated that some of their members "believe that certain other measures, such as rigorous blockades of foodstuffs essential to civilian life, and obliteration bombing of civilian areas, however repugnant to humane feelings, are still justifiable on

Christian principles, if they are essential to the successful conduct of a war that is itself justified."[16]

The majority of public opinion on killing enemy civilians was probably accurately represented by the reactions to Brittain's article, ranging between avid support for vengeful urban attacks and resigned acceptance of a regrettably unavoidable practice. The average American might not have been aware of the extent of the destruction that bombing wreaked on cities; posters depicted Allied bombers attacking factories instead of people, and periodicals described B-17s dropping explosives down industrial smokestacks. Even if Americans had known the exact results of bombing, it would not have made much difference. Most families had experienced the deaths of loved ones, friends, or neighbors; if bombing enemy civilians would speed victory and save American lives, it had to be done.

ATTITUDES OF LEADERS IN WASHINGTON

Many Americans were comforted, however, by the belief that the AAF avoided indiscriminate killing of civilians whenever possible. In turn, AAF leaders perceived a public opinion in line with the position of publications like the *New Republic*, which stated that it did not approve of terror bombing but added that to the best of its knowledge most bombardment was directed at military objectives.[17] A subtle, important interaction was maintained between public perceptions of American strategic bombing and the attitudes of the leaders carrying it out. Air Force planners interpreted public opinion as favoring precision attacks on industrial and military targets without indiscriminate civilian casualties, one of the influences that shaped AAF bombing doctrine. Military reports and news releases designed to demonstrate the accuracy and effectiveness of pinpoint bombardment in turn shaped public opinion. This use of information exemplifies a trend that can be traced to the American Civil War, and "management of, or compliance with, public opinion" has become "an essential element in the conduct of war."[18] In World War II, American leaders worked persistently to dispel any impressions of American terror bombing.

This effort often caused men in high places to present different public and private positions on the bombing of enemy civilians; the commander-in-chief, Franklin D. Roosevelt, is a good example. When the Germans invaded Poland on 1 September 1939, he immediately issued a plea to all belligerents to cease "the ruthless bombing from the air of civilians in unfortified centers of population" that "has sickened the hearts of every civilized man and woman, and has profoundly shocked the conscience of humanity." He asked for a public affirmation that all parties would avoid such acts, "upon the understanding that these same rules of warfare will be scrupulously observed by all of their opponents."[19] This plea was largely a political ploy. A week earlier, Ambassador William Bullitt had proposed that such an appeal should be made at the start of hostilities. The assumption was that Britain, Poland, and France would agree but that Germany would not, thus showing the moral superiority of the Allies and swaying world opinion against Germany. After consultation with Cordell Hull, Roosevelt agreed to send the message.[20] The Allies did indeed respond favorably, but so did Germany. And the Germans were able to claim by 11 September that the Poles were violating the rules of warfare by resisting in open cities and shelling their own people, thus justifying retaliation from the air.[21]

FDR's true feelings are probably better demonstrated by a statement he made to Henry Morgenthau on 4 August 1941 about defeating Hitler: "Well, the way to lick Hitler is the way I have been telling the English, but they won't listen to me. . . . I have suggested again and again that if they sent a hundred planes over Germany for military objectives that ten of them should bomb some of these smaller towns that haven't been bombed before. There must be some kind of factory in every town. That is the only way to break German morale."[22] Although factories would be the technical targets, FDR's actual objective was to smash civilian will, not the economy. (Operation CLARION, similar in concept, was mounted in 1945 and generated much controversy over its aims.) Roosevelt revealed as early as 1938 that he believed the morale of the German people could be cracked by the terror of aerial bombardment.[23]

The President did emphasize the distinction between obliteration and precision bombing in his message to Congress in 1943, but he revealed no such awareness during the controversy over Brittain's pamphlet. Stephan Early, Roosevelt's secretary, responded to "Massacre by Bombing" with a letter on behalf of the president. Although FDR was "disturbed and horrified" by civilian air-raid casualties, "the bombing is shortening the war, in the opinion of an overwhelming percentage of military authorities." Brittain replied that the president's response was "irrelevant, unjustified, and destructive of the very ideals with which the American people went to war."[24] A bit later, FDR sent a note to Secretary Stimson taking an even harsher stand, stating that "the German people as a whole must have it driven home to them that the whole nation has been engaged in a lawless conspiracy against the decencies of modern civilization."[25]

At least in private, FDR showed a willingness early in the war to attack civilian morale from the air. So did AAF Chief of Staff Gen. Henry "Hap" Arnold, who had what one aide called "an open mind" on terror bombing.[26] In 1941 Arnold wrote that "bombing attacks on civil populace are uneconomical and unwise" because "bombers in far larger numbers than are available today will be required for wiping out people in sufficient numbers to break the will of a whole nation."[27] Arnold kept his options open for future civilian bombardment, and his memoirs and diaries reveal even more flexibility on the subject. He was impressed by the damage and civilian listlessness that a relatively small number of Luftwaffe bombers had caused in London, and he envisioned great results from larger fleets of American planes.[28]

In public Arnold called terror bombing "abhorrent to our humanity, our sense of decency," a policy he himself did not support.[29] In private he told his air staff that "this is a brutal war and . . . the way to stop the killing of civilians is to cause so much damage and destruction and death that the civilians will demand that their government cease fighting." He added, however, that "this doesn't mean that we are making civilians or civilian institutions a war objective, but we cannot 'pull our punches' because some of them may get killed." He did confide to reporters once that the AAF could bomb to destroy a city "as well as anybody else" and did sometimes carry out "pattern bombing," which could be used to break morale though that was really not a preferred AAF objective.[30]

In order to support his desire for a postwar independent air service Arnold wanted to avoid alienating the public with an improper image, but he also needed impressive results to prove the effectiveness of airpower. Though he was not really involved in running day-to-day combat operations, his authority to relieve field commanders gave him leverage to influence their actions. Poor health limited his effectiveness late in the war, however, and after he suffered his fourth heart attack in January 1945 his involvement in key decisions was especially limited.[31] But his pressure for more raids despite bad weather led to increased use of less accurate radar-directed bombardments in Europe, and his demand for increased efficiency in Japan inspired the use of fire raids. His main goal was to make the largest possible contribution to winning the war and to ensure that the AAF received credit for it through proper publicity.

Thus he demanded much from his field commanders in the area of public relations. He wrote to commanders in 1942, "Within the borders of continental United States, two most important fronts exist, namely, aircraft production and public opinion." He thought that the American public was entitled "to see pictures, stories and experiences of our Air Force in combat zones," and he sent out personnel from his staff to gather such information. A year later he complained to his commanders that too much information was being withheld because of secrecy; it was more important that the people be kept informed of the major impact the Air Force was making on the enemy's war effort, an impact that could save millions of lives in ground combat. "For whole-hearted and official support of our Air Forces in their operations, . . . the people [must] understand thoroughly our Air Force precepts, principles, and purposes. . . . In short, we want the people to understand and have faith in *our way of making war*."[32] Field commanders protested when Arnold tried to get them to replace a machine gun from their bombers with a camera to provide combat film footage, but their objections had little effect on his drive for media coverage. Arnold exerted even more pressure for publicity once the Allies invaded Europe and the war seemed to be winding down. He complained that ground and naval commanders such as Gen. George Patton and Adm. William Halsey got the publicity but that the contribution of airpower was ignored. He emphasized to the field that he considered "the whole subject of realistic reorientation of the public's concept of the effect of air power upon the outcome of the war so important" that he would "scour the country" to find public-relations experts to reinforce press representatives in the theater. Because of his push, by November 1944 fully 40 percent of the total film released by the Army to newsreels came from AAF combat camera units.[33] Even this increased output did not please Arnold, who wanted more front-page stories and sent out to all commanders a list of fifty points applicable to writing proper news releases. Thinking ahead about the future of the AAF, he was determined that "through proper presentation to the press" the American people could get the facts necessary to make "a correct evaluation of the part air power has played in this war" so that "the United States should not make the mistake of allowing through lack of knowledge the tearing down in post-war years of what has cost us so much blood and sweat to build up."[34]

Though Arnold did stress the advantages of precision bombing to his commanders, pushing for increased accuracy and refined tactics to achieve "the maximum attainable with the forces and facilities available," he was also "the prophet and proponent of the most terrifying technologies of war."[35] He emphasized that his commanders "must be ever on the alert to accept new ideas, must have flexible minds on procedure and technique in our missions."[36] He liked to glean such new ideas from the minds of experts; gadgets and "hot ideas" fascinated him. In keeping with the impression given in his early writings that he would try almost anything if he had enough aircraft, Arnold commented favorably on plans to bomb volcanoes around Tokyo and schools of fish off the coast of Japan.[37] He was fascinated with pilotless flying bombs like the German V-1s and wanted to retaliate for German booby traps in North Africa by dropping explosive devices in fountain pens and pocketbooks onto German territory. Foreshadowing a tactic eventually adopted by the Japanese, Arnold also had his staff investigate a plan to use "Vinylite" film balloons to drop incendiaries on Japan.[38]

There seemed to be little consideration for ethics in Arnold's decisions, but he did espouse the traditional moral position of airpower theory that bombing would cost fewer lives than land warfare and end the war quickly. Like other air leaders, he sincerely believed that the decisive power of modern aerial technology could prevent a repeat of the deadlocked carnage of World War I and achieve swift and relatively bloodless victory. He told his commanders that "when used with the proper degree of understanding, [the bomber] becomes, in effect, the most humane of all weapons." He also realized the political costs of indiscriminate bombardment, writing in 1942 that "careless inaccurate bombing intensifies and spreads those hates which will be stumbling blocks to international amity for years after the war is over."[39] Yet as the war continued and he pushed more and more for decisive results to support his dream of an independent air service, considerations of humanity were never a priority with Arnold.

In contrast, at least one leader in Washington, Secretary of War Henry L. Stimson, did consistently oppose the intentional killing or terrorizing of enemy noncombatants. Repelled by the barbarism of indiscriminate attacks on civilians, he had been instrumental in U.S. government protests against such raids during the 1930s and tried to keep a close watch on American strategic air operations during World War II. Stimson's diary is filled with references to atrocities and war crimes and occasionally with concerns for enemy civilians. He was convinced that the Nazi leaders and the secret police, not the German people, caused the war. The same sentiment motivated those critics of strategic bombing who concluded that workers in Berlin were no more evil than the airmen ordered to bomb them.[40] Stimson complained that only Gen. George Marshall supported him in that view: "It is singular that the man who had charge of the Department which did the killing in the war, should be the only one who seemed to have any mercy for the other side."

Lt. Gen. H. H. Arnold traveling with Secretary of War Henry Stimson. Unlike Arnold, Stimson consistently expressed moral opposition to indiscriminate attacks on enemy civilians.

The secretary of war believed that in general Army officers had a better sense of justice on the issue of "responsibility of peoples" than civilians.[41]

Though Stimson called the Japanese "barbarians" in speeches, he did work to restrain "the feeling of war passion and hysteria which seizes hold of a nation like ours in prosecution of such a bitter war." Reports of the fire raids against Japan evoked a strong reaction; Stimson felt he had been misled by Robert Lovett, assistant secretary of war for air, and by AAF leaders who had promised to restrict operations there to "the precision bombing which [the AAF] has done so well in Europe." In his diary he wrote, "I am told it is possible and adequate. The reputation of the United States for fair play and humanitarianism is the world's biggest asset for peace in the coming decades."[42] Discussing the topic later with President Truman, Stimson realized the validity of Air Force arguments that the omnipresence of dispersed Japanese industry made it difficult to prevent area bombing, but he "did not want to have the United States get the reputation of outdoing Hitler in atrocities." He often agonized over sanctioning bombing raids and wondered about the lack of public protest. Robert Oppenheimer recalled that Stimson thought it was "appalling" that no one protested the heavy loss of life caused by the air raids against Japan. "He didn't say that the air strikes shouldn't be carried on, but he did think there was something wrong with a country where no one questioned that."[43]

Ronald Schaffer is especially critical of Stimson for not being more effective, pointing out that his protest of the fire raids came almost two months after they started and that he could have inquired more into the bombing of Japan and Dresden. Schaffer speculates that Stimson might have been too old, ill, and misinformed or that he simply chose not to know what the AAF was doing.[44] Stimson was suffering from poor health and often could not work full time, and he was not kept informed on day-to-day operations. But in his role as secretary of war he was more concerned with administrative matters than with strategy. As the war went on his diary deals increasingly with the problems of manning and supplying his forces as the sources of recruits and replacements dried up and as public enthusiasm for the war began to wane. The AAF did respond when Stimson showed strong interest in a subject, such as the sparing of Kyoto from the atomic bomb or the Norwegian complaints about stray bombs from raids on heavy-water plants, but they did not feel obligated to brief him on operations. Stimson remarked once of Robert Lovett that "his youngsters have run away with the ball without apparently attracting his attention," but the military treated the civilians in the War Department in just such a manner.[45] Stimson probably learned more about specific operations from the newspapers than he did from soldiers in his department. The war was planned and directed by the Joint Chiefs of Staff and fought by the operational- and tactical-level commanders in the field.

ATTITUDES OF FIELD COMMANDERS

One field commander effective in restraining indiscriminate bombardment was Lt. Gen. Carl Spaatz, commander of the United States Strategic Air Forces and an officer most historians credit with continuing to raise the moral issue in opposition to British attempts to enlist American participation in terror attacks and deviations from precision bombing. Russell Weigley calls him "a pillar of common sense," whom ground commanders could always talk to. Although Spaatz believed that "we have proven the precision bombing principle in this war," he realized that with the limits of technology, "our precision . . . is in a relative not a literal sense," and he continued to strive for "pickle barrel accuracy."[46] He also had a more realistic view of Arnold's publicity campaign, and though he supported his chief, he was wary that "the people back home are getting the idea now [April 1944] that the War is won and apparently we have unintentionally given the impression that more has been accomplished than has actually been accomplished." While Arnold pushed for optimistic reports of the triumphs of airpower, Spaatz wanted to "lean a little on the side of understatement" to avoid false confidence at home and mistrust of superiors by the airmen who had to engage the German fighters supposedly destroyed by the AAF.[47]

Weigley also claims that "Spaatz was an airman genuinely troubled over the moral questions raised by aerial bombardment."[48] The USSTAF commander wrote in his diary after the dropping of the atomic bomb, "I have never favored the destruction of cities as such with all inhabitants being killed." In an often-quoted 1962 interview, however, he claimed, "It wasn't for religious or moral reasons that I didn't go along with urban area bombing."[49] One must be careful in interpreting this statement; Spaatz was emphasizing in the interview that the AAF bombed strategic military targets because that was the quickest way to win the war, not because the United States was morally superior to the British. From the beginning of the war, Spaatz condemned efforts to "belittle the RAF and their bombing effort" even though he was not "an enthusiastic supporter of all they do."[50] Spaatz had helped develop precision-bombing doctrine and pursued it dog-

Maj. Gen. Jimmy Doolittle in the cockpit of his plane in 1943. He often flew his own aircraft to visit units under his command. Doolittle served under Carl Spaatz from 1942 until the end of the war in Europe and supported him in his efforts to restrict strategic bombing to precision targets.

gedly in Europe. Although he did emphasize the efficiency of such tactics, he also continually expressed concern over civilian casualties caused by bombing.

Spaatz's primary objective was to make the maximum contribution to winning the war in Europe. He cooperated with the ground effort, but he believed that precision bombing of economic targets, especially oil, made the best use of his bombers. His subordinate commanders supported his goals and AAF doctrine, though their attitudes demonstrated varying degrees of concern for morality, efficiency, and public opinion, depending on their background and training. Lt. Gen. Jimmy Doolittle, commander of the Eighth Air

Force in 1944–1945, seemed to share Spaatz's attitude toward morality in strategic bombing. A famous air racer and aeronautical engineer before the war, Doolittle was not a career military man like the rest of the commanders. Wartime biographers emphasized "his superb sense of fair play and his constant observation of the rules of human decency." He restricted his objectives to purely military targets during his famous Tokyo raid and carefully avoided religious shrines in his 1943 bombings of Rome. He wanted to be the first to bomb Berlin, too, but he supported Spaatz in resisting obliteration attacks on that city.[51] In his recent autobiography, Doolittle remarks that, in his opinion, the Americans who supported daylight precision bombing instead of the night area attacks used by the British did so not because pinpoint methods were significantly more effective than RAF tactics but because "to us, it was the most ethical way to go."[52]

Maj. Gen. Frederick L. Anderson, eventually USSTAF deputy commander for operations, was a proponent of efficiency. He was young, a 1928 graduate of West Point, having risen from first lieutenant to brigadier general in less than six years, and unlike Arnold, Spaatz, Doolittle, or Eaker, he had no experience from World War I or the 1920s to draw on. He was, however, the AAF's leading bombardment expert. As a captain in 1939, he was put in charge of the Bombardier School at the Air Force Technical School at Lowry Field, Colorado. He had not developed precision-bombing doctrine, but he trained bombardiers to put it into practice. When the AAF needed someone to evaluate crew training and bombsights in England in early 1942, Anderson got the assignment. He helped develop the justification for daylight bombing when it was questioned early in the war, emphasizing the efficiency of precision bombing and how it complemented British area bombing. Another strong proponent for an independent Air Force equal to the other branches, he believed "that for the efficiency of our fighting forces a reorganization is needed."[53]

Achieving an independent Air Force was also paramount in importance to Lt. Gen. Ira Eaker, who commanded both the Eighth and the Fifteenth Air Forces at different times during the war and eventually became Arnold's deputy. Favorable public opinion was essential for this goal, and Eaker was deeply concerned about the AAF's image, both current and future. He warned the assistant chief of air staff for intelligence to keep criticism of operations out of official exchanges because "we have a mass of historians at both ends watching all this correspondence and these things cannot but creep into the official documents unless we are all on guard." He supported Arnold's drive for publicity about the importance of airpower, promising, "We are making certain that every American newspaperman we can get our hands on has these facts hammered home to him."[54]

Eaker was extremely intelligent; he had a journalism degree and had taken some law courses at Columbia. Among the AAF leaders he came closest to being a true public-relations expert. After serving as the records custodian for Brig. Gen. Billy Mitchell's court-martial, he saw the dangers of confrontation and "deliberately set out to become army air's most persuasive spokesman." He worked hard to develop his writing and speaking skills, and his efforts paid off at the Casablanca Conference in January 1943. Plagued by a slow build-up of forces in Europe, lack of proper fighter escorts, and poor selection of target systems, American daylight bombers in 1942 had not been able to match the night efforts of RAF Bomber Command, which included 1,000 plane raids. Eaker made the presentation that convinced Churchill and others of the merits of a Combined Bomber Offensive (CBO) involving round-the-clock bombing, thus preserving the AAF's chance to vindicate precision-bombing doctrine. Arnold also often sent Eaker to make presentations to the Joint Chiefs of Staff for the AAF. Eaker had written books and articles with Arnold, and the latter frequently asked his editorial advice. When an article criticizing daylight bombing appeared in *Reader's Digest* and caused a stir, Eaker wrote an official reply defending American air strategy that was released by the War Department.[55]

His comments to Arnold and other sources reveal that Eaker was not as committed to precision bombing as Spaatz or Anderson. He advised Arnold to put in a prewar *Saturday Evening Post* article that it was "probably uneconomical to bomb civil populations unless in extreme cases such as London or Paris, where it would be done for the morale effect in the hope for a short war." He admitted in a 1972 interview that he was not "completely sold" on daylight precision bombing when he took over the Eighth Air Force in England in 1942 and viewed his operations as a test of the concept, though he felt that Arnold and Marshall were "relying on him to make it work." If he had failed to save daylight precision bombardment at Casablanca, he was prepared to shift his forces to night bombing in three to six months after installing flame dampeners, taking out unnecessary machine guns, and retraining crews.[56] In late 1944 General Spaatz criticized diversions of Eaker's Fifteenth Air Force from oil targets, but Eaker advocated dispersed attacks to destroy German morale, suggesting that such tactics might also pull defenses away from oil targets. When Eaker did oppose terror attacks in early 1945, his position was based on his fears about the political and historical ramifications of "throwing the strategic bomber at the man in the street."[57]

Eighth Air Force B-24 Liberators bombing harbor installations at Dunkirk, France, on 15 February 1943. Raids such as this one contributed to the dispute between American and British airmen over risks to civilians in occupied nations. (Special Collections Division, U.S. Military Academy Library, West Point, N.Y.)

DIFFERENCES WITH THE BRITISH

The attitudes of American leaders committed to daylight precision bombing were bound to clash with the views of their RAF counterparts dedicated to "dehousing" German workers and obliterating whole cities. From the early days of the war, U.S. military attachés in England had been sending reports criticizing the inaccuracy of night bombing, yet AAF personnel understood the rationale for RAF tactics.[58] They knew that aircraft capabilities and German countermeasures rendered British daylight precision attacks ineffectual, but public pressure demanded that the RAF strike back at Germany. Night raids on urban areas seemed the only viable alternative. If the British had possessed the long-range escort fighters that eventually made daylight bombing practicable, their campaign might have developed differently. But by 1942 AAF leaders realized that British aircraft, with their heavy bombloads, inaccurate bombsights, and sparse defensive armament, were primarily adapted to night attacks and that the heavily armed American planes, with smaller bombloads, good bombsights, and no flame dampers, were chiefly suited to daylight operations.[59]

Until they could prove the viability of their own tactics, AAF leaders were wary of criticism. British leaders or journalists who criticized daylight bombardment were often invited to go on American missions. Joint statements were issued to emphasize the complementary nature of RAF and AAF campaigns. Articles in the American press advocating night bombing also evoked nervous reactions, and a proposed film on RAF bombing exhibits in early 1943 was tabled because the AAF staff felt that "we should do nothing to stress night area bombardment to the American public."[60] Yet throughout the war, even after daylight bombing had proved so successful, the Americans continually discouraged any public criticism of the British obliteration raids, believing that "odious" comparisons between bombing techniques only assisted German propaganda and caused resentment between the two Allies.

In private, however, sharp differences often existed over the bombing of civilians, especially about the attacks on countries conquered by Germany. From the onset of war, Spaatz was sensitive to civilian casualties in occupied areas. He was probably also aware of the strong anti-British feeling resulting from RAF raids on targets such as the Renault Auto Works in Paris. To avoid such reaction to AAF bombing, on 6 October 1942 a special broadcast to France was made on "America Calling Europe," warning the French that though the United States had "only the greatest sympathy" toward them, "all factories in France that are working for Germany are susceptible to being bombarded." Because bombs dropped from high altitudes often fell short of or beyond the target, "all those who live within two kilometres of factories working for Germany are advised to move." Even with this warning, casualties from a raid on Lille dismayed Spaatz; later in the month, to avoid similar results, he gave orders to his Eighth Air Force that if their primary military target was obscured they could not attack Paris as an alternate objective.[61] The responsibility for "political matters" such as bombing in occupied countries was left to the British Air Ministry, and on 29 October their office issued a restrictive bombardment policy that limited targets in occupied countries to military objectives located far away from populated areas.[62]

The 29 October directive established a double standard that would exist throughout the war, allowing far more latitude for air attacks within Germany than in occupied zones. The policy presented no problems to the RAF since they were targeting German morale and cities. In contrast, confident in their own accuracy, chafing to attack the enemy and its support structures, and seemingly unappreciative that airpower had "political as well as military" effects, the Americans were not happy with the restrictions that limited attacks against lucrative targets in occupied countries.[63] Such objectives were much

Gen. Carl Spaatz and Gen. Dwight Eisenhower maintained a close relationship throughout the war in Europe even though they sometimes disagreed about the proper application of American airpower. Here Spaatz and his staff brief Ike on the initial deployment of the Eighth Air Force to England in 1942. Back row, left to right: Brig. Gen. Ira Eaker, Brig. Gen. Frank Hunter, Brig. Gen. Robert Candee; front row, left to right: Spaatz, Eisenhower, Maj. Gen. Walter Frank.

closer to British bases, not as heavily defended as targets in Germany, and provided better opportunities to perfect daylight-bombing techniques with less risk.

And not only the airmen were unhappy. In March 1943 Assistant Secretary of War Lovett had to explain to Judge Patterson, undersecretary of war who often did special work for FDR, why the AAF was restricted to bombing "admittedly impossible targets" at submarine bases while "the RAF accomplishes the end result by bombing out the working community."[64] The next month saw an exchange of letters between Sir Charles Portal, Britain's chief of air staff and the Combined Chiefs of Staff chief agent for the CBO, and Major General Eaker, now commanding the Eighth Air Force and the senior American air commander in England while Spaatz was serving as commander in chief, Northwest African Air Forces, for Eisenhower. Spurred by complaints from the Belgian ambassador to the United States, the British again tried to restrict any attacks that could result in civilian casualties near targets in occupied zones. Eaker, with additional emphasis from Arnold, stressed that although the Allies had to avoid unnecessary civilian casualties and limit objectives in occupied countries to key factors in Axis strategy, all civilians employed "willingly or otherwise" in Axis industry were assisting the enemy and should accept the risks "which must be the lot of any individual who participates directly in the war effort of a belligerent nation." This policy applied to German workers as well as to the French and showed a consistency in thought independent of political considerations. Axis employees were no longer viewed as noncombatants, an important step in the escalation to total war. Yet it must be noted that this combatant status applied only to workers in factories being bombed; the AAF strategic campaign, unlike that of the RAF, did not target laborers in their homes.[65]

One can only speculate whether Spaatz would have been more receptive to Portal's pleas than Eaker, but when Spaatz returned to England and was named commander of the newly created USSTAF in November 1943 he continued bombing precision targets near conquered cities. Also in January 1944 Doolittle, who had commanded the Northwest African Strategic Air Force, replaced Eaker as commander of the Eighth Air Force. Spaatz and Doolittle continued to debate the British over the issue of civilian casualties in occupied countries, this time concerning the air campaign to support the impending cross-channel invasion.

Some civilian advisers to the British Air Ministry had studied operations in Italy and concluded that the best support for the invasion would result from mass attacks by all available air resources to completely disrupt the transportation system in Europe. The plan was supported by Deputy Supreme Commander Air Chief Marshal Tedder and Allied Expeditionary Air Force (AEAF) Commander Air Chief Marshal Leigh-Mallory. Spaatz's planners developed a counterproposal to attack the German oil industry, and the USSTAF position was also favored by "Bomber" Harris. The Transportation Plan offered greater promise of "immediate effect on the success of OVERLORD in its initial period," and Eisenhower eventually adopted it. But the plan also threatened considerable civilian casualties and evoked severe protest from USSTAF personnel.[66]

Spaatz resisted the Transportation Plan for many reasons. Because so much unused capacity existed in the rail system, damage to French and Belgian lines would really not restrict key troop movements. From his own experience in Italy, Spaatz knew that the destruction of choke points such as tunnels and bridges was the best method to block movement and isolate the battlefield, and Anderson wrote letters to the British to recommend this course of action. USSTAF also believed that attacking oil targets promised the quickest way to cripple the German economy and end the war and made the most efficient use of strategic bombers. But Spaatz, especially, complained most vociferously that the Transportation Plan would "jeopardize the good will of the French and Belgian people by the resultant loss of civilian lives in the attack of rail centers in populated areas and all for a very slight effect."[67]

Americans were left out completely in the planning and target selection for the AEAF transportation attacks, and the USSTAF director of plans, Brig. Gen. Charles Cabell, believed that this was all part of a scheme by the British "to have some of the odium" for area bombing and indiscriminate air attacks shared by the United States. He and Spaatz feared that bombing the French might even jeopardize their support, needed for the invasion. The two airmen sent letters to Eisenhower and cables to the JCS for "fact-finders" to ensure that the U.S. government would "not accept any responsibility for that loss of friendly civilian lives, except with the best of knowledge as to its extent, with full understanding of its implications, and without any illusions as to the gain to be expected from it." When Spaatz's pleas were ignored and Eisenhower overrode any objections, the USSTAF commander did what he could to limit civilian casualties. He emphasized "very strongly" to his subordinate commanders that there was "great need for care in all operations against French targets." He directed that "the best lead bombardiers would be used, no indiscriminate bombing would be permitted, no H2X [radar] bombing permitted, and crews must be impressed with the need for air discipline in order to avoid needless killing of French personnel." Through his efforts, civilian casualties were considerably reduced. Although the Americans may have accepted the killing of some French noncombatants in attacks on individual military and industrial targets of strategic worth, widespread attacks on transportation with vague objectives were not worth the ethical and political costs.[68]

The attitudes of American leaders toward the bombing of urban areas were affected to varying degrees by concerns for ethics, efficiency, and public relations. Perhaps the best summary of a collective AAF approach appears in a letter titled "Suggested Reply to Letter Questioning Humanitarian Aspects of Air Force," composed in response to the letter from a concerned mother to the AAF chief of staff (see Appendix). It is impossible to determine who wrote the reply (it was probably composed by someone on Arnold's staff), but it had traveled from Arnold to Spaatz to Anderson and been reviewed by each man. The letter combined the themes of public relations, ethics, and efficiency stressed by those leaders. It began by emphasizing that air warfare differs from more traditional forms only in its massive potential for destruction. "Law cannot limit what physics makes possible. . . . We can depend for moderation only upon reason and humane instincts when we exercise such a power." It pointed out, however, that "the precision which is the keynote of America" was more efficient than terror bombing and at the same time more humane. By allowing reason and humanity to curb the "bestial instincts" released by "the awful weapon at our disposal," the AAF showed "that humanity pays and that Air Power is the most powerful urge for peace."[69]

None of these leaders professed to be moralists, yet all of them wrestled with the dilemmas resulting from good ends and bad means. They tried to strike a balance between the extreme views that war legitimizes all means or that suffering and death are absolute evils that can never be justified. Most of these men professed to be in favor of limiting "unnecessary" casualties and destruction, but they held different opinions as to what that entailed. And as the distinguished British historian Michael Howard has noted, "Those responsible for the conduct of state affairs see their first duty as being to ensure that their state survives; that it retains its power to protect its members and provide for them the conditions of a good life." When in doubt, leaders tended to do what was best to win the war and protect American citizens, whether those citizens were factory workers or bomber pilots.[70]

4. ATTITUDES AND PERCEPTIONS OF AMERICAN AIRMEN

> War shall yet be, and to the end;
>   But war-paint shows the streaks of weather;
> War yet shall be, but warriors
> Are now but operatives; War's made
>   Less grand than Peace,
> And a singe runs through lace and feather.
> —*Herman Melville*[1]

> The more mechanical become the weapons with which we fight, the less mechanical must be the spirit which controls them.
> —*Maj. Gen. J. F. C. Fuller*[2]

In his influential work *Men against Fire*, S. L. A. Marshall wrote that "war is always an equation of men and machines. Efficiency comes of a proper balancing of the equation." There are limits, however, "to the uses of the machine in war," and ultimately its effectiveness depends on "the efficiency, intelligence, and courage of the relatively few men who must take the final risks of battle."[3] Many observers, though, would agree with Herman Melville that the technology of modern war has reduced the importance of soldierly qualities and produced an impersonal combat with no sense of humanity. One scholar argues that American airmen "were technicians and professionals who happened to be waging war" and that few saw themselves as warriors. They possessed an elite status and image, were most concerned with mastering technique, and "their consuming goal" was completing their quota of missions. Their existence on the ground and in the air "created a curious sense of unreality and alienation" that also contributed to their sense of detachment from both the enemy and the real effects of AAF bombs. Other writers, however, acknowledge the risks airmen accepted and lived with:

"The constant presence of death was bound to affect the way air officers felt about killing people of enemy nations." Accordingly, airmen were fatalistic and hardened to losses, whether their own or the enemy's.[4]

The AAF did get preferential treatment at induction centers, especially earlier in the war, ensuring that their recruits generally scored higher on the Army general-classification test and mechanical-aptitude test than those soldiers sent to other branches. These test results were used along with more evaluations to classify candidates further into categories such as groundcrew or aircrew. Standards for officers' positions such as pilots, bombardiers, and navigators were even more stringent. This process did reinforce a sense of the superiority of the AAF over branches such as the infantry, though the actual quality of air recruits diminished as the war went on because of the large numbers of men required by the expanded AAF. The airmen's perception of their elite status was also shaped by the greater proportion of officers and higher ratings of enlisted men who flew as well as by the recognition from the press and the general public of the courage and contributions of combat flyers.[5]

Yet the basic differences between infantrymen and airmen were environmental, not genetic. Most "grunts" of World War II would not have claimed to be warriors and were most concerned with completing a disagreeable job and going home; moreover, their attitudes about noncombatants were similar to those of the airmen. American servicemen tended to be much harsher with civilians of Axis nationalities than with those citizens of occupied areas, though soldiers and airmen usually found it hard to stomach the sight of any dead civilians. To maintain their sanity, infantrymen often rationalized such casualties by blaming enemy artillery. Aircrews rarely had to view dead or wounded enemy civilians, but many fliers would have agreed with a former World War II bomber pilot, now a Tulane professor, who claims, "I don't believe that I could have faced seeing people killed close up." Airmen who returned from the first great fire raid on Tokyo and who had observed from low-level the carnage they caused "handed in their reports with hands that shook, with shock and horror still reflected in their eyes."[6] Despite such reactions, B-29 crews carried out more incendiary raids, since the airmen were convinced that such attacks were the only way to destroy strategic objectives and end the war quickly.

Although airmen did not face the constant exposure to danger experienced by front-line infantrymen, air combat was particularly intense, especially in Europe. On missions an aircrew was more concerned with survival than with technique; they fought many enemies. Aerial combat has been called "the most frightening warfare of all" because in the "unnatural habitat"

Flak hits could be catastrophic. This unlucky B-17 had its nose shot off just after completing its bomb run on a target near Budapest, Hungary. Accompanying aircraft watched helplessly as it crashed and counted only five parachutes from its ten-man crew.

of the air, one is "marooned aloft in an aluminum capsule" and cannot run or hide. Enemy fighters closed in to attack at speeds of up to ten miles per minute to deliver cannonfire, rockets, or bomblets. On the most widely used B-17, the G model, almost everyone except the pilots also served as machine gunners. In addition to enemy fighters, antiaircraft fire (flak) was a deadly threat; on deep-penetration missions it could last up to four hours.[7] During May and June 1944 almost 8,000 American aircraft were damaged and 300 more destroyed by flak alone. Crewmen who operated in a sitting position usually sat on one protective flak suit and draped another over their lap, "for the ultimate in physical and psychological protection." Not surprisingly, flak was a greater source of aircrew anxiety than enemy fighters, which could be shot down or outmaneuvered.[8] Weather and the elements also had to be endured. At bombing height, temperatures in B-17s and B-24s sometimes reached fifty degrees below zero, and even for airmen wearing heated cloth-ing, severe frostbite claimed many casualties. Oxygen masks could freeze up as well. One bombardier wrote to his parents about his concerns regarding being wounded at high altitudes: "The pressure inside your body is so much greater than outside that you bleed profusely." And crewmen worried about mechanical failures of their aircraft or human failures from fatigue.[9]

These factors affected bombing accuracy, focusing the airmen's attention on the air space around them and not necessarily on the target. Commanders found, however, that the best way to bolster morale when the crew returned to base after the mission was to produce immediate photographic results of their attack to show the worth of the hell they had just been through. Personnel reporting to the Eighth Air Force in spring 1943 were told that B-17 and B-24 aircrews completed only an average of five and one half missions. A study done for Spaatz in early 1944 indicated that of 1,000 airmen assigned to the Eighth Air Force, only 216 could be expected to finish twenty-five missions. This figure may have been optimistic; data from the Office of the Air Surgeon for the European theater during the first half of 1944 revealed that AAF battle-casualty rates for heavy-bomber crews were 712 killed or missing and 175 wounded out of each 1,000 men who served for six months. This 89 percent casualty figure matches the finding of William Fili, a B-24 crewman in Europe, that only 27 out of the 250 men in his July 1943 gunnery class completed their quota of missions. The average airman's prayers consisted of a simple, constant repetition of the words, "Please God, I don't want to die."[10]

Because of the high casualty rate, American airmen in the European theater were critical of missions they believed were wasteful or that entailed risks beyond the perceived worth of the target. Indiscriminate attacks on cities with no clear objectives also violated the precision-bombing doctrine airmen had been taught. They especially criticized the long and dangerous raids on Berlin. Typical complaints in a June 1944 survey were that the city "is not a military target" and that it was bombed mainly for "headlines," and "I don't believe in spite bombing." Almost three-quarters of veteran flyers stated they "occasionally" or "quite often" had gone on missions "not worth the cost."[11] Nor did airmen like humanitarian gestures that raised their risks, such as General Doolittle's April 1945 warning to workers at the Skoda Works in Czechoslovakia of an impending raid in order to reduce civilian casualties. Although depleted defenses offered no resistance to the planes that dropped 500 tons of bombs on the factories, the disgruntled aircrews felt that their leaders had exercised "greater concern for the safety of civilian workers than their own."[12]

Combat conditions were not as severe in the Pacific. Only four of the crewmen on B-29s were gunners, and they fired their weapons by remote control. The rest of the eleven-man crew could concentrate on their own particular technical tasks. For the fire raids in 1945 LeMay even stripped out all the ammunition except that for the tail-guns to allow a heavier bombload. By that time the Japanese Air Force was no longer a threat, and antiaircraft fire over Japan never reached European intensities. Moreover, most of the long flight from bases in the Marianas to Japan, sometimes as long as eight hours one way, was over undefended waters. The B-29 also had a pressurized and heated interior lacking on other bombers, considerably increasing the crew's comfort.

On the other hand, the plane had been rushed into action before it was fully perfected, resulting in many technical problems, especially engine fires. The accident rate for the Very Heavy Bombers was much higher than the AAF average. One pilot mused, "Sometimes we wondered whether the battle was with the Japanese or the B-29." As another result of the rush to get the bombers into combat, too few planes were available for training. Crews often did not get enough time flying the aircraft in the United States before deploying overseas and thus had to finish training on combat missions. An additional problem on the long flights to Japan was fatigue. A mission from initial briefing to final debriefing usually lasted twenty-four hours. Despite the liberal use of coffee and even amphetamines, some aircraft actually crashed because exhausted crews fell asleep. With fewer distractions from enemies and harsh cold and with much longer missions, airmen in the Pacific could have considered themselves as technicians more than as warriors, focusing on the mechanical problems of flying their aircraft and delivering their bombload.[13] Though they witnessed the nightly conflagrations they caused, they might not have sensed what bombing cities really entailed; unlike airmen in England they could not go on pass and observe the results of the Blitz or of V-weapons firsthand or talk to air-raid victims.[14]

Unfortunately, few diaries or memoirs to verify these impressions are left behind by the crews who carried out the fire raids. Many reasons are possible for this scarcity of sources. The incendiary campaign was relatively short, lasting less than five months. In contrast, the American daylight-bombing offensive over Europe lasted almost three years. Possibly the shorter Pacific air campaign, with its more boring missions, did not provide the material or the inspiration for published memoirs, or perhaps B-29 crews were indeed aloof technicians and therefore less likely to express their feelings in writing. Another factor could have been the B-29 itself. Different crews often shared the same aircraft, and few airmen seem to have felt close to an airplane with so many technical problems. The best explanation, however, may be that the crews who carried out the fire raids did not want to remember them or had little pride in the destruction of Japanese cities and the deaths of Japanese civilians their bombs caused. LeMay wrote extensively about his recollections, but he never seemed to be bothered by the results of his campaign. On the other hand, Wilbur H. Morrison, another veteran of the Twentieth Air Force who has written about its experiences, relates that crews often watched the holocausts they had created "in utter horror."[15] The emphasis in LeMay's after-action reports that the object of the incendiary attacks "was not to bomb indiscriminately civilian populations" but to destroy "industrial and strategic targets" might have been intended to ease the troubled consciences of airmen sickened by the stench of death lingering in their planes.[16]

OTHER INFLUENCES ON ATTITUDES
TOWARD BOMBING CIVILIANS

Just as varying factors of combat and technology in each theater could influence airmen's attitudes toward bombing civilians, so too could their individual training and position. Diaries and memoirs from the European air war support the contention that crew members' positions in the air were a primary factor in determining individual attitudes toward what happened when bombs hit the ground. The officers on the bombers in particular—pilots, bombardiers, and navigators—underwent considerably different training.

For example, when as a captain, F. L. Anderson set up the curriculum for his bombardier school, he ensured that students received eleven hours of instruction on military law and the laws of war as well as classes on national policy and current events.[17] Technical training focused on targeting and accuracy; students practiced bombing day and night in order to achieve the average miss distance of 230 feet necessary for graduation. With this training and their responsibilities in combat, bombardiers seem to have been the crew members most concerned about the effects of indiscriminate bombing. One man was able to keep his sanity only by following his chaplain's advice to "keep it impersonal" and not to focus on what happened on the ground. He rationalized that he was doing his best to hit military targets, helping to shorten the war and save lives in the long run. Yet he was still troubled throughout his tour by recurrent thoughts of an incident in which he had almost hit a city amphitheater with an errant bomb. Despite pleas from his nervous pilots, another lead bombardier took his wayward formation over most of Berlin through heavy flak to hit railroad yards when their primary target was obscured instead of dropping his bombload onto a convenient built-up area of the city.[18]

On the other hand, the pilots who commanded the bombers concentrated most on what happened in the air. Fatigue, fear, and concern for their crew could wear pilots down quickly. In Lord Moran's classic study *The Anatomy of Courage*, he found that more pilots broke from mental strain in Bomber Command than in any other section of the RAF.[19] The 1949 movie *Twelve O'Clock High* illustrates how the pressures and responsibilities of command could cause a nervous breakdown in the toughest air officer if he really cared about his men. John Muirhead, a B-17 pilot in the Fifteenth Air Force, saw many of his friends display the gaunt signs of fatigue or become comatose with the "clanks," their term for stress casualties. Muirhead tried to shield himself by ensuring that he did not know his crew or any other airmen. Psychiatric studies found that the loss of friends in aerial combat was the second most important source of stress, (enemy activity was first), and Muirhead reasoned, "If I didn't know them, I would not grieve." Actor Jimmy Stewart, who rose to be a World War II squadron commander, said in an interview that airmen never talked about their odds of survival. "We all prayed a lot, though," he admitted. "I didn't pray for myself. I just prayed I wouldn't make a mistake" that could cost the lives of his crew. He thought about civilians on the ground, but he also remembered the defenseless civilians the Germans had been bombing throughout the war. The memoirs of pilots like Philip Ardery are full of incidents in which pilot errors destroyed aircraft and crews. Haunted by the possibility of error, pilots did not seem concerned so much with the target they were attacking or with where bombs fell as with bringing their plane and crew back in one piece.[20] The best reason to hit a target right the first time, especially the tough ones, was to ensure it would not have to be attacked again.

Copilots shared the pilots' burdens. Locked into uncomfortable postures on long flights, they suffered physical and mental stress along with the pilots. Other crewmen could move around, but the pilot and copilot had to stay at the controls. They often had to switch positions during flight, especially while maneuvering into tight formations where the effects of vertigo could quickly interfere with the ability to coordinate controls properly.[21] Copilots lacked the overall command duties of pilots, but they felt responsible for their aircraft and could be especially frustrated if forced just to ride along while everyone else kept busy. Perhaps the best account of a copilot is found in *Serenade to the Big Bird* by Bert Stiles, who was killed in 1944 after transferring to fighters when he had completed thirty-five bomber missions in Europe. After his first bombing mission, he could think only about how fatigued he was, how lousy his flying had been, and how close he was to his crew, concerns that dominate his writings. Once he did muse about the "senseless ugliness" of

Squadron Cmdr. Jimmy Stewart after receiving the French Croix de Guerre with Palm. Typical of pilots and leaders, Stewart worried about making a mistake that could harm the airmen under his command. (Northwest and Whitman College Archival Collections, Penrose Memorial Library, Whitman College, Walla Walla, Wash.)

bombing Berlin through overcast, questioning why the AAF wanted "to knock hell out of some city with the vague hope that some day that city will be rebuilt for some people we can get along with," but in general he seemed not to care about specific targets. After the D-Day landings, his primary focus was to win the war "and win in a way so there is never another one."[22]

The most self-centered and individualistic aircrew officers seem to have been navigators. They plotted courses and kept a log of events; someone else flew the plane and dropped the bombs. The memoirs of Elmer Bendiner, a navigator on the Schweinfurt raids, differ from the accounts of pilots or bombardiers and resemble the image of the technician in combat. Bendiner writes less about the rest of the crew and more about his own experiences, noting that while planes fell all around him in combat he remained detached, "scribbling in the log the time, place and altitude of flak, of rocket bursts, of kills and fallen comrades, of headings and checkpoints." Surviving to complete "the magic number of twenty-five" missions was his primary goal. More cynical than most airmen, he believed that precision bombing was a "semifiction," but he also believed that any terror was permissible in response to German terror and that the Allies' just cause set them apart from the Axis, no matter what tactics were used. He surmised that Eighth Air Force crews would have attacked cities as did the British if trusted AAF leaders had said that in their judgment this was the best way to win the war and to get home safely. Yet like most of his comrades, he preferred "a surgical technique by which we could excise the vital organs of Nazi Germany without unnecessary bloodshed."[23]

Except for Stiles, however, in writing about their experiences these other airmen had the benefit of considerable hindsight in their judgments. A good example of a navigator's attitudes untainted by editing or rethinking can be found in the letters of Earle C. Cheek. He wrote to his girlfriend about every two weeks from March 1944 until his death near the end of the war, and his descriptions uniquely portray the European air war through a navigator's eyes. He constantly mentioned crews dying in crashes, even in training, and his consuming goal was to complete his quota of missions quickly and safely. He even arranged a transfer from the Fifteenth Air Force in the Mediterranean to the Eighth because it lowered his required missions from fifty to thirty. He showed little loyalty to any crew and was continually switching planes to get in more missions. For his thirtieth mission in April 1945, he hooked on as an extra navigator on a plane dropping supplies to British paratroops. He was killed when it was downed by ground fire.[24]

Cheek was a "technician and professional" more than he was a warrior. Trained on new radar navigational gear, he was extremely confident in its ability to see through overcast, and he eventually became a Pathfinder navigator leading missions. His letters rarely discuss the results of bombing, though "the high point of my combat tour" came when he led "the greatest raid of the war" on Berlin. When he did mention the effects of his work he emphasized precision bombing of factories, oil, and transportation. He wrote in March 1944 that "the only men who can be said to be fighting this war are the men who constantly face death," infantrymen in the front lines and "airmen flying combat missions." He changed his views, however, after meeting some infantrymen from Patton's Third Army, who had "nothing to look forward to except one action after another and living in the mud and cold. . . . They make me ashamed of any complaining I've done." Such admiration for ground troops was common among airmen. Cheek said of enemy flak and fighter attacks, "There isn't a thing you can do about it except fly through it at 30 degrees below zero with the sweat running off your face and freezing on your clothes and the exploding shells blowing the ship around like a cork in a stormy sea." Only once did he mention bombing civilians, after he had viewed bomb damage in London: "I suppose that in modern war civilians must suffer." But he rationalized what he was doing to Germany: "Civilians in countries under German occupation have endured much more than the English, of course."[25]

American doctors conducting psychiatric studies of World War II airmen found that bomber pilots, concentrating on safety and on accomplishing their missions, bore an especially heavy burden of responsibility. Researchers were surprised to find that, contrary to the image of unfeeling technicians indiscriminately dropping high explosives, heavy-bomber crews could not "tolerate well the guilt of killing" even though victims were "remote, almost abstract." Although fighter pilots who strafed ground targets were seldom affected by concerns for the casualties they caused, studies discovered that "many a bombardier tosses in his bunk at night to think what his bombs may have done to the civilians miles below his plane." The increased stress on bomber crews was alleviated somewhat by the "banding together" of combat crews and their reliance on each other, almost like the closeness of a family. The pilot was seen as a father figure and other crewmen as brothers, a feeling of camaraderie and teamwork that usually took between five and ten missions to develop. This process was especially evident in the Eighth Air Force, where command policies encouraged the consistent use of standard crews.

The Fifteenth Air Force had different practices and often seemed to expect airmen to perform like interchangeable parts as they were shifted between planes. The rationale for such actions seems to have been to lessen the effects on morale of death and wounds in close crews, but the result was to increase the number of psychoneurotic casualties from stress. Flyers in the Fifteenth retained the peculiar burdens and attitudes of their positions on the crew without being able to rely on the strong bonds of comradeship existing among the members of a well-established combat team. Many Eighth Air Force airmen identified so much with their crew that they suffered more fear and tension "when they are on the ground and their crew is flying without them on a combat mission than when they are flying."[26]

Although more study of the attitudes of aircrews is warranted, my research indicates that navigators cared most about technique and finishing their mission quota, pilots about bringing their crews home safely, and bombardiers about accurate bombing. Like the American public, airmen in Europe probably would have tolerated bombing cities indiscriminately if they had thought it was necessary, but they believed in the precision doctrine that so many had died to prove. Some units even instituted lecture programs to reinforce the commitment to AAF doctrine.[27] If the leaders in Europe and in the Pacific had been more alike and if conditions in the two theaters had been similar, there would have been American fire raids on Germany. But such similarities did not exist, and those intentionally indiscriminate attacks on enemy civilians did not occur.

One difference in attitude between the two theaters, however, disturbed American leaders: the feelings of AAF airmen about the enemy. Bombardment crews in Europe did not seem to hate the Germans enough; reports in FDR's files complained that U.S. flyers had "no particular hatred of Germans." Surveys showed that almost three-quarters of heavy-bomber crews harbored no vindictiveness toward the German people and wanted only to punish their leaders. This feeling matched the attitude Stimson had complimented in Marshall. A commander wrote in an after-action report, "Like every American who flies to Europe for combat duty, I regretted my failure to get the desired crack at the Jap. I failed to possess any real enmity toward Jerry and sensed a certain repulsion to European bombings where non-combatant Axis life might be involved." He claimed that he soon learned to hate the Hun, but others did not. Stiles wrote that he felt fighters and flak were just "shooting at whole formations. There's nothing personal in it."[28] Psychological studies of the Eighth Air Force during its first year of operation revealed that only 29 percent of successful combat airmen had any personal hatred for the enemy, including the desire to kill enemy fighter pilots and even then "not always, but at least when they are in the air!"[29]

It was much easier to hate the enemy in the Pacific theater. Racism played a part as did the sneak attack on Pearl Harbor and reports of Japanese atrocities. Perhaps hatred would have been more intense in Europe if more had been known about the concentration camps. When briefed on the Malmedy Massacre, FDR said, "Well, it will only serve to make our troops feel towards the Germans as they already have learned to feel about the Japs." Airmen, however, again reflected the attitudes of society. Public hatred was directed at Hitler and Mussolini rather than at their subjects, but it was aimed against the Japanese people as well as the emperor. Ground troops echoed public opinion, too; officers and enlisted men in all theaters expressed considerably more vindictiveness toward Japanese citizens. AAF feelings toward the Germans were more a product of the home front than a result of the aloofness of technicians. And such attitudes were reinforced by respect for enemy soldiers who seemed to be fighting hard but cleanly and who treated AAF prisoners of war rather well in accordance with the Geneva and Hague conventions.[30]

LEADERS' PERCEPTIONS OF AIRMEN

AAF leaders realized that the attitudes of their airmen reflected those of society, but they perceived the public as abhorrent to any indiscriminate bombardment and supportive of precision doctrine. As with AAF press releases, official AAF publications proclaimed a commitment to precision bombing and also demonstrated its effectiveness. Probably the best source to illustrate the perceptions of their soldiers that AAF leaders in Washington held and to cover the course of the airman's war from combat photography is *Impact* magazine. Assistant Secretary of War Lovett saw the publication as a way to keep units informed of current developments, and General Arnold endorsed it as a means to spread "knowledge of the technique and accomplishments of your fellow members of the AAF" and to provide "information of the enemies you are fighting." Arnold thought that photographs were the easiest form of information to absorb, hence his emphasis on combat photography for newsreels and for filling 90 percent of *Impact*. With the assistance of Henry Luce, Lovett found some veteran *Life* editors to run the classified magazine, which was dis-

tributed by the assistant chief of air staff for intelligence to intelligence officers at AAF units around the world.[31]

Impact highlighted the effectiveness of precision-bombing doctrine; the
text reflected Arnold's views by emphasizing efficiency and public relations,
not ethics. "Expensive planes and highly skilled personnel" had to be used to
attack the enemy's ability to wage war directly instead of being dissipated
against area targets such as residential districts, "which are relatively un-
important from a military standpoint." An article touting the accuracy of
Doolittle's bombing of Rome displayed the maps designating religious centers
to be avoided, boasting, "It was a test of what our bombers could miss as well
as what they could hit because of the crocodile tears Axis propagandists
would be sure to shed if we had hit any religious edifice." Another article
showed the military targets hit by the Doolittle Raid on Tokyo to justify the
"universal rage" over the execution of airmen captured on that mission. The
avoidance of outright ethical statements might have been the result of the
AAF's desire not to appear critical of the RAF. When British area bombing of
cities was discussed, *Impact* emphasized that they "didn't invent [it,] nor did
they start it. But it certainly taught the boys who did start it that they never
belonged in the big leagues." By the end of the war, the magazine claimed
that with British improvements in training, equipment, and tactics, the RAF
night-bombing technique had become so accurate that it "no longer could
correctly be called area bombing."[32]

From the editorial themes emphasized in *Impact*, one can deduce which
beliefs and practices AAF leaders in Washington had decided needed reinforcement in the field. Americans have traditionally favored a strategy of
annihilation and direct assault over indirect or partial approaches, and airmen seemed distrustful of any tactic that detracted from visually observed
precision attacks on important military targets. The accuracy of radar-directed attacks through overcast was often touted with magazine captions such
as "Radar Performed Miracles." The use of leaflets instead of bombs was explained at great length in articles supporting "psychological bombing." One
article boasted that 77 percent of German prisoners captured in France "either carried leaflets in their pockets or had used them to surrender"; (some
units also used their lecture program to justify such tactics). Raids involving
religious shrines were carefully explained as well. Besides the famous bombing
of Rome, a raid on Florence was used to illustrate "the effort that is made to
avoid hitting structures of historical or cultural interest." When the Mediterranean Allied Air Forces (MAAF) "yielded to the military necessity of bombing German troops from the famous Abbey at Monte Cassino," an article

justified the action by explaining in detail that exploding ammunition and fleeing Germans demonstrated "that this was indeed a military installation."[33]

Impact mounted an especially intensive campaign to explain and support the fire raids on Japan. Coverage of the first such attack, on Tokyo the night of 9 March, was preceded by eighteen pages of articles describing Japan's economy and society, emphasizing that weather limited precision bombing and that concentrated industries and workers were more vulnerable to saturation raids. The proliferation of home industries, "small, feudal-type" family workshops creating "sub-contracting area complexes," necessitated area bombing to reinforce precision attacks by "interrupting the flow of components into final assembly." A common theme was that the fire raids were "destroying Japan's big industrial areas." Later issues of the magazine added that the low-level night raids were also safer for B-29 crews. When burned-out areas were shown, the destruction of individual factories was emphasized. One article pointed out 111 "small and medium-sized plants" ruined in one small area of Tokyo. In the summary of the campaign, *Impact* acknowledged that the objectives of incendiary attacks "were basically the same as those of British area bombing" but they were necessary to save lives and end the war. The fire raids were also legitimized as consistent with American practice and as increasing the effectiveness of precision attacks. Airmen were reminded that area bombing and precision bombing were both types of strategic bombing and were told, "Against Germany, the American doctrine was pinpoint precision bombing against key factories in key target areas. Against Japan, the American doctrine is the same plus the complementary incendiary program." Significantly, although the fire raids dominated actual B-29 operations during the last months of the war, precision attacks on Japan continued to receive equal coverage in the pages of *Impact*.[34]

The editors of *Impact* and the military bosses who approved their work obviously had an image of American airmen consistent with their view of the American public. Airmen were seen to support the precision doctrine taught in service schools and emphasized in unit lectures. Area bombing that did not concentrate on important targets and methods to bomb through overcast or at night when targets could not be clearly seen were suspect. Additionally, AAF leaders perceived that airmen would not tolerate the indiscriminate bombardment of civilians or the destruction of targets with historical or religious significance, hence the lengthy explanations about Tokyo and Cassino and even the justification and defense of RAF area bombing.

The view from Washington was partially correct. Airmen in general did believe in and support precision doctrine, and diversions from that accepted approach were suspect. General Doolittle confirmed that the morale of his personnel was adversely affected "by having to do a lot of things that they feel are not basically sound," such as using strategic bombers to attack tactical targets or bombing through overcast.[35] However, though many airmen had misgivings about bombing civilians and shrines, protecting their crews and winning the war were also important. When Doolittle said he would excuse any of his Catholic airmen from the mission to Rome who could not in good conscience bomb their Holy City, not one accepted his offer. Peer pressure, as well as confidence in the accuracy of precision bombing, was undoubtedly a factor, but the majority of those airmen concerned probably believed that their duty to their crews and the desire to gain the quickest possible victory outweighed any considerations of accidental damage to religious buildings.[36] Most Americans were not as callous as the officer who wrote after Cassino, "If the enemy intends to use Italian cities as fortresses, we should feel no qualms in using our Air Force to level them thereby saving countless lives."[37] Most airmen did feel qualms at one time or another, but they were convinced that their actions were the best means for winning the war and saving American lives, on the ground and in the air. And they believed that their bombing methods were the most efficient, and humane, possible.

5. THE LURE OF TECHNOLOGICAL INNOVATION—BOMBING AIDS

We are becoming increasingly aware of our inability to achieve accurate bombing on some of our top priority targets. Leuna and Politz are two examples. When the weather is good, these are covered by a smoke screen which effectively obscures the target for visual bombing. . . . Our air war is becoming a radar war.

—*Lt. Gen. Carl Spaatz*[1]

Even during World War I, technology was perceived as the solution to the stalemate of trench warfare. Poison gas, heavy artillery, and tanks were developed and used in attempts to restore maneuver to the battlefield and bring victory. The airplane, too, was seen as a means to avoid such costly land warfare; thus, between the wars tactics and doctrine were developed to match the promise of aerial technology. It became apparent early in combat, however, that the tactics and technology of American precision bombing would need further refinement to realize its full potential.

Many critics of precision bombing have argued that it was too inaccurate to merit that title. Even Lieutenant General Spaatz agreed privately in 1944 that USSTAF precision had meaning "in a relative not a literal sense"; but that did not stop him from striving for the continuing development of bombs and bombsights and the training of bombardiers to achieve "pickle barrel" accuracy in all weather. General Arnold pushed his commanders by telling them, "Efficiency in winning the war is our goal, and, in bombing, efficiency and precision are synonymous." AAF equipment was capable of "precision beyond the fondest dreams of a few years ago," but this potential could not be realized without "tactics and techniques to match the equipment." The result of this combination would be increased accuracy, meaning more bombs on target, "one mission per vital target instead of two or three," and an "actual saving in lives and effort."[2]

Early in the war, improvements in bombing accuracy were mainly the result of improved tactics and techniques, not of technological innovation. American airmen had confidence in their equipment, especially their Norden bombsights, estimated to be six to eight times more accurate than the "simpler, less precise" Mark XIV bombsights used by the RAF. Only about 5 percent of the British bombs landed within a mile of their aiming point under combat conditions early in the war, but the cocky Americans expected 90 percent to get that close and 40 percent within 500 yards.[3] They had much work to do to refine their bombing methods, however. During the first half of 1943, the Eighth Air Force put only 14 percent of their bombs within 1,000 feet of their targets. Poor visibility, fighter attacks, inexperience, poor training, flak, and camouflage led to errant attacks. The rapid increase in the number of American airmen in Britain made training aircrews and maintaining their proficiency especially difficult. Sometimes bad luck contributed: The lead bombardier might be shot down or his bombsight could malfunction. Other problems resulted from the inherent difficulty of handling large bombing formations, as following groups always bombed with less accuracy than leading groups. Varying ballistics of incendiary and high-explosive bombs also caused errors. But by 1945 diligence, experience, refined tactics, and innovative techniques eventually brought accuracy up to 44 percent of all bombs falling within 1,000 feet of the target and 73 percent within 2,000 feet.[4]

These results were even better than predictions early in the war and probably represented as much accuracy as could be expected from well-executed formation-bombing techniques with unguided bombs under combat conditions. Normally the twelve to eighteen planes of a group dropped their bombs simultaneously, on the signal of the lead bombardier, a tactic with many advantages. The best group bombardiers could aim for everyone; the mass bombing operation would be carried out more rapidly than individual drops, lessening exposure to flak, and the groups could retain a tight defensive formation. The bomb impacts would be as dispersed as the formation, but commanders believed that a well-disciplined group could produce a tighter bomb pattern to smother any target more efficiently than several aircraft could, bombing on their own. Sometimes to ensure hitting a target, aircrews would use an intervalometer setting of 400 feet for a normal bombload of twelve 500-pound bombs; thus bombs were released to impact 400 feet apart on the ground, producing a string of explosions 4,400 feet long for each plane. This technique offered more chances for hitting an obscured target or for inflicting greater damage to a large objective such as a marshaling yard, but it also could result in widely scattered misses. At the other extreme, some groups routinely

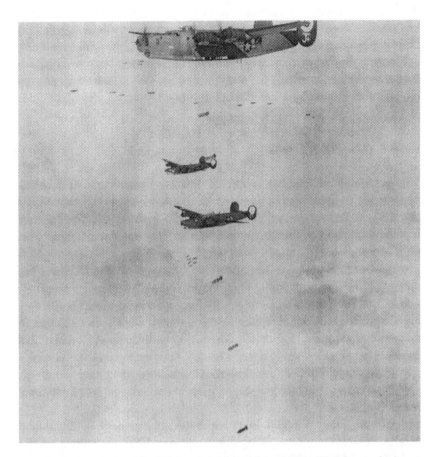

B-24s bombing Frankfurt through flak and clouds in February 1944. The plane in the fore-ground has dropped its bombs with a moderate intervalometer setting, while the tight bomb pattern in the center of the picture shows no spread at all.

achieved phenomenal results. Perhaps the best performance was by an eleven-plane squadron bombing submarine pens in Wilhelmshaven that used a combination of radar and visual sightings to put 90 percent of its bombs within a 50-foot radius of the aiming point and the rest within 150 feet. Commanders really did not expect such tight bomb patterns, but the significant improvements in bombing accuracy achieved by the AAF in Europe through training and experience between 1943 and 1945 reinforced the faith that airmen had in precision-bombing capabilities.[5]

Yet General Arnold warned his commanders not to "complacently tell ourselves that our methods and efforts have begun to reach a peak of perfection beyond which we cannot go." Jealous of the impressive tonnage dropped on Germany by Bomber Command, he began very early to push his commanders in Europe to find ways to increase their number of missions. Considering the European weather, especially in fall and winter, an increase meant that methods had to be devised to bomb through overcast.[6]

RADAR AIDS TO BOMBING

The problem of overcast was countered primarily by using various forms of radar, either to guide aircraft to targets or to allow bombardiers to see their objectives through the cloud cover. Most of the devices were developed by the British to assist in their night area attacks. Navigational aids came first. GEE appeared in 1941, a system by which a navigator could determine his position by calculating the time it took to receive pulse signals from three different ground stations in Britain. German jamming negated its usefulness by late 1942, and it was replaced by OBOE, a radar pulse sounding like that musical instrument. Variations from course caused recognizable changes in the pulse; a second signal then told the bombardier when to release his bombs. These systems were limited in range, however, because of the curvature of the earth.[7] For deep-penetration missions, the Americans had to rely on radar scanners that could be carried in their aircraft to present a picture of the ground below.

Spaatz and Maj. Gen. Ira Eaker had begun experiments to circumvent overcast conditions in late 1942 but became frustrated by limitations in GEE and OBOE. By March 1943 the Eighth Air Force had turned to H2S, "a self-contained radar device transmitting a beam which scanned the ground below and provided a map-like picture of the terrain on its cathode ray tube indicator." Eaker boasted to the JCS that with these new devices the notorious English weather "would actually become an aid rather than a hindrance" because it would enable Allied bombers to exploit conditions that severely hampered enemy defenses. Much of this enthusiasm was fueled by optimistic reports on H2S from military attachés in London. American versions of this device were called H2X; by fall 1943, enough were available to mount the first major raids to test the radar's effectiveness. Ronald Schaffer has inaccurately called the use of these nonvisual bombing methods "tantamount to urban area attacks," but USSTAF planners did recognize that these techniques involved some compromise with precision tactics. Targets had to be carefully selected. At first, leaders picked objectives in city areas on coastlines or estuaries because of the verifiable distinction between water and land on radar screens. This technique allowed a large increase in raids during the testing period in late 1943 and early 1944 and thereby relieved much of the intense pressure Arnold applied for maximum bombing.[8]

The first H2X mission on Wilhelmshaven in October 1943 proved a resounding success, and in December the Eighth Air Force announced in a press release the "development of a new day bombardment technique employing latest scientific devices enabling bombing through solid cloud cover. . . . While accuracy is not equal to that usually attained in high altitude attacks when the target can be seen, . . . accuracy is satisfactory and gives promise of improvement. . . . The new technique is regarded as a logical outgrowth of American bombardment doctrine made possible by scientific advances and does not involve any basic change in the American conception of bombardment."[9] Presumably, a public that seldom questioned such military pronouncements accepted this position, but the release also seemed to be an accurate representation of Eighth Air Force beliefs.

Arnold, however, was not initially convinced of the effectiveness of such techniques. His staff advised him that radar bombing had not been tested thoroughly and that much training and experimentation were still needed. Ever mindful of the AAF image, Arnold particularly feared that the term "blind-bombing" then in use would create the wrong impression and directed the Eighth Air Force to drop that phrase. Press censors in Europe had already begun stopping any news items implying deviations from precision bombing, ostensibly to keep the Germans from finding out that the Allies had new bombing equipment. When Brig. Gen. Curtis LeMay, who had led the pioneering raids, came to the United States on a public-relations tour, he was prohibited from even mentioning overcast bombing.[10]

Eaker, then commanding the Eighth Air Force, was especially enthusiastic about the nonvisual attacks. Never as committed to the idea of precision-bombing doctrine as Spaatz, he saw great possibilities for H2X and worked hard to persuade Arnold of the rightness of his views. Coast ports were easy to recognize, and destroying them through overcast would lower enemy morale and force the Luftwaffe out to defend them. He justified his assaults on lower-priority targets: "The material destruction by these overcast attacks in workmen's homes and in harbor facilities and allied war industries is considerable and is certainly alone worth the effort." At this point in the development of radar bombing tactics and procedures, Eaker was willing to compromise precision targeting in order to keep pressure on the enemy, but through "experiment and test and trial," he was confident that eventually small point targets would also be attacked successfully using radar techniques. In correspondence to both Arnold and Lovett Eaker emphasized the increased number of raids resulting from the ability to bomb nonvisually. This last argument in particular eventually swayed Arnold to wholehearted support of the continued development and use of such methods.[11]

The first nonvisual missions on recognizable docks and shipyards in coastal cities such as Wilhelmshaven and Kiel encouraged the believers in radar bombing and converted the doubters, but the early successes turned out to be beginner's luck. They "gave an unfounded hope of potential accuracy; and it may therefore have contributed to an unfortunate tendency to treat H2X as a rival of visual bombing rather than a supplement to it." The successes may also have helped to make the Eighth Air Force complacent about the increased rate of operations that the new equipment made possible through the winter. But by early 1944 it was evident that new training and equipment would be necessary to achieve acceptable accuracy.[12]

DEVELOPMENTS CONTINUE

In late December 1943 Spaatz returned to Britain from the Mediterranean. A disappointed Eaker, replaced by Maj. Gen. James Doolittle, was reassigned from his beloved Eighth Air Force to command all air forces in the Mediterranean, including the strategic bombers of the American Fifteenth Air Force. Along with policies concerning the bombing of civilians in occupied countries, Spaatz inherited Eaker's and Arnold's commitment and program to pursue nonvisual bombing. Initially Spaatz was enthusiastic about the performance of H2X Pathfinder aircraft in leading bombing missions, calling them "the most critical need of the Strategic Air Forces." In January he successfully defeated attempts by the Combined Chiefs of Staff to force him to cut back on radar attacks before OVERLORD, arguing that it would be "wasteful" not to use radar methods if cloud cover prevented visual bombing. He admitted in a March press conference that radar attacks were primarily made on "area objectives" but stressed that they had "resulted in considerable pressure on the German Air Force, combined with the destruction of a number of his vital factories."[13] For USSTAF, area objectives meant concentrations of factories, shipyards, or marshaling yards, not residential zones hit in RAF raids. Unlike Eaker, Spaatz did not consider workers' houses suitable targets. Yet the use of less accurate nonvisual bombing techniques in urban areas resulted in an increase in the risk to civilians in targeted cities.

Beginning in 1944, Lt. Gen. Carl Spaatz and Maj. Gen. James Doolittle often pleaded with Gen. H. H. Arnold for better radar equipment to replace their H2X sets, but the priority for the improved APQ-7 Eagle radar remained with the B-29s in the Pacific. Here radar operator Sgt. W. C. Yoder of the XX Bomber Command searches for targets on his Eagle scope over Omura, Japan, on 21 November 1944.

By April Spaatz's enthusiasm for current radar technology and tactics had begun to wane. He complained to Arnold that "the inherent accuracy and presentation of H2X equipment is not satisfactory enough for precision bombing of high priority strategic targets." Sparked by complaints from Doolittle that the radar pictures needed more detail, Spaatz asked for new radar equipment; Doolittle and Spaatz would continue such pleas until the end of the war. The new Eighth Air Force commander had little faith in radar bombing and waited for good weather instead of using nonvisual methods during his "Big Week" attacks in February that greatly helped to break the back of the Luftwaffe.[14]

After six months of nonvisual raids, problems were apparent with both personnel and equipment. Daily USSTAF intelligence summaries reveal that the results of most nonvisual raids remained unobserved; the same poor weather that limited accuracy and visibility also limited damage assessment. When results were readily available, they were sometimes embarrassing. On 1 April

1944 the Second Bombardment Division mistakenly bombed Schaffhausen, Switzerland, in "particularly unfavorable" weather conditions. An investigation revealed that "the advent of GEE and H2X had caused a let-down in the standard of dead-reckoning navigation because of a misconception that these aids to navigation constituted in themselves a means of navigation." After completing his training course on these radar aids, navigator Earle Cheek wrote, "There is very little error with this equipment and it makes no difference to the navigator whether the ground is visible or not." The Schaffhausen incident proved that judgment wrong. Classes were instituted throughout the Eighth Air Force to highlight each crew member's specific tasks with radar and to prevent any more decline in visual bombing skills.[15]

Meanwhile, coverage of radar bombing in *Impact* emphasized that the new methods allowed the Eighth Bomber Command to drop a record tonnage of bombs in November 1943, ordinarily a month of bad weather and few missions, and showed pictures of damage to Wilhelmshaven. Articles pointed out to airmen that the cloud cover also improved the crew's safety by providing protection from flak and fighters. The *Official Guide to the Army Air Forces*, printed for the public in spring 1944, proclaimed, "Accurate high level bombing has been accomplished through more than 25,000 feet of overcast."[16] Apparently, Eaker's early enthusiasm and bomb-tonnage figures had convinced the Air Staff in Washington of the usefulness of bombing through overcast. Although Spaatz and Doolittle did not share this optimism about the strategic effectiveness of nonvisual methods, the coming of OVERLORD focused their attention on tactical applications for the new technology. Placed under the direction of General Eisenhower for the Normandy campaign, the airmen now had to consider ways to support the ground troops and the land campaign directly with heavy bombers in addition to the usual lighter tactical aircraft.

The lessons learned in trying to perfect nonvisual bombing for strategic bombers paid dividends in tactical applications and in support of the invasion. Using H2X on D-Day, 1,365 Eighth Air Force bombers dropped 2,798 tons of bombs nonvisually behind the beaches thirty minutes before the landing, with more raids during the day. Concerns for safety meant that many bombs fell up to three miles inland, but the air bombardment did help the assault on UTAH Beach especially and caused no friendly casualties. Effects on the morale of German troops were significant.[17] Ground forces were disappointed with the results of the bombing since a deliberate delay of several seconds in releasing bombs, ordered by Doolittle to prevent damage to assault craft, also meant that beach defenses were spared. Only later was it apparent that the heavy bombing had destroyed important mine fields and rocket pits and that the damage caused behind the beaches had severely restricted the movement of reinforcements.[18]

With the troops ashore, radar bombing tactics, techniques, and procedures initially developed for the strategic air campaign soon became essential to support the ground drive across Europe. The Ninth Air Force, concerned with tactical missions, pioneered numerous advances in the use of radar to guide in air strikes, eventually using Microwave Early Warning Stations (MEWS) and SCR-584 control radars at Forward Director Posts to lead planes to their targets. These techniques, combined with GEE and SHO-RAN, the latter a new directional guidance system from ground stations, enabled light and medium bombers to provide ground support even in winter weather. Because of developments in radar and tactical improvements, Ninth Air Force planes operated in support of the advancing armies for 139 days between 1 October 1944 and 9 May 1945. Accuracy increased, and friendly casualties from bombs dropped short of targets were lessened. Tactical instrument bombing, based on many of the lessons of strategic attacks, allowed increased and sustained air support for the successful Allied ground campaign.[19]

The crews of the heavy bombers, however, did not like hitting tactical targets. The men were not suited to such a role, having had training in organization, tactics, techniques, and procedures that differed from that of the light- or medium-bomber units. The heavy crews did not like bombing through overcast, either. General Doolittle claimed that his airmen considered those missions "not basically sound." They wanted to get back to bombing Germany, visually observing their bombs destroying key military and industrial targets and thus shortening the war.[20] By fall 1944 the heavy bombers were released from Eisenhower's direct control and had more freedom to hit strategic objectives. But because of typical German fall and winter weather, nonvisual bombing remained an essential part of the USSTAF air campaign.

Spaatz relied heavily on a team of advisers on radar bombing methods sent out by Arnold to prepare for the coming air campaign. He asked for advice on the use of new beacon systems arriving in October 1944 and received details on advances in nonvisual aids used by B-29s. He pushed Doolittle to use "originality and initiative" in order "to take advantage of the fleeting opportunities for bombing during the winter season." With the German Air Force broken and Allied armies advancing, Spaatz wrote, "We cannot allow the advantages gained by the very successful operations during the past summer to slip out of our hands during the winter season."[21] Much of the impetus for increased radar bombing at this time came from Gen. George C. Marshall, who visited the

European theater in October 1944 to formulate plans to bring about the defeat of Germany by 1 January 1945. The chief of staff was not satisfied that the air effort was exerting full pressure in the right places, and he therefore suggested that USSTAF abandon its long-range objectives in favor of an all-out effort to force an early surrender. As a result of this prodding, Doolittle, who had a strict policy prohibiting secondary or last-resort attacks on German towns or cities without identifiable military objectives, modified it to allow secondary overcast-bombing attacks on "towns and cities large enough to produce an identifiable return on the H2X scope" since they generally contained appropriate military targets. This move was a departure from USSTAF's record on avoiding indiscriminate bombardment. Spaatz and Doolittle were not pleased with their options, but they agreed that pressure had to be maintained on Germany through winter weather and wanted to comply with Marshall's intent to end the war as soon as possible.[22] During this period, the USSTAF staff was also working on other operations to end the war with a blow from the air that involved yet more compromise of precision doctrine. These plans will be discussed later.

RESULTS OF RADAR BOMBING

Approximately 80 percent of Eighth Air Force missions during the last quarter of 1944 used some type of radar bombing devices, either for navigation or targeting. Although winter raids did prevent sectors of German industry and the Luftwaffe from getting any respite, accuracy was disappointing. Analysts estimated that about 50 percent of blind missions were "near failures or worse." The Eighth Air Force Operations Analysis Section estimated that bombing under good visual conditions was 6 times more accurate than with GEE or with a beacon combination with H2X called Micro-H and 150 times more accurate than with H2X through complete overcast. Poor results stemmed from false returns from cloud static, increased crew fatigue from adverse weather conditions, and the difficulty of briefing radar missions.[23] The USSTAF staff was also concerned with the difficulty of getting any poststrike photo reconnaissance of targets after attacks since cameras, unlike radar, could not see through overcast; without good pictures, the value of attacks could not be assessed. Maj. Gen. F. L. Anderson proposed using smaller formations or single aircraft, but there were too few trained crews and radar sets for that. Moreover, Doolittle complained that the bad-weather operations were producing more accidents and safety hazards. In December 1944 Spaatz again pleaded with Arnold for new and better radars, whatever the cost: "We are . . . willing to pay the high price of introduction of new and complicated apparatus because the return is proportionately high."[24]

Perhaps the Eighth Air Force's poor record was to some degree a self-ful-filling prophecy. Strategic Mediterranean Allied Air Forces bombers under Eaker, an enthusiastic supporter of nonvisual bombing from the beginning, performed more successfully during this same period under similar weather conditions. For the last three months of 1944 the percentage of Eighth Air Force bombs falling within 1,000 feet of the target was 38, 25, and 25; for the same months the Fifteenth Air Force in the Mediterranean achieved a percentage of 40, 36, and 36. The latter continued with a better record throughout the war. The Eighth Air Force tried to equip two bombers in every group as H2X Pathfinders to lead blind missions; the Fifteenth assigned four each to half its groups. These specially equipped groups carried out deep attacks on Germany and flew overcast missions, and the remaining groups bombed visually closer to Italian bases, specialization that seemed to pay off in greater accuracy. Eaker also sustained pressure on the enemy with Lone-Wolf raids by single bombers or small groups (as Anderson had proposed) and was especially successful with attacks on oil refineries. His surprise attacks, often at night and in bad weather, "hit the refineries when they are working and more vulnerable."[25]

Eaker proclaimed his successes to USSTAF and Washington, whose attitudes he thought were too "gloomy" about radar bombing. He pointed out that during ten days of bad weather, Lt. Gen. Nathan Twining's Fifteenth Air Force had shut down all synthetic oil refineries within its range. He admitted that his Pathfinder techniques were not as accurate as visual bombing; "However, enemy smoke screens are becoming increasingly effective making blind bombing attacks mandatory even in good weather." Such concealment was especially effective on a target such as an oil refinery or an important factory. Eaker gave the credit for his success to "an emphasis on training that it does not appear has been duplicated elsewhere." His commanders at all levels were "absolutely enthusiastic about this technique and their ability to do a worth-while job employing it." Neither this training nor this faith in nonvisual techniques seemed to exist in the Eighth Air Force, with the possible exception of Curtis LeMay's Third Bombardment Division.[26]

The Army also apparently had faith in nonvisual bombing, perhaps because of Ninth Air Force successes. The ground forces also remembered the contributions of heavy bombers to the breakout from Normandy during Operation COBRA. Though Spaatz was no longer under Eisenhower's direct control, the airman preferred working with Ike to the British, and there were abundant air assets available to support Supreme Headquarters, Allied Expeditionary Forces (SHAEF), when called upon. Arnold also wanted to stay friendly with the ground forces so that he could count on their support in his drive for an independent service. Airmen sometimes had to restrain soldiers from calling for blind attacks on impossible targets, such as the time when Gen. Jacob Devers demanded that Brissac and its bridge be heavily bombed, "blind or otherwise." Spaatz's deputy chief of staff had to go to the deputy supreme commander to keep the target's priority for visual bombing only. Usually, however, USSTAF supported ground demands, and Doolittle complained to Washington that he "desired better aids from radar for bombing thru the overcast at front lines. At present we are killing too many of our own men."[27]

The correspondence to Washington had some effect. Spaatz was sent a few new APQ-7 Eagle radars, but priority remained with air units assigned to bomb Japan. Lt. Gen. Barney Giles, Arnold's deputy commander and chief of air staff, cautioned Spaatz, however, that new radars probably would not solve his problems. The Air Staff knew that the Fifteenth Air Force was performing much better than the Eighth, and Giles told Spaatz to look internally for "the cause of the large errors in your present H2X bombing." To assist in lowering the risk to ground troops in bombing near their lines, Giles suggested that Spaatz look at SHORAN, another line-of-sight beaconing system that had been tested in Italy and that had been called "the real precision blind bombing system."[28]

Spaatz accepted the advice. He soon acknowledged the superiority of SHORAN in bombing efficiency over self-contained units such as the APQ-7 Eagle. Bombing accuracy increased significantly from February to May 1945, resulting from "improvement in weather, defeat of the German Air Force, greater exploitation of fighter escort, bombing by smaller forces, and further improvement in technique and equipment." USSTAF training improved so much that Brig. Gen. Lauris Norstad of the Twentieth Air Force requested that Spaatz send some radar lead crews to the Pacific to train and guide missions there.[29]

The contention that American nonvisual bombing was the equivalent of area bombing is not supported by the record of European air operations. During the early RAF night attacks on the Ruhr, less than one-tenth of British bombs fell within five miles of the aiming point. By the end of the war, the average error for the most accurate RAF raids, using OBOE, was a little over 2,000 feet; Eaker's airmen actually had a better record using only H2X. But

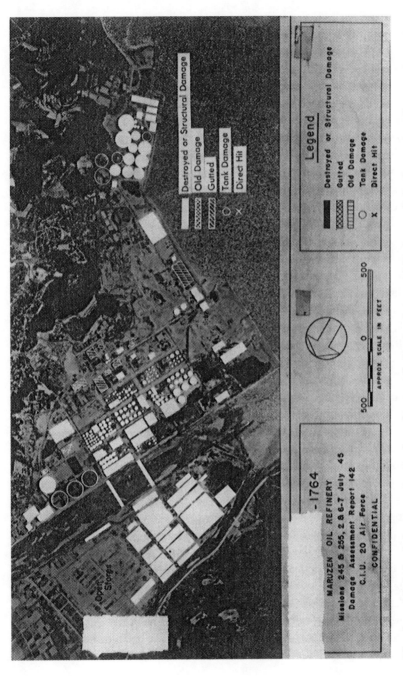

This photograph for bomb-damage assessment shows the potential of perfected nonvisual bombing methods. Using radar techniques, the 315th Wing destroyed 95 percent of the oil refinery at Maruzen in only two raids in July 1945.

the key difference between the two air forces lay in their targets. RAF area attacks aimed at the center of residential districts; American H2X attacks, the most inaccurate nonvisual method, usually targeted docks or marshaling yards that operators could detect on radar scopes. There was a large difference between the RAF and the AAF both in intent and effort as to the number of civilians killed. Exceptions occurred, such as LeMay's attack on Münster and raids on Berlin, which will be discussed later, but generally the Americans consciously avoided indiscriminate nonvisual assaults that airmen considered wasteful.[30] Yet it is undeniable that USSTAF's extensive use of radar bombing was a departure from the spirit of precision bombing and implied the acceptance of greater civilian casualties to achieve strategic objectives. As the war continued, such a trend would become more evident.

Perhaps the most important contribution of radar bombing to the war was in Ninth Air Force tactical support for ground troops, but there were significant strategic benefits as well. An assessment of Eighth Air Force operations concluded that nonvisual methods permitted many extra visual missions by guiding aircraft through overcast to targets, that these methods were fairly accurate when H2X was combined with some visibility and beacon guidance, and that the technology permitted bombing of targets through total overcast or smoke screens that would otherwise have gone unbombed. Even the poorest H2X missions against isolated oil plants like Leuna eventually produced significant results that airmen felt were worth the many wasted bombs. In addition, operating in bad weather caused severe problems for responding German fighters, which had no instruments for blind flying, no cockpit deicers, and little training for such conditions. Adolph Galland, general of the Luftwaffe Fighter Arm, admits that his winter losses were "appalling." Hitler himself attributed Allied air superiority to the development and use of radar. The H2X campaign against marshaling yards did have a major impact on the German economy, especially regarding coal transportation. Developments in Europe also contributed significantly to strategic successes in the Pacific. Equipped with new Eagle radars and using special training learned from missions over Germany, the 315th Wing managed to obtain results with nonvisual bombings on Japanese oil refineries that were 98 percent as accurate as visual bombings.[31]

Yet the use of nonvisual techniques did contribute to the escalation toward total war that would culminate in the Pacific. Although Spaatz and Doolittle did not like radar bombing, they acknowledged the need for it to keep pressure on the enemy and to win the war. Accepting less accurate bombing methods also meant accepting increased risk for civilians. While in Europe the majority of American strategic air attacks were still in daylight under visual conditions; in Japan the opposite would be true. B-29 crews deployed to the Pacific were trained in night radar-bombing methods supposedly perfected in Europe, and it proved difficult to revert to daylight precision methods.[32] Eventually LeMay would devote his main effort to night fire raids on cities portrayed on radar scopes and marked by radar Pathfinders. Whereas the adoption of nonvisual bombing techniques in Europe signified that civilian casualties were a matter of decreasing concern, by the time such methods were applied against Japan, civilian casualties were of no concern at all.

6. THE LURE OF TECHNOLOGICAL INNOVATION—BETTER BOMBS

> It seems to me that this whole project [APHRODITE] is put together with baling wire, chicken guts, and ignorance.
>
> —Lt. Gen. Jimmy Doolittle[1]

Developing better techniques for more accurate bombing was not the only way to improve bombing effectiveness. Research on better bombs with more accurate guidance or with greater destructive power was also pursued in a series of projects that would climax in World War II with the development of the atomic bomb. Except for nuclear developments, however, and to some extent incendiary bombs, these projects did not contribute significantly to the escalation to total war. Examining them in detail emphasizes the persistence of the belief in precision bombing among USSTAF leaders and how that commitment sometimes clashed with the attitudes of leaders in Washington.

According to Ronald Schaffer, one of the programs that "appeared to conflict with the official policy against indiscriminate air attacks" was the War-Weary Bomber project, a plan involving the use of explosives-laden, worn-out aircraft as guided missiles against European targets. "AAF leaders recognized that War-Weary planes would fall on the Germans indiscriminately," but the leaders wanted to use them anyway. Indeed, only British fear of retaliation stopped the program.[2] The AAF official history acknowledges that the project was a sign that "opposition in the AAF to area bombardment had actually weakened" by early 1945.[3] These observations are generally accurate if one considers only the attitudes of leaders in Washington, but an examination of the actual testing and use of the war-wearies in Europe provides more evidence that the belief in precision bombing remained strong at both the operational and tactical levels.

It is not surprising that the main force behind the project was Gen. Henry

"Hap" Arnold. Along with his interest in new gadgets, he was intrigued by the idea of pilotless flying bombs like the German V-1s. During World War I, Arnold had been closely involved with the testing of the Kettering Liberty Eagle, a rather primitive and flawed pilotless bomber.[4] He retained his interest in such weapons, and according to his memoirs by December 1941 an American radio-controlled model had been developed with a range of 200 miles. Attracted by their inexpensive price tags—he claimed that 500 of them could be purchased for the price of one B-17—Arnold believed that their range and accuracy were capable of rapid improvement. Nonetheless, despite the additional appeal that these "Bugs" might save the lives of many aircrews, he abandoned the project when the war started because with Britain as a base, "we could not get at the real heart of our enemy—interior Germany itself." His recollections are inaccurate, however. The Bug program actually lasted until 1943 and even then never showed much promise.[5]

Predictably, Arnold reacted enthusiastically to Spaatz's request on 20 June 1944 to provide support for a special project to destroy hardened German V-1 launching sites that were "practically invulnerable to normal bombing attacks." Spaatz mentioned special bombs or radio-controlled aircraft as possibilities and asked that the Army Air Forces Proving Ground Command at Eglin Field, Florida, select and test some methods. At the same time, he reported that his units were initiating a program to equip war-weary B-17s with radio-control equipment "for the purpose of carrying a heavy explosive load and diving it into the target."[6] Spaatz was convinced that his heavy bombers were being wasted in attacks on the V-1 sites, code-named Operation CROSS-BOW, and was searching for a more effective method to destroy them.[7] The difficulties experienced by American airmen hunting missile launchers in Europe in 1944 foreshadowed similar problems encountered by their successors seeking Scuds in the Iraqi desert in 1991.

Response in Washington was swift, and the Navy also immediately offered men and equipment. Soon special units from the U.S. Navy's assault-drone station at Traverse City, Michigan, and the Army Air Corps Signal Division's Castor unit at Wright Field, Ohio, arrived at the secret staging field at Fersfield, England.[8] The AAF chief of staff also informed his subordinate field commanders of Spaatz's plan, which to Arnold suggested "an effective method of disposing of our great and growing numbers of war weary aircraft of all types in all theatres" since they could be expended against targets in the Far East as well as in Europe. From the Mediterranean Eaker replied that if the Germans retired within a heavily defended "inner ring," then "one of our most effective weapons . . . would be masses of pilotless aircraft with sufficient range."[9] Perhaps the most enthusiastic reaction came from Lt. Gen. George Kenney, commanding the U.S. Far East Air Forces and the Allied Air Forces, Southwest Pacific Area, who pledged "100% cooperation" if Arnold would send him the engineers and equipment to take advantage of his area's "many suitable targets . . . for high explosive war-weary B-24's."[10]

In Europe Spaatz gave the responsibility for the project, now code-named APHRODITE, to Doolittle's Eighth Air Force. Beginning in July 1944, nine old B-17s in Britain were loaded with ten tons of TNT and one B-17 with ten tons of jellied gasoline. By then the Allies had already lost 2,900 men and 450 aircraft trying to knock out the rocket sites, and pressure for results was intense. As the more technically advanced Navy and Castor units prepared their equipment, an Eighth Air Force team under Maj. Henry James Rand was already prepared to go. They flew the first missions with a rather primitive double-Azon (azimuth only) control system, with an operator on a mother ship flying the pilotless aircraft much like a radio-controlled model airplane. A two-man crew had to get the robots into the air, set their controls, and then bail out. The AAF flew six Azon aircraft missions against missile-launching sites in early August but managed only two ineffective attacks on targets, the nearest hitting about 500 feet away. One enterprising controller, finding that he could not dive his robot, flew it around an unsuspecting German flak battery until a direct hit destroyed both the war-weary and the battery. One of the robots went out of control and disappeared but was found circling the English town of Ipswich; a frantic controller barely managed to dump it into the North Sea. The missions were especially hard on bail-out crews; one pilot was killed in a crash, and seven others were hurt in jumping. When Doolittle, who surveyed each mission in his personal fighter, saw the results and the casualties of the double-Azon sorties, he stopped those missions and released Rand's team.[11]

The Navy was also involved in APHRODITE, initially with one PB4Y robot (a Navy B-24) and two PV-1 Ventura control aircraft. The Navy assault-drone contingent, now dubbed Special Attack Unit 1, had been working on remote-controlled aircraft since 1937. They had a more sophisticated system, involving FM equipment, a block to better handle the robot's controls, and a TV camera and monitor to enable the operator to aim the B-24 he was controlling more accurately. Their first mission, on 12 August 1944, ended in disaster when the robot disintegrated from a premature explosion, probably from a faulty electrical arming panel. One of the pilots killed was Lt. Joseph P. Kennedy, and fears of his father's reaction caused much consternation at many military headquarters. The Navy then suspended its project in order to

AZON TAIL FOR 1000 lb. BOMB

AZON TAIL FOR 1000 LB. BOMB   28565 AC

The Azon system initially used on APHRODITE was derived from a similar method for controlling bombs. These diagrams illustrate the workings of this rather crude but pioneering guided munition.

find another drone and perfect its equipment; among other things the faulty electrical detonators were replaced with manual arming. By the time the unit was ready to go again, the Germans had abandoned hardened launch sites in favor of mobile ramps, and the primary targets for the project now became submarine pens at Heligoland. The next mission went well until it was close to the objective, but the block operator misidentified his target and then lost his picture because of a flak hit.[12]

After the initial failures, Spaatz began to lose his enthusiasm for the use of war-weary aircraft, informing Eaker of his belief that RAF 12,000-pound bombs were more promising as a method to eliminate the missile sites. After the Germans switched to mobile launchers, Spaatz stopped the procurement of worn-out aircraft and released the naval unit. Apparently, the only reason for keeping the project going was the knowledge that, in the words of one disgruntled officer, "this is the Old Man's baby," referring to General Arnold's continuing interest. General Doolittle of the Eighth Air Force had already collected eleven planes for the missions, and Spaatz directed him to use them up and file a report with any recommendations for their use. The AAF now had the use of its Castor control equipment, similar to the Navy system, and results improved. Seven robots were flown against docks, sub pens, and an oil refinery, with the first two hitting very close to their targets, though bad weather spoiled the other sorties. One lost war-weary exploded in southern Sweden, but Swedish military authorities just sent a polite note with regrets that they could find no trace of any crewmen. Spaatz directed Doolittle to expend the last four aircraft "in attacks on industrial objectives in large German cities as far inland as practicable" to test their effectiveness on deep-penetration missions against softer targets more susceptible to the weapon's blast effects. These aircraft were used against marshaling yards at Herford and the thermal-power station at Oldenburg in December and January, but bad weather again negated their effectiveness. The main result of these deep missions was to cause fears that the program had been compromised when carburetor icing forced one robot down intact behind enemy lines. For three weeks fighters and bombers went back to find and destroy the plane, but not until after the war did Allied intelligence learn that a German infantry patrol had destroyed the robot, and themselves, battering in the plane's door.[13]

The final report on the APHRODITE project was quite critical; the "Weary Willies" were a failure as a strategic weapon. They were ineffective against heavily defended targets and severely hindered by adverse weather, and the few allotted radio frequencies limited the number of "Willie Mother" and "Baby" aircraft that could go on a mission. The report concluded that if the weapon was to be used in Europe, "it should be used as a tactical rather than a strategic weapon with its launching base well forward." In November 1944 the Ninth Air Force had begun to test this concept in Project WILLIE ORPHAN. During this operation, the aircraft was to be flown to within thirty-five to fifty miles of the front lines, where the pilot would bail out and a ground-control station would then guide the robot onto its target. Encouraged by preliminary tests against area targets at Eglin Field, Arnold sent personnel to Europe in mid-November to support this phase of testing. Despite advice to the contrary, Spaatz accepted the project, telling Arnold that he envisioned the use of the Weary Willies "against fortified German cities or other suitable area targets" that would supplement the tactical air forces' ground-support effort.[14]

But the commander of the Ninth Air Force viewed things differently. Shortly after Spaatz took the project, Lt. Gen. Hoyt Vandenberg notified him that the weapon was "not sufficiently accurate when controlled from the ground to be effectively employed against normal precision tactical targets." He maintained that his unit could not afford to waste time with a weapon "still under development" and requested that the Eighth Air Force fly some airplane-guided missions to learn if that was a more accurate technique. Some ground commanders also had misgivings, fearing that there was more danger to friendly troops along the worn-out aircraft's flight path than to any enemy in the target area. In December General Eisenhower told Arnold that he would give WILLIE ORPHAN a limited try but only after more training on safety checks to ensure that no accidents would occur over friendly territory.[15]

Meanwhile the Joint Chiefs were developing their own concept of a plan to use the Weary Willies, a move highlighting the lack of communication between Washington and the field. While all this rather dismal testing was going on in Europe, Arnold had already announced to the Joint Chiefs that the AAF was preparing a plan "for the launching of over 500 loaded war-weary U.S. bombers against large industrial target areas in Germany." This project involved a weapon similar to Arnold's Bugs, far different from Spaatz's original concept. The AAF chief of staff did not even mention television or radio control, and when the British chiefs inquired about it, the Americans replied that any possible improvements in accuracy by using such controls "did not justify the additional time and personnel which would be required in further research or in the movement to the theater of specialized technicians and equipment." The JCS envisioned the project not as precision bombing but "as a means of requiring continued mobilization of enemy civilian defense services, interrupting industrial production and producing economic-industrial disruption." Fearing retaliation with similar weapons from the Germans, in January the British announced that they could not agree to such a proposal, and all further testing in Europe was halted.[16] There was some justification for British fears; the Germans had already used their own explosives-laden, war-weary Junkers 88 bombers in attacks on shipping. These robot bombs were guided strictly by automatic pilot, but captured Allied technology could have been used to improve their performance. When Maj. Gen. Lawrence Kuter assailed Sir Charles Portal for "Indian giving," the British airman blamed "politicoes" for the decision against using the Weary Willies.[17]

A few weeks after presenting his plan to the JCS, Arnold sent a preliminary report to Spaatz on the results of war-weary tests at Eglin Field. He seemed to ignore the outcome of Spaatz's tests and gave a general outline of his plan to use the Weary Willies "as an irritant and possibly a means of breaking down the morale of the people of interior Germany." Arnold saw "very little difference" between this operation and British night area bombing (as if that were a justification for the project) and asked for the USSTAF commander's reaction to the proposition. In his reply, Spaatz was diplomatic but presented his position clearly. He described the problems of APHRODITE and concluded that the use of the robots for strategic deep-penetration raids "had good chances of success against Japanese targets" despite their failure in Europe, presumably because of better weather there and because long flights could be made over open, undefended waters. As for WILLIE ORPHAN, Spaatz wrote that he could "see no reason why we should not attack towns if they have military targets or industries associated with them." But he was referring to robots guided by ground stations of limited range into targets near the front, a tactic to assist the ground advance and not necessarily to attack civilian morale. He argued that limitations on aircraft and trained personnel would prevent any volume of war-weary aircraft from being launched and that the AAF had to "be reasonably sure of hitting the target" to achieve any significant effect. Arnold's plan to "turn them loose to land all over Germany" would therefore be impossible to support and a waste of effort.[18]

It is difficult to know the effect of Spaatz's letter on Arnold, but after the British rejected the use of Weary Willies, Arnold changed his position somewhat. In February Arnold instructed Eglin Field to send a letter to Spaatz explaining all the control techniques that had been developed for the robot aircraft, and at a JCS meeting the AAF tried to reopen the issue with the British.[19] Major Generals Laurence Kuter and Frederick Anderson argued that there had been a "misunderstanding on the part of the British as to the employment of the weapon" and that the AAF never intended to launch the robots indiscriminately against Germany. Recent developments in guidance had now proven that "explosive-laden aircraft could be directed against military targets with considerable accuracy." Their arguments must have been persuasive as they convinced Adm. William Leahy, a staunch opponent of indiscriminate bombing who had considered the war-wearies "an inhuman and barbarous type of warfare with which the United States should not be associated," that the missiles "could be usefully employed."[20]

Eventually the Joint Chiefs persuaded Roosevelt to intervene with Churchill after Leahy wrote FDR a memo describing the improvements and arguing that the "highly concentrated areas of the Japanese homeland" were especially vulnerable to the Weary Willies if enough combat experience could be gained in Europe. The president used the same logic in his letter, but by the time Churchill reluctantly agreed, Roosevelt was dead and the war in Europe was almost over. "Due to the tone of the message [from Churchill] and the circumstances on the Western Front," Truman directed that the project not be "pressed further" in Europe. Arnold's staff continued experimentation in the United States, but nothing came of it.[21] Kenney never did get the support he had requested for the Pacific, but the plan JAVAMAN was later devised using Weary-Willy technology to guide robot boats with B-17s. The boats were designed to destroy the Kammon Tunnel in Shimonoseki Straits in September 1945, isolating the area in Japan to be invaded, but of course they were not needed.[22]

AMERICAN GLIDE BOMBS AND BUZZ BOMBS

The record shows a considerable difference between the views of the AAF chief of staff and the opinions of his field commanders in Europe on the employment of Weary Willy. Their intent was to use the war-weary aircraft as a tactical or strategic missile of some precision, not as an indiscriminate weapon of terror. A similar gap between Arnold and his field commanders can be seen in his other attempts to force new weapons particularly on Spaatz, beginning as early as 1942 when the AAF chief of staff tried to get Spaatz to use a new "stabilized glide bomb" that could hit "an area the size of Dayton, Ohio, from 25,000 feet" while the bomber stayed out of flak range. Unimpressed with the new weapon's accuracy, Spaatz declined. Even Kuter, who worked for Arnold, believed it was "a bomb to do indiscriminate bombing the hard way." Yet during Eaker's command of the Eighth Air Force in 1943, he arranged with Arnold to test it. When Spaatz returned, the trials were discontinued. Eventually, despite protests from Doolittle and Spaatz,

Two GB-1 glide bombs slung under a B-17 for testing. The results of experimental attacks on Cologne with these munitions in 1944 were disappointing, and the GB-1s were never used in combat again.

"chair-borne" leaders in Washington insisted that the Eighth Air Force test the GB-1, an unguided and unpowered 2,000-pound bomb with stubby wings. On 28 May 1944 the 384th Bomb Group launched a strike with the glide bombs against targets in Cologne. None of the GB-1s even hit the city, and the only significant effect of the attack was to increase the confidence of German flak gunners who were sure that the glide bombs exploding throughout the countryside were really downed B-17s. Engineers at Wright Field in Ohio continued to work on improving the GB-1, but the Eighth Air Force never again had to test them.[23]

Eaker retained his interest in such technology, which eventually produced a bomb guided in azimuth by radio, a system used in APHRODITE. A transmitter emitted signals that varied the pitch of the bomb's stabilizing fins, allowing the bombardier to reduce deflection errors. In May 1944 Eaker arranged for a test raid on the narrow Avisio bridge, a difficult target that bombs usually straddled but key in the Brenner Pass rail system. Four special B-17s dropped twenty-four 1,000-pound Azon bombs and took out a seventy-foot stretch of the bridge with four direct hits. There was some dispute about these results, however, and European tests were generally disappointing. Kenney also used these weapons in the Pacific, and the 7th Bomb Group in the China-Burma-India theater destroyed about forty bridges with them, estimating that Azon bombs were ten times more effective than conventional munitions against such targets. Azon bombs were not widely used in World War II because the technology was limited in availability and reliability and because pilots did not like the requirement to fly straight and level after bomb release so that bombardiers could guide the Azons to the target, a particularly dangerous tactic against heavily defended objectives such as important bridges. Even with limited use, the Azon bombs showed some promise, especially in Burma. Further development was neglected after the war, however, and American airmen would not get effective guided bombs until late in the Vietnam War. These weapons can be seen as the predecessors of the "smart bombs" perfected in Vietnam and that received such glowing publicity during DESERT STORM.[24]

Arnold continued to pursue new weapons, and his fascination with the German V-1 culminated in a project to copy it. During a trip to England in June 1944 he calculated that "if the Germans were as efficient as we were" they would be able to launch as many as 1,440 cheap V-1s per hour, to "cause consternation, concern, and finally break the normal routine of life in Britain and dislocate the war effort."[25] He also examined salvaged V-1 parts, and on 12 July 2,500 pounds of them were shipped from Great Britain to Wright Field. Within three weeks the AAF had completed its "Jet Bomb 2," a so-called "Chinese copy" of the V-1. An attempt to develop a purely American-designed flying bomb, the JB-1, was initiated at about the same time, but that project never made much progress.[26]

During the first few months of the project, Arnold was engaged in a battle with the Ordnance Corps and Army Service Forces over control of research and development of guided missiles. The ground services wanted a weapon with missile range and artillery accuracy; Arnold did not seek such precision. In January 1945 Arnold won his victory when Marshall gave the AAF sole responsibility for developing the JB-2. That same month, *Impact* announced the existence of the new weapon.[27]

Spaatz and Eaker had been told about the weapon in October in a message admitting that plans for accurate guidance were "proceeding slowly" but asking that the European commanders cable their estimated monthly requirements for the new missile. Twice Spaatz "reiterated his lack of immediate interest" before Arnold sent an emissary to change his mind. The Air Staff in Washington thought that the JB-2 could be effective only "against a large urban area" like the Ruhr and only in great quantity, an opinion that assuredly contributed to Spaatz's lack of enthusiasm. To appease Arnold, in December the USSTAF staff finally sent him an estimated need of 1,000 missiles per month but added that the project should have no special priority. In other words, they really did not want the missiles.[28]

About the same time, probably at Arnold's urging, Marshall sent Eisenhower a cable on the JB-2. The chief of staff admitted that with current inaccuracy it was a "terror weapon when used on a small scale," and for any decisive strategic effect 500 to 1,000 per day would have to be launched at a major target like the Ruhr. He was concerned that such usage would be prohibitive in cost, might cut into artillery-ammunition production, and would tie up too much shipping. Marshall added, however, that possible radar control to improve accuracy would lower the launch rate and make the weapon useful on strategic and tactical targets. He asked Eisenhower for his opinion. In Marshall's view, the main problems with employing the JB-2 were "logistical not tactical" and seemingly not moral, either. Eisenhower proposed a plan to produce 100 JB-2s a day and to launch 300 a day, ten days a month. Arnold's staff called this wasteful of manpower on idle days and developed a counter plan to fire 300 every day of the month; this increased possible conflicts with other production, however. The Air Staff's final plan proposed the expenditure of 1,000 JB-2s per month.[29]

Meanwhile, Lt. Gen. Barney Giles, Arnold's chief of air staff, wrote to Vannever Bush of the Office of Scientific Research and Development (OSRD) to garner support for the AAF plan and rightly prophesied, "We believe the JB-2 to be representative of a new family of very long range weapons whose capabilities will profoundly affect future warfare." But he still could not overcome OSRD's "lack of interest" in the project.[30]

Arnold's and Lovett's Scientific Advisory Group in Europe was slightly more successful. They presented a paper to Spaatz explaining their plans to apply Weary Willie control technology to the JB-2 along with ground control by SCR-584 radars,[31] which would bring the weapon "into the class of very flexible, extremely long range artillery." When Spaatz found out that JB-2s could not be deployed until September, he agreed to support the program then. This shift did not signify any weakening on his part; rather, he reasoned that if the war was still going on in Europe in September it would be because "some new developments by the Germans have made it impossible for us to continue to operate the VIII Air Force on the present scale." If that were the case, drastic measures such as the JB-2 might be needed, but he did not really believe this would happen. His acquiescence in a later date was also a conve-

The American JB-2 buzz bomb, set for launching from a rail system. It closely resembled the German V-1 that inspired it. Though the JB-2 was built and tested, it was never deployed to the field for a number of reasons.

nient way to appease Washington at no real cost. Ground commanders Omar Bradley, Courtney Hodges, and George Patton agreed with Spaatz that the weapon had great possibilities for siege warfare, but they were also "affected by an undercurrent of conviction that the war would be over before these weapons could be brought into operation." Leaders at SHAEF remained skeptical about the weapon, believing that it was unsuitable for both strategic precision use and tactical bombardment; however, that position was subject to review as more test data became available.[32]

As the European field commanders had foreseen, the JB-2 was never needed there. A month after V-E Day in 1945, the Air Staff cut back its order of weapons to 7,000 for development, training, and combat testing and continued its procurement of auxiliary equipment to set up one Special Weapons Unit to fire them. At the same time, Eaker, now Arnold's deputy commander, approached Kenney about putting the JB-2 into operation in the Pacific. If Kenney's response to Weary Willies was any indicator, he would have been an avid supporter of the new project, but the war ended before the American buzz bomb could be used in combat.[33]

GAS AND INCENDIARY BOMBS

Giles's prediction that guided missiles could revolutionize future warfare was correct. Today such weapons are especially deadly because of the nuclear, biological, or chemical warheads they can carry. These extreme methods of warfare were all available in World War II as well, the use of any of them signifying a new escalation in the move toward total war, but they were never viable options for field commanders in Europe. Of course the atomic bomb was not ready before V-E Day, and apparently Spaatz and his subordinates were not aware of the biological-warfare program spurred on in Britain and the United States by fears of Axis developments in that area.[34] They did get involved in the issue of chemical warfare, however.

The main impetus to use gas warfare in Europe came from the British, especially Winston Churchill. FDR's known opposition to such weapons contrasted sharply with his British counterpart's attitude, especially after German V-weapons began raining down on England in 1944. As early as January of that year, Brig. Gen. Charles Cabell of the USSTAF staff had participated in meetings of the British War Cabinet Inter Service Committee on Chemical Warfare. Committee members agreed that "the destruction of an industrial city or area by incendiary or high explosive attack offers a more direct and lasting diminution of Germany's capacity to make war than the more or less temporary contamination of the same locality . . . with . . . gas." The group did propose a contingency plan for retaliatory use of gas, however, involving "six major area attacks with Mustard Gas and two with Phosgene Gas per month."[35]

Arnold had already directed the preparation of such plans for retaliation against Japan, and he kept Spaatz informed about new developments in chemical bombs and agents.[36] The USSTAF commander had first seen British plans for gas attacks by air on Germany in December 1943 and at that time had generally indicated that he was willing to use such tactics if the Germans did it first. By May, when he was asked to provide recommendations to SHAEF on this course of action, Spaatz had considered his position in more detail. He advised Eisenhower that despite governmental threats, "we should assume no *obligation* to conduct retaliatory gas attacks." Even if the Germans used gas, the most effective response would be determined by the "situation at the moment." Spaatz believed "a strong effect on morale could be obtained through the continuance of the threat alone. Punishment might be meted out more strongly through other bomb loads." With the number of strategic targets he had to hit and the few good bombing days he had available, Spaatz did not want to waste missions on relatively ineffective gas attacks on cities. His logic was not completely pragmatic since he strongly emphasized that the use of gas by the Germans "on military personnel does not justify our unrestricted use of it" on civil populations. He was especially adamant about the use of gas in occupied areas: "The repercussions of gas use against satellite populations would outweigh the slight advantages to be gained." He did acknowledge, however, that a threat of use in those areas might tie down defensive equipment. It is clear from Spaatz's recommendations to SHAEF that he did not favor gas warfare, and since Hitler never resorted to it and Churchill's military advisers forced him to yield on his plans for first use, the USSTAF commander never had to face a challenge to his convictions.[37]

Only one aspect of the search for better bombs in Europe actually contributed to the escalation toward total war in World War II, and its effects would come to fruition in the Pacific—the development and use of incendiary bombs for American strategic bombing. Ironically, the impetus for this new bomb can be traced to Col. Crawford Kellogg, head of the Eighth Air Force Chemical Section, who was initially responsible for ensuring that his units had sufficient protection against German gas attacks. Once this mission was completed in summer 1942, he turned his attention to expanding the role of the Chemical Warfare Service (CWS) in the impending American air campaign against the Axis. Considering the U.S. position on the use of gas, he realized that the only hope for any CWS contribution would be through the use of incendiary bombs controlled and developed by the chemical branch.[38]

After ensuring that the CWS supply division at Edgewood Arsenal had enough incendiaries to supply his expected needs, Kellogg enlisted the help of the British to persuade American airmen in England to use these bombs. The British were enthusiastic and provided demonstrations in England and reports for distribution to the War Department in Washington. Initially, Arnold and his staff were not convinced of the usefulness of incendiaries, agreeing with the views of most American airmen that demolition bombs were more effective for precision bombing, especially when resources were limited. Incendiaries worked well for mass-area raids of 1,000 aircraft but not for pinpoint bombardment with smaller numbers of planes.[39]

By April 1943 Arnold saw three uses for Eighth Air Force incendiary raids: to burn down precise industrial objectives that could not be damaged as effectively with an equivalent tonnage of high-explosive bombs, to start fires to act as night beacons for the RAF, and to burn down cities "when the occasion warrants." He directed his staff to determine the effectiveness of incendiaries on industrial targets, and they provided a rather dismal assessment of the bombs' capabilities against German factories. But research and development went into high gear, motivated especially by the CWS, which built a five-square-mile complex of German and Japanese towns at Dugway Proving

Ground that included authentic furnishings. Dropping bombs on this site led to the development of special incendiaries that could penetrate German roofs. A small, delayed-action incendiary called a Braddock was even invented, designed to be dropped into Germany and used for sabotage by disgruntled workers. Thousands were dropped, along with leaflets advertising them, but their main contribution to the war effort seems to have been in keeping Nazi security forces busy picking them up.[40]

Despite CWS efforts and British successes such as the fire storm at Hamburg in July 1943, American strategic air forces in Europe never embraced the incendiary as a replacement for high-explosive (HE) bombs. Airmen complained about wasted space in bomb bays that reduced the destructive power they could carry and about the difficulty of aiming the new bombs. Ballistic problems plagued the lighter munitions. Incendiaries also proved vulnerable to damage in shipment. The CWS solved these problems with aimable clusters and improved packaging procedures by 1944, even claiming in official histories that the AAF in Europe "began to scream for incendiaries," an assertion not borne out by the record, however. Colonel Kellogg did persuade Curtis LeMay to use them in quantity and the British continued to push for increased use, but the Eighth and Fifteenth Air Forces dropped high-explosive bombs predominantly, 87 percent and 98 percent of their total tonnage, respectively. In Europe, incendiaries remained supplements to HE bombs that could at times increase damage and presented a different threat to enemy efforts to protect strategic precision targets. Even in raids on the center of Berlin, the AAF chiefly used HE bombloads. The full effect of new developments in incendiaries would become evident only when they were used in mass-area attacks on Japanese cities. Approximately two-thirds of the bomb tonnage dropped by the Twentieth Air Force in the Pacific would be incendiaries.[41]

The fire raids on Japan would set the stage for the use of the atomic bomb, the culmination of World War II technological innovation. That weapon also promised to achieve the dream advocated by airmen from Douhet to the writers of AWPD/1: to end the war in one final deathblow from the air, thus realizing the potential of technology by preventing a costly stalemate on the ground.

7. THE LURE OF THE DEATHBLOW IN EUROPE

Timeliness of attack is most important in the conduct of air operations directly against civil morale. If the morale of the people is already low because of sustained suffering and deprivation and because the people are losing faith in the ability of the armed forces to win a favorable decision, then heavy and sustained bombing of cities may crush that morale entirely. . . . It is believed that the entire bombing effort might be applied toward this purpose when it becomes apparent that the proper psychological conditions exist.

—*AWPD/1*[1]

The vestige of Douhet's theory that remained in AWPD/1 lingered in the minds of ground and air commanders in Washington and in the European theater of operations. Army leaders hoped to save the lives of their men by bombing the Germans into capitulation, and the AAF hoped to bolster their postwar position by bringing the war to an end with victory through airpower. Once the Allies were firmly established on the Continent, these desires produced a number of plans for an aerial *Todestoss* that increased pressures to stray from the doctrine of precision bombing against Germany and established precedents and a state of mind that would influence the air war against Japan.

These plans were also fueled by leaders' perceptions of the results of similar air attacks aimed at breaking morale in the Mediterranean theater, especially against Italy, where Douhet's theories about the effects of air bombardment on morale seemed particularly applicable to his own countrymen. The surrender of the Italian garrisons on the islands of Pantelleria and Lampedusa in June 1943 was due almost completely to intensive bombing of military installations there, and this victory caused some airmen to claim that no place and no force could hold up under a concentrated aerial bombardment. Future operations would show this claim to be false, but ground commanders such as

93

George Patton continued to resort to intensive air attacks against stubborn enemy strongholds throughout the war.[2]

More significant were the effects and perceptions resulting from Doolittle's July 1943 attack on Rome. The marshaling yards there were the key bottle-neck for Axis supplies flowing south, but many leaders feared the backlash from Catholics, artists, architects, and other concerned parties that might result from attacking the Holy City. Roosevelt and Stimson wanted Rome declared an open city, not to be bombed, but the Italians procrastinated. Churchill believed that the decision to mount a daylight attack should be left to Eisenhower, and Arnold supported that view, recommending that Ike "should not be influenced by religion or politics" in his decision. Eventually the JCS persuaded the president to allow the mission, and it was scheduled for 19 July 1943.[3]

In accordance with the views of both Churchill and Roosevelt, crews were carefully briefed on the location of historic and religious sites in Rome. Press releases were prepared for quick issuance to get information out before enemy propaganda could exploit the attack, and warning pamphlets were dropped. The crews fully understood the importance of their mission. "I never briefed crews quite as carefully and flew a bombing run through flak as meticulously as on this raid," one group commander wrote.[4]

The immediate effect of the attack brought Italian rail traffic to a standstill; the yards were demolished by 1,000 tons of bombs. The Vatican protested, but only one shrine, the Basilica of San Lorenzo, was significantly damaged. Spaatz even reported to Arnold that the raid was "too easy"; there was little opposition. The long-term results of the attack were even more important. Factory workers fled or failed to report for work, producing a noticeable de-cline in war production and clear evidence that the civil populace was tired of war. The air strike influenced King Victor Emmanuel to desert Mussolini a week later, and the Fascist Grand Council deposed him. Seven weeks later, in early September, a new Italian government signed a peace treaty. Diplomats and commanders recognized that the bombing of Rome had contributed di-rectly and significantly to the Italian surrender.[5]

The easy elimination of Italy led planners to consider the vulnerability of Balkan targets. In October Maj. D. Dalziel, deputy assistant chief of staff for Spaatz's Northwest African Air Forces, submitted a plan to knock Bulgaria out of the war. Basing his claims upon interviews with a Yugoslavian officer, Dalziel argued that the Bulgarian people were not afraid of any ground ad-vance but that "the very possibility of air attack by U.S. Forces has them

A sample of the destruction caused by Doolittle's attack on the marshaling yards near Rome. Note the undamaged building in the left background, a result of careful targeting and precision bombing.

practically terrified." He proposed that the capital, Sofia, should be "bombed in its entirety" by day and by night, which would probably cause the collapse of the country. Within five days after successful completion of these attacks, Bucharest, Romania, would receive the same treatment.[6]

There is no evidence that Dalziel's plan received any consideration from Spaatz, but similar operations were being developed at higher levels. The Joint Planning Staff of the British War Cabinet had studied the problem of forcing the German Balkan satellites out of the war and had also decided that Sofia was the best target. Support of the land campaign in Italy and the Combined Bomber Offensive would retain priority over attacks on Balkan capitals, but such raids could be mounted during bad weather or lulls in other campaigns. Psychological warfare operations would be launched to "unnerve Bulgarian opinion," along with a propaganda campaign to emphasize the military importance of Sofia since military and communications targets were "so small and so situated within the town that their attack would result in the destruction of the city proper." Instructions to propose this plan to the Combined Chiefs of Staff were transmitted to the Joint Staff Mission in Washington.[7]

As a result, the Combined Chiefs of Staff directed Eisenhower to pursue the Balkan attacks when sufficient resources were available. Ronald Schaffer in particular criticizes the raids: "American flyers were expected to terrorize Balkan civilians without appearing to use terror tactics," and he cites the acceptance of these attacks by leaders as an important step in the escalation to total war.[8] Yet airmen always expected some psychological impact from any air raid, whether on ground troops or factory workers, and valid military reasons existed for bombing Balkan communication centers, especially as the Russians moved closer. If secondary effects on morale could be obtained from precision attacks, as in Rome, and if bombing Bulgarian marshaling yards could influence that government to leave the war, then so much the better. Still, American airmen in Europe resisted such attacks when they were seemingly targeted primarily at morale and saw the Balkan city missions as a diversion from more important targets, such as the oil refineries at Ploesti. This AAF position was bound to produce friction with the British, who were determined to exploit the political possibilities of bombing cities such as Sofia and Bucharest.

Sir Charles Portal had the authority to set priorities for strategic air forces on behalf of the Combined Chiefs of Staff, and he continued to emphasize the Balkan raids while the Americans tried to establish a stable chain of command for European air operations. In early 1944, the American air command structure in Europe was in some turmoil as Spaatz and Doolittle moved to England and Eaker settled in as commander of Mediterranean Allied Air Forces. In January Anderson told the USSTAF director of intelligence to prepare a policy directive covering the bombing of Balkan cities "similar to that used by forces operating from the United Kingdom . . . applied to cities in the occupied countries." The next month Budapest, Sofia, Bucharest, and Vienna were listed as a secondary priority for "over-the-cloud" area bombing. But few such raids were mounted because Spaatz and Anderson resisted the diversion of strategic bombers to "the intangible attempt to break civilian morale."[9]

The British, however, continued to press for more Balkan attacks. The Air Ministry provided tempting intelligence reports describing Bulgarian offers of surrender and intimating that one or two more raids might knock them out of the war. Other reports promised Russian diplomatic pressure and emphasized the assistance to OVERLORD that would be provided if the Germans had to garrison the Balkans.[10] Portal also tried to bypass the recalcitrant USSTAF headquarters by having the commander in the Mediterranean theater, Gen. Sir Henry Maitland Wilson, give "strategical directions" to the Fifteenth Air Force, a move that brought strong protests from Spaatz, who possessed that authority as commander of USSTAF. Portal apologized to Spaatz and Arnold, but he also strongly urged the AAF chief of staff to support more attacks on the Balkans. At this time, the JCS was also doubtful whether attacks on Bulgaria would achieve the desired effects. Arnold cabled Spaatz that the CCS had approved attacks on political targets in Southeastern Europe, "when highly important results might be expected and the situation warrants it" but did not tell Spaatz to make them a priority.[11]

Spaatz continued to clash with Portal over the choice of Balkan targets, repeatedly asking to adjust strategic priorities to emphasize the oil refineries at Ploesti instead of the marshaling yards in cities. The USSTAF staff complained bitterly that when the issue was referred to the Combined Chiefs, they left the decision in Portal's hands. "Accordingly... Portal enforced his own" desires.[12] Since Spaatz could not ignore Portal completely because of his CCS influence, the USSTAF commander apparently employed the assistance of the American ambassador to Great Britain. Ambassador John Winant informed the president in April that the attacks being forced on United States Air Commands in the Balkans were militarily unsound, creating ill will against the Americans and helping the Russians politically. He complained that targets were being selected by the Joint Intelligence Committee, which had no U.S. representation, and forwarded by Portal. Decisions were based on British political judgment and "not subject to political review by us although carried out by United States Military Commands." Winant concluded, "I believe that British political considerations are integrated in military decisions and that they do not conform necessarily with United States long term interests." Roosevelt referred the problem to his advisers; the Department of State and the JCS agreed that the AAF should not have to make such politically oriented attacks and proposed to the CCS in July that "strategic priorities for bombing operations in the satellite countries (Hungary, Bulgaria, and Romania) will be strictly limited to military objectives." The British tried to amend the policy to allow Portal and Wilson to designate political targets as well, but the CCS adopted the American proposal. The British may have given in so easily because Romania had already surrendered and Bulgaria was also about to defect from the German orbit. Some American raids were launched on Balkan marshaling yards after this, but they were designed to assist the advancing Russians or to tie in to systematic assaults on

Axis transportation. The British continued to express interest in Balkan operations throughout 1944, including recommending a landing there to support OVERLORD instead of in southern France.[13]

Some international agencies also complained about the air attacks on Balkan cities. In September 1944 the International Red Cross protested AAF bombing attacks on Romanian civilians in Bucharest. Eaker had already visited the city and discovered that due to a series of unforeseen occurrences, 12,000 people had been killed in one attack. Six thousand foreign workers had died in trains passing through the marshaling yards, and many Rumanians had ignored air-raid sirens because of an advertised practice drill shortly before the raid. Surprisingly, the people showed no resentment toward the Americans, perhaps because of recent German dive-bombing attacks on city streets. Romanians and Russians described American bombing accuracy as remarkable and obviously "after purely military objectives." Eaker's perceptions were seconded by his inspector general and incorporated into Stimson's reply to Secretary of State Hull concerning the Red Cross charges. The secretary of war expressed his regrets over any civilian deaths and reiterated his assurances "that the Army Air Forces has not condoned, and will not condone, any wanton slaughter of non-participants in the war."[14]

The 1944 attacks on Balkan cities did not influence American airmen to adopt terror tactics. Though the campaign was perceived as a British attempt to divert valuable strategic bombers to attain questionable political objectives, the AAF believed that it had attacked primarily military objectives with the maximum precision possible. The only legacy from these attacks for future operations was the reinforcement of the belief that marshaling yards in cities were viable precision targets.

PURSUING A DEATHBLOW AGAINST GERMANY

Meanwhile, other plans to deal an aerial deathblow to the Axis were being pursued against Germany. The Americans had been reluctant participants in such operations in the Balkans, but they could not resist the temptation to try to end the war against the Nazis. Although Omar Bradley and other ground commanders had hoped that air bombardment might defeat the Germans as early as winter 1943, AAF leaders did not really pursue a systematic *Todesstoss* until mid-1944, after the Allies were firmly established on the Continent and the enemy appeared close to collapse.[15]

In August 1941 FDR had proposed that the British could demoralize the

Germans by bombing small towns across the nation. In December his coordinator of information, William J. Donovan, who worked on special projects against the Nazis with the British, completed a study of German morale predicting that the universal realization "that ultimate defeat is inevitable" would bring national collapse, unless the propaganda ministry could instill a sense of "last-ditch defense" in the face of adversity.[16] Col. Edgar Sorenson, Arnold's assistant chief of air staff for intelligence, concluded in a report two years later that although "present evidence indicates that air bombardment alone can not decisively reduce the morale of the civilian population," the indirect results of air bombardment or impending military catastrophe might push the German army or the industrialists to "revolutionary action" against the Nazis to preserve the existing social order from irreparable damage.[17]

A more realistic view of the chances of ending the war through aerial attacks on morale was expressed by Spaatz in his exhaustively documented plan submitted in March 1944 to counter the Transportation Plan in support of OVERLORD. It recognized how completely the Nazis controlled German society and that even refusal to work would just result in resisters being shot. The army was the only group with the potential to challenge the Nazis, and it was more concerned with factories than with workers. The report concluded, "Attacks on industries of direct military importance, therefore, are far more capable of producing significant effects on Army political moves than attacks on non-industrial areas."[18] At the same time, Spaatz directed the Eighth and the Fifteenth Air Forces to prepare operations to attack profitable and relatively undefended industrial targets throughout Germany, an idea he apparently adopted from a rather informal 1942 letter sent to him by a Londoner named E. Frey. Spaatz expected to spread or avoid German ground defenses, extend operational days, and improve accuracy by bombing targets at lower altitudes. He also saw the opportunity to overcome external censorship and impress people and officials throughout Germany with "the fact of Allied air mastery and its impact." He cautioned his commanders, however, that official or civilian morale was "not worthy of being the primary objective" of these operations, which would mainly increase "chances for drawing extra dividends from our regular target systems." The assignment of USSTAF to SHAEF's control for the duration of OVERLORD prevented these "bomber sweeps" from being carried out at that time, but Spaatz continued to refine his concept.[19]

With the successful invasion and the lodgment at Normandy in June 1944, air commanders in Washington and Europe began seriously to consider ways to achieve victory through airpower over Germany. For many leaders, the time seemed right for an aerial *Todestoss*. Three weeks after the landings, a captain at USSTAF headquarters, probably inspired by the deputy director of intelligence, Col. Lowell Weicker, submitted a plan to the USSTAF director of intelligence to break military and civilian morale by bombing 100 German cities in one day. Attacks would be made by heavy bombers on government buildings, transportation facilities, or minor industries "to free such an operation from the stigma of being merely retaliatory terror bombing"; but psychological warfare through leaflets and broadcasts would also be used to emphasize the defenselessness of the Reich to air attack. The plan, Operation SHATTER, was analyzed in detail by Col. Charles P. Cabell, USSTAF director of plans. He thought that attacks against "priority non-morale targets" of a military or economic nature held more promise and that obvious terror attacks would assist German propaganda, while the effect on world opinion "would be detrimental to the interest of the AAF and the US government." Cabell did not recommend the plan.[20]

In July Cabell was promoted and sent to head the Operations and Intelligence Section for the Mediterranean Allied Air Forces under Eaker. Cabell's successor, Col. Charles G. Williamson, immediately became embroiled in a bitter dispute within USSTAF headquarters over plans like SHATTER coming from the Office of the USSTAF Director of Intelligence. Although Brig. Gen. George McDonald signed the proposals, his deputy, Colonel Weicker, was responsible for them, and he was opposed by the chief of his own Target Section, Col. Richard Hughes. Hughes was a former British army officer who became an American citizen in the 1930s. He has been described by one of his subordinates as "one of those selfless men, of high intelligence, integrity, and dedication, who play major roles in great enterprises but, operating at a middle level of authority, leave little trace in the formal records of history." Hughes argued that Weicker based his proposals on questionable assumptions and that his plan pursued the same "Will of the Wisp" of morale that had been sought so long in the Balkans, deviated from fundamentally sound doctrine, and diverted resources from more important objectives. He also devoted great attention to morality:

> Hypocritically sometimes, Polly Anna-ishly frequently, but yet none the less fundamentally rightly, America has represented in world thought an urge toward decency and better treatment of man by man. Japs may order our prisoners to be shot, but we do not order the shooting of theirs. Hot blood is one thing—reason and the long view is another. As Mr. Lovett stated very strongly the other day, silly as it may seem to some of us realists here, there is definite and very genuine concern in both the Senate, Con-

gress, and the country about the inhumanity of indiscriminate area bombing, as such.[21]

Weicker replied that Hughes had "a closed mind and a prejudiced point of view." The deputy director thought the target selection was based on an orderly system of military requirements and necessity. He agreed that Americans wanted to use "Marquis of Queensberry's rules" to protect civilians, but this approach was not feasible against the brutal Nazi regime. His program was not a new way to kill women and children, he contended, but a method to press home fundamental ideas to the German people about their defenselessness that could end the war. He did argue, however, that if his program saved a few Allied lives, any price paid by the enemy should "not be a factor of sober and practical consideration." When Col. Charles Taylor, Williamson's deputy, saw Weicker's plan and the attached arguments, he agreed with Hughes, adding that it went against his own perceptions of General Arnold's desires as well. Williamson agreed, and Taylor penned "Never sent, Thank God!" on the proposal that was to be submitted to Air Chief Marshal Sir Arthur Tedder, SHAEF deputy supreme commander. One week later Taylor killed another psychological-warfare plan that proposed to destroy "Nationally Famous Monuments of Industry" to sap morale and to attack the power and transportation infrastructure in 116 cities. His comments, reflecting his growing irritation with such plans, noted that the proposal "leaves the door open for civilian bombing and the needless destruction of industrial monuments." If the "industrial monument" was "a major factor in keeping Germany in the war," it would be destroyed anyway as part of the strategic-bombing campaign. He concluded testily that if the target was not that important, "then to hell with it. Let's get on with the war."[22]

Contrary to Taylor's perceptions of the AAF chief of staff, Arnold was indeed considering *Todestoss* at this time. By mid-July he began to believe that a well-timed strike by ground or air units would destroy the "increasingly shaky structure" of German resistance. Although he and Kuter, now the assistant chief of air staff for plans, saw some promise of weakening German morale with air attacks concentrated on one or two cities, Spaatz and Anderson, USSTAF deputy commander for operations, envisioned widely dispersed raids similar to Spaatz's earlier ideas for bomber sweeps.[23]

Meanwhile, the British Air Ministry circulated a memorandum entitled "Attack on German Civilian Morale" that proposed to break the morale of the army and the civil population primarily with an intensive bombardment of Berlin, concentrated on the administrative center of the city and contin-

ued "without respite so long as operational factors permit." Clearly they
wanted to replicate the urban destruction and civilian dislocation of the July
1943 raids on Hamburg. Approximately 45,000 people had died there, the
vast majority from the devastating RAF firestorm of the night of 27 July, the
first such conflagration caused by bombing. Most of the dead had heeded the
advice of local authorities to stay in basement shelters, where they were as-
phyxiated by carbon monoxide or crushed by collapsing buildings. But those
who took to the streets sometimes died even more horribly, sucked into fires
by high winds or caught in molten asphalt. The Eighth Air Force made two
daylight raids on precision targets as part of the series of attacks on the
city. They were responsible for less than 1 percent of civilian casualties but
achieved poor bombing results since targets were obscured by smoke from
fires induced by RAF incendiaries. Because of this experience, the Americans
learned that they could not follow Bomber Command in attacking a target, a
lesson seemingly forgotten by the time of the Dresden raid in February 1945.[24]

The Americans were generally disappointed with their performance against
Hamburg; bomber losses were heavy and bombing accuracy was poor. Eaker
was evidently impressed with the destruction of the RAF attacks, however. He
believed that the fear of another Hamburg "apparently has the Germans in a
great dither," and he wanted to exploit the situation with a similar attack on
Berlin with the RAF. Some American commanders perceived that Hamburg
had affected the will of the German people and wanted to mount spectacular
precision raids to further demonstrate Nazi weakness. Anderson, then commander of VIII Bomber Command, thought an American daylight attack on
the capital would increase German panic and demonstrate the power of the
AAF in the European theater. Yet the mass raid on Berlin did not occur.
During the remainder of 1943 Eaker and Anderson mainly focused on other
ways to prove the worth of precision daylight bombardment, and Eaker was
reassigned to the Mediterranean by the end of the year. Arnold's emphasis
remained on precision attacks, especially on German aircraft factories and
facilities. Spaatz and Doolittle had been engaged in Sicilian operations at the
time of the Hamburg attacks and seemingly took little notice of them. Hamburg did not move the AAF toward carrying out similar attacks on civilian
morale; key leaders in the European air war remained committed to the ideas
of precision-bombing doctrine.[25]

This commitment was evident in the response of American air leaders to
the British proposal to attack German civilian morale. It produced "diverse
reactions," but most of them at AAF headquarters in Washington were negative. Kuter echoed Spaatz's fears when he wrote to Anderson that "we

should consider whether the recent buzz-bomb attacks have not instilled in the British government a desire for retaliation in which American air units will be called upon to share with RAF Bomber Command the onus for the more critical features of night area bombing." He reiterated that it had been American policy to bomb military and industrial targets in accordance with the precision doctrine he had helped develop. Apathy and discouragement resulting from morale bombing "are not the qualities to pressure revolt," and people in the Nazi police state were not in a position to influence national will as much as in a democracy. "Furthermore," Kuter added, "it is contrary to our national ideals to wage war against civilians." AAF headquarters found several other aspects of the British plan unacceptable. Contrary to Anderson, Kuter thought that "attacks against impressed labor of non-German origin are unsound." In regard to strikes against civilians he emphasized, "We do not want to kill them—we want to make them think and drive them to action."[26]

Kuter told Williamson, visiting Washington, that the AAF had been and would continue to be "employed exclusively against military objectives until the time when it is broadly accepted that morale attacks including the killing of German civilians will tip the scales causing the cessation of hostilities." The decision to make such an attack "would be the unquestioned prerogative of the commander in the field." Even someone as devoted to precision doctrine as Kuter was willing to depart from it for *Todestoss* and conceded that such a course of action should be based on operational, not policy, concerns. Though Williamson believed that the adoption of civilian morale as a primary target would be "regrettable," he thought that Spaatz's ideas on the subject were more "acceptable" and more "likely to succeed" than British proposals. Williamson managed to get Arnold's concurrence for USSTAF to prepare a plan based on Spaatz's concepts that would entail an "all-out, widespread attack, of perhaps six or seven days duration." Arnold did not yet favor obliteration attacks, even on Berlin. No one in the AAF thought the time for *Todestoss* had arrived, but everyone agreed that contingency plans should be prepared.[27]

The time for executing these plans would soon arrive. As the war in Europe dragged on through 1944 and into 1945, the temptation to end it with the aerial deathblow against morale envisioned in AWPD/1 became almost irresistible. For Arnold, it would demonstrate the decisiveness of airpower and virtually ensure his dream of an independent air force. For members of the Joint Chiefs of Staff and other leaders in Washington becoming increasingly anxious about the will of the American people to sustain the war, a swift *Todestoss* against Germany was essential to facilitate the timely shifting of emphasis and resources to Japan. For ground commanders facing a seemingly revitalized German army, any victory through airpower would save many lives, an argument that even the most devoted advocate of precision bombing had to consider. Arguments about the inefficiency of area bombing of cities could be waived for this special case, in which a set of unique circumstances, however vaguely defined, promised decisive results from an attack on civilian morale. Some leaders who retained strong scruples against killing civilians, such as Spaatz, would try to develop and execute a plan capitalizing on the inherent psychological shock effects of air attacks, designed to terrorize without killing by collapsing enemy morale through a widespread assault on military or economic targets. Other leaders less committed to precision doctrine would go to almost any lengths to end the war and still be comforted by the belief that any expedient against civilians at this critical phase of the conflict would save many more lives in the long run. Once the precedent for such attacks was established in Europe, *Todesstoss* inevitably would be directed at Japan as well.

8. DELIVERING THE DEATHBLOW TO GERMANY

If the time ever comes when we want to attack the civilian populace with a view to breaking civil morale, such a plan as [CLARION] is probably the way to do it. I personally, however, have become completely convinced that you and Bob Lovett are right and we should never allow the history of this war to convict us of throwing the strategic bomber at the man in the street.
—*Lt. Gen. Ira Eaker to Lt. Gen. Carl Spaatz*[1]

The reactions of the people of Berlin who have been bombed consistently will be very different from the people of London who have not experienced a heavy raid in years. Terror is induced by the unknown. The chances of terrorizing into submission, by merely an increased concentration of bombing, a people who have been subjected to intense bombing for four years is extremely remote. We will, in what may be one of our last and best remembered operations regardless of its effectiveness, violate the basic American principle of precision bombing of targets of strictly military significance for which our tactics were developed and our crews trained and indoctrinated.
—*Lt. Gen. Jimmy Doolittle to Lt. Gen. Carl Spaatz*[2]

Your comments on the decisiveness of results achieved by air power lead me to believe that you might be following the chimera of the one air operation which will end the war. I have concluded that it does not exist.
—*Lt. Gen. Carl Spaatz to Gen. H. H. Arnold*[3]

While Americans in Washington discussed contingency plans for *Todestoss*, the British in Europe were pushing their own proposals. They developed a new plan for a combined effort to destroy the Ruhr, Operation HURRICANE, to go along with Operation THUNDERCLAP, the attack on Berlin. The name HURRICANE caused some confusion, since Spaatz had chosen the same designation for the plan he was developing. As a result, the operations were initially known as HURRICANE I (British) and HURRICANE II (American), until the Americans changed theirs to CLARION late in 1944.[4]

The detailed plan for THUNDERCLAP came out on 20 August, and immediately USSTAF commands complained. Cabell wrote a scathing letter to Hughes, sarcastically calling the plan "the great opus" and "a combination of retaliation and intimidation for the future." Cabell thought that German morale was still very strong but realized that USSTAF needed its own "morale plan ready to offset the baby killing schemes." He proposed that widespread objectives be selected for attack that were symbolic of German industrial, economic, or military strength. Reflecting his subordinates' concerns, Spaatz wrote to Arnold outlining his own opposition to the British proposal: "I feel that a case may be made on the highest levels for bombing of the city of Berlin." Any deviation from policies of precision bombing of military objectives, "even for an exceptional case," would be "unfortunate" since "there is no doubt in my mind that the RAF want very much to have the U.S. Air Forces tarred with the morale bombing aftermath which we feel will be terrific." Spaatz also pointed out that his position "so far has been supported by Eisenhower," who still had overall direction for strategic air forces.[5]

Spaatz informed Eisenhower about THUNDERCLAP on 24 August, stating that he opposed the operation as it was planned. He was willing to participate in an attack on Berlin but would "select targets for attack of military importance." Eisenhower's mixed reply must have alarmed Spaatz: "While I have always insisted that US Strategic Forces be directed against precision targets, I am always prepared to take part in anything that gives real promise to ending the war quickly." Ike told Spaatz not to change current operational policies yet but to bring the paper to SHAEF for a discussion. When they conferred on 9 September, the military situation was at a critical stage. The Germans were broken and fleeing across France, but the Allied pursuit had ground to a halt during the first five days of September. Transportation was not adequate to keep the fast-moving columns supplied, and logistical shortages threatened the victory that seemed so close. This dilemma must have influenced Eisenhower to favor operations such as THUNDERCLAP, which promised to exploit the recent successes on the ground by breaking the apparently crumbling German morale from the air. Ike directed that the Eighth Air Force be prepared to bomb Berlin "at a moment's notice." Following this order, Spaatz told Doolittle "that we would no longer plan to hit definite military objectives but be ready to drop bombs indiscriminately on the town." USSTAF was now officially committed to THUNDERCLAP.[6]

The idea of a devastating attack on Berlin to shatter German morale was not new to American leaders. In 1943 Eaker had wanted to mount a three-day combined operation with the RAF against the city to compound the effects of the firestorm on Hamburg; in early 1944 Arnold's staff had prepared an inconclusive study of the effects on morale of bombing the enemy capital.[7] Berlin was a unique target with much symbolic value. Seversky's predictions of the possible benefits of bombing cities had been realized in Berlin; daylight attacks on the enemy capital harmed German prestige, forced the Luftwaffe to defend it, and demonstrated Allied might. American planes had participated in a giant raid on Berlin as recently as 21 June 1944 (the British also were supposed to provide heavy bombers but withdrew because of insufficient fighter support). The British intended the attack to achieve the goals of THUNDERCLAP, still being developed; but with Eisenhower's support, Spaatz targeted only military objectives: aircraft factories, railroad facilities, and government areas. Forty-four bombers were lost, a high casualty rate typical of such deep-penetration raids. Resistance to THUNDERCLAP from the rank and file of USSTAF was bound to be fierce. Eaker was in the minority with his enthusiasm for such attacks. Airmen did not like the long and dangerous Berlin raids, and most agreed with the commander who said, "[Hitler] has made the morale of the German civil population highly invulnerable to either propaganda or morale attacks." Part of the opposition of American air commanders in Europe to THUNDERCLAP stemmed from the realization that their subordinates had no desire to attack such a dangerous target for the vague and probably unachievable objectives of breaking morale and destroying the German will.[8]

The plan was also causing a stir in Washington. In mid-September the Combined Chiefs of Staff deferred a British proposal to endorse morale bombing after Adm. William Leahy, FDR's chief military adviser, said it would be a mistake to "record" such a decision,[9] an apparently diplomatic way to avoid offending the British and endorsing a distasteful proposition. But pressure for THUNDERCLAP began to mount after the Battle of the Bulge in December. General Marshall, already concerned with American staying power for the war with Japan still ahead, began "pressing for any and every plan to bring increased effort against the German forces for the purpose of quickly ending the war." He suggested that Munich also be bombed as part of THUNDERCLAP, to demonstrate to civilians evacuated to that city "that there is no hope." By the end of January, Bradley's headquarters staff, facing a bloody assault into Germany, were also pressing for THUNDERCLAP. Arnold acknowledged that these pressures were causing him to stress "some very marginal projects," but "we will not know just where the breaking point may be."[10]

With improving weather and the availability of more fighter escorts, a reluctant Spaatz could delay no longer. Acceding to Marshall's and Eisenhower's desires, he scheduled the operation for 3 February 1945. He also ordered the Fifteenth Air Force to plan to bomb Munich.[11] True to form, Doolittle resisted to the end. On 30 January he sent a long message to Spaatz explaining his reservations. Besides the dangers to his crews, he complained, there were few "important strictly military targets in the designated area." He argued that the chance of terrorizing Berliners was remote since they had been subjected to intense bombing for four years and were used to it. What would be "one of our last and best remembered operations" violated American doctrine and principles, and American crews were not trained for such area bombing. Doolittle pleaded with Spaatz to let the RAF hit the city while the Eighth Air Force bombed precision targets that would ensure effectiveness and lower losses. Spaatz cabled back some partial replies, emphasizing the priority of visual oil targets and redefining the purpose of the operation by telling Doolittle to stress in news releases the "effort to disrupt reinforcement of Eastern Front and increase administrative confusion."[12] Not satisfied, Doolittle sent another message: "Is Berlin still open to air attack? Do you want priority oil targets hit in preference to Berlin if they definitely become visual? Do you want center of City in Berlin hit or definitely military targets, such as Spandau, on the Western outskirts?" Spaatz replied that Doolittle should hit oil targets if good visibility existed for them; otherwise, the center of Berlin would be the target. Spaatz would carry out his assigned operation but only when it would not interfere with his oil campaign. Just as Spaatz was interpreting his orders as he saw fit, so did Doolittle. He bombed the center of Berlin as he was told, but he still had his crews target transportation facilities and government areas more in keeping with his concept of how Americans should bomb. Accuracy was fairly high, though aircraft did have to evade murderous flak that downed twenty-one heavy bombers. Nevertheless, the density of that part of the city resulted in high civilian casualties, and since the raid coincided closely with the attacks on Dresden, it contributed to the ensuing controversy over whether the AAF was adopting terror tactics.[13]

OPERATION CLARION

Spurred by a sincere desire to end the war and by the realization of the need for an alternative to THUNDERCLAP, USSTAF leaders continued to work their own plan for *Todestoss* throughout late 1944 and early 1945. On 1 October 1944 Spaatz wrote to Lovett that he had "started the development of a plan for the full-out beating up of Germany with all the Air Forces at our disposal."

He believed it represented the only means to end the war that year since the weather would limit operations by November. In a similar message to Arnold, he explained that HURRICANE would use bombers and fighters to attack "the most critical target system or targets inside Germany within the tactical capabilities of the forces involved" and was designed "to impress the German High Command with the might and destructive power of Allied Air Power."[14]

At the same time, Anderson was attending a conference on HURRICANE at the British Air Ministry, along with Hughes and Col. Alfred Maxwell, USSTAF director of operations. The British expected the Americans to present a plan based on SHATTER; instead they proposed a widespread attack on oil targets. USSTAF conceded that the best objectives for tactical forces would be rail targets but destroying these would facilitate the oil campaign by forcing more use of motor transport. The British offered to let USSTAF bomb oil targets in the Ruhr as part of their own operation. The meeting concluded with both parties committed to both concepts, HURRICANE I, the British plan to obliterate the Ruhr, and HURRICANE II, the American plan for widespread attacks on oil targets. Meanwhile Arnold had replied to Spaatz's cable, which had been inspired by Anderson. Though USSTAF still willingly took direction from Eisenhower, it was now technically under the supervision of Arnold as the agent for the Combined Chiefs, and his support would help in executing the American plan. Arnold endorsed it wholeheartedly, though he believed that "everything with military importance," no matter how small, should be attacked, since "all sections of Germany should have opportunity to be impressed by overwhelming superiority and destructive power of Allied Air Forces." And he rebuked the British for their plan; "I will not condone attacks on purely civilian objectives."[15]

The plans Anderson brought back were circulated among the USSTAF staff. Maxwell criticized the British proposal for ignoring the "dividends of wide-spread fighter strafing" and for selecting targets for U.S. air forces that could be knocked out at any time, not just during a special operation.[16] Hughes's Target Section was even more critical of HURRICANE II, concluding that only oil objectives offered "ample targets suitably geographically located" and also "immense, quick, military returns"; rail transportation and morale were not suitable target systems for such an operation. Despite this recommendation, the section was told to prepare a plan to attack German transportation. Using SHATTER as a guide, they looked at 100 cities with transportation targets to destroy but again presented objections, emphasizing that transportation was best disrupted through attacks on oil. Such an attack on so many cities "might subject our commanders to the criticism of having espoused a combination of morale and terror bombing."[17]

There were many forces at work that would produce the final American plan, Operation CLARION. The realization of the limitations of tactical fighters and of Bomber Command focused USSTAF's attention on transportation. Although transportation systems had been low on the list of precision-bombardment objectives, many leaders in SHAEF believed that widespread attacks might collapse the German economy and assist the ground forces as well. Tedder emphasized that the biggest dividends were to be gained by bombing small railroad stations because of the effects on railway personnel and the signaling system. Maj. Gen. Elwood Quesada of the Ninth Tactical Air Command had also impressed the Advisory Specialists Group with his plans to loose fighter-bombers across Germany, an idea transmitted to the

The shadow of a B-24 over the shattered marshaling yard in Munich. Such transportation objectives were included in AWPD/1 and targeted as a means to weaken the German economy, but their location within urban areas meant increased risks for enemy civilians. (Northwest and Whitman College Archival Collections, Penrose Memorial Library, Whitman College, Walla Walla, Wash.)

War Department. Lovett became an especially avid supporter of these "Jeb Stuart" units. Transportation targets such as trains were especially vulnerable to strafing.[18]

"The General Plan for Maximum Effort Attack against Transportation Objectives" was published by USSTAF on 17 December. It was designed to disrupt the enemy's lines of communication and transportation system, thereby assisting the ground forces, depleting oil supplies for motor transport, and perhaps even precipitating a crisis among railway workers. As a secondary benefit, the attack would bring home the effects of the war to German industry and the people to push them "over the brink" and perhaps cause the Germans to further spread their flak defenses. Targets included bridges, marshaling yards, railway stations, signaling facilities, and locks. Undefended or lightly defended targets were to be selected, and they were to be attacked with bombs, machine guns, and napalm. Actual "development of a scheme which will insure a maximum efficiency in the use of forces" was delegated to Air Force commanders. It was hoped that RAF Bomber Command would attack the Ruhr, but they would not participate directly in the operation. The Americans and the British were now pursuing their ideas of *Todestoss* independently.[19]

The plan raised violent objections from USSTAF commands, especially from key officers in the Mediterranean Allied Air Forces. Though in October Cabell had proposed his own plan to cause German collapse by attacking their rail system, he penned on his copy of CLARION, "This is the same old Baby killing plan of the get-rich-quick psychological boys, dressed up in a new kimono. It is a poor psychological plan and a worse rail plan." Lt. Gen. Nathan Twining, commanding the Fifteenth Air Force, was confident that he could execute the plan, but he thought that low-altitude bombing and strafing by valuable heavy bombers was dangerous and unsound. He also was concerned with "how the enemy and our own people will react to our attacking these types of targets and the resultant heavy losses to the civilian populace." Eaker echoed these concerns in a personal letter to Spaatz, adding that the attack would convince the Germans that the AAF were "barbarians" since 95 percent of those people killed would be civilians. Eaker did think the plan was the best way to attack civil morale, if such a plan were needed, but he was now convinced "that you and Bob Lovett are right and we should never allow the history of this war to convict us of throwing the strategic bomber at the man in the street." Eaker's apparent softening on such attacks might have resulted from working with Cabell or possibly he decided that with the war almost won, the AAF should not risk tarnishing its image.[20]

Doolittle expressed similar objections to CLARION, adding that outraged German civilians might take out their anger on Allied prisoners of war. He was also concerned that the plan risked heavy losses of low-flying aircraft "to attack objectives with results of such uncertain permanent value." The Ninth Air Force offered some minor suggestions, though no air force said it could not accomplish the mission if so ordered. The Air Ministry added to the cacophony of complaints, its greatest concern being that diverting resources to CLARION might affect the fulfillment of the plan to destroy oil supplies![21]

Before the execution of CLARION, Spaatz moved to alleviate his subordinates' concerns. He not only understood the validity of their arguments, but he also had lost faith in the possibility for *Todestoss*. In January he wrote Arnold that Germany was far from ready to crack and on 5 February announced to his chief that he had given up "following the chimera of the one air operation to end the war." He now expected that the attack would paralyze German transportation for only a few days. The same day he sent a message to his subordinate commands concerning their questions about the operation. Explaining that the plan they had seen was but a guide and that it was up to them to balance risks against the objective to attack widespread communication facilities, he delegated the resolution of all questions back to the units that had asked them. In effect, he left the complete execution of CLARION to his field commanders and abandoned any concept of a concerted attack aimed at morale. To ensure that his intent was understood by his own units and by outside agencies and to prevent any public perception that the AAF was engaged in terror bombing, he cabled all commanders on the night before the operation, directing them to emphasize the military nature of targets and not to give the impression in any releases "that this operation is aimed at civilian populations or intended to terrorize them."[22]

On 22 February the weather cleared enough to leave most of Germany vulnerable to air attack, and for two days strategic and tactical bombers pummeled German railroads, primarily. Ronald Schaffer argues vehemently that CLARION was a terror attack, citing among other items instructions to a briefing officer emphasizing that the attacks, striking throughout Germany, would "provide a deterrent for the initiation of future wars."[23] Yet deterrence was considered a side effect by the officers involved, and the units engaged in the attack did not purposely target morale in any way. The subject was not covered in lower-level plans, and no information on it was available in poststrike air force intelligence assessments. Even fighter-bomber pilots were briefed to stick to communications targets for bombing or strafing. Reports from participating units concentrated on the destruction of railways and rolling stock.

Situation maps in FDR's war room primarily highlighted bridges and marshaling yards.[24] German observers stated after the war that the February air attacks "had been indistinguishable from any others."[25] Reports on the operation were mixed; even today studies differ radically in their assessments of CLARION. Not surprisingly, Portal and the British Joint Intelligence Committee perceived little serious damage and recommended total suspension of such operations. SHAEF was pleased and the USSTAF summary called it "a spectacular success." Doolittle made a film showing that CLARION "materially aided in the break-through of the armies to the Rhine." The official American history claims Spaatz also thought CLARION was useful, but when the operation was scheduled again for 3 March, he personally stopped it.[26]

THE RAID ON DRESDEN AND ITS AFTERMATH

The basic focus of CLARION, attacks on enemy transportation, was not a departure from precision-bombing doctrine. Even AWPD/1 planned to attack transportation objectives but recognized that large facilities such as marshaling yards, because of their dispersed nature and easy reconstruction, required repeated area bombing. The American method of area bombardment differed significantly from RAF attacks on major residential zones. Still, the selection of such a large objective within a city usually resulted in predictably increased civilian casualties, as evidenced in the earlier raid on Bucharest. American formation-bombing techniques often covered a wide zone, a tactic that kept formations tight for defense and increased chances of hitting the objective but that also produced a bomb pattern dispersed according to the arrangement of aircraft and spread out by varying intervalometer settings. Planners and commanders reasonably expected that most bombs would fall on or near the target, but results, as air force leaders knew, were never as precise as articles on the home front claimed. Rail centers were also popular nonvisual targets since large marshaling yards could be discerned on H2X radar screens. And as large industrial targets were destroyed or dispersed and more heavy bombers became available, strategic attacks on transportation objectives increased significantly. Such air strikes also helped the rapidly advancing Russians. Alfred C. Mierzejewski argues that the bombing of marshaling yards was actually the decisive factor in creating a "moribund" economy in Germany by the end of the war. Disrupting marshaling "severed the coal/transport nexus, demolished the division of labor, and contributed heavily to the disorganization of [Albert] Speer's administrative system."[27]

Ruins of Johanne Strasse in central Dresden after the controversial raid of 14–15 February 1945. This picture was taken more than a year later, reflecting not only the interest of the press in the bombing of the city but also Russian and German desires to exploit the destruction through propaganda. (Special Collections Division, U.S. Military Academy Library, West Point, N.Y.)

An example of the deadly effect of formation bombing on such a target within a major city occurred a week before CLARION during the 14–15 February American raid on Dresden, planned in conjunction with massive British night area bombardments. Poor visibility over the target, in part due to the many fires started by the RAF, compounded the errors. U.S. bombing was good the first day but very poor later, after targets were obscured by smoke.[28] The lessons of Hamburg concerning the problems of hitting precision targets after RAF fire raids seem to have been forgotten. The majority of the 25,000 to 35,000 people killed in Dresden died from inhaling hot gases or carbon monoxide in the tornado of the firestorm caused by RAF incendiaries, though inaccurate USSTAF bombing of marshaling yards in the city probably contributed to the casualties to some degree. British tactics were especially deadly since they mounted a follow-up attack with mostly high-explosive bombs just as the firestorm burnt itself out and before citizens could flee from their cellars to surrounding suburbs. For years after the raid, German and Russian propaganda estimated deaths as high as 135,000 and contributed to the horror associated with the raid.[29]

The best studies dealing with the attack lay much of the blame on Churchill and the confusion over Russian desires for support. At the Yalta Conference on 4 February, General Antonov and Marshal Stalin asked for Allied air attacks on communications centers to prevent the shifting of German troops to the Russian front; this request led to the Allied bombing of Dresden. Antonov specifically mentioned the junctions of Berlin and Leipzig, but Allied planners also had identified Dresden and Chemnitz as appropriate objectives to meet the Russian needs. On 8 February, SHAEF instructed RAF Bomber Command and USSTAF to prepare an attack on Dresden because of its importance in relation to movements of military forces to the eastern front. Contrary to later reports, the city did contain important industrial and transportation targets worth destroying.[30] Like the intelligence summaries, newspaper accounts emphasized the communications and industrial features of Dresden and the support the attack gave the Russians, though military reports did not ignore the residential devastation. General Doolittle was quite disturbed about the destruction from the raid, telling assembled SHAEF air commanders with the "greatest reticence" that smoke from the burning city rose to 15,000 feet.[31]

The targeting of Dresden fueled two controversies, one involving SHAEF, USSTAF, and AAF headquarters before the actual attack and another that included the media and War Department afterward. When control of the strategic air forces reverted to the CCS in September 1944, directives governing the operations of USSTAF and Bomber Command were drafted by Spaatz and Air Marshal Bottomley, delegates for Arnold and Portal. Oil was the main priority of Directives 1 and 2, and in October 1944 transportation was elevated to second place in Directive 2. These remained basically as the top two priorities for Directive 3, issued on 12 January 1945. Though Spaatz was pleased that oil retained its importance, in reality air force commanders still possessed great latitude in choosing their targets. Weather was often the main arbiter in deciding whether to bomb an oil refinery, a marshaling yard, or a tank factory. The situation was muddled even more when Allied air leaders meeting at Malta, anticipating Russian needs and requests at Yalta and with the approval of General Marshall, revised the directive on 30 January. Second priority became "Berlin, Leipzig, Dresden, and associated cities where heavy attack will cause great confusion in civilian evacuation from the east and hamper reinforcements." Attacks on communications came third.[32]

Kuter was visiting Eaker at MAAF and immediately sent a copy of the directive to Arnold. Bottomley claimed that Spaatz had agreed with the plan, and Kuter, an architect of precision doctrine, was troubled by USSTAF's apparent shift to city bombing. In response to Kuter's cable, Giles sent a message expressing concern over the high priority given the bombing of cities and supporting Kuter in his queries to Spaatz on the issue. In reply, Spaatz assured Arnold, recovering from his fourth heart attack, that USSTAF was continuing to follow Directive 3 and that he had not issued a revision of it because he felt none was necessary. The Malta message basically "reflected the differences in capabilities" between the RAF and USSTAF and was more in accordance with operations that Bomber Command could actually carry out. USSTAF continued with business as usual. Arnold said he was satisfied, though he emphasized that he would not accept "the promiscuous bombing of German cities for the purpose of causing civilian confusion"; it was acceptable to bomb transportation targets in those cities, however.[33] The same attitude was evident on the USSTAF staff. Brig. Gen. George McDonald, director of intelligence, published a memorandum for Anderson on "Target Value of Berlin, Cottbus, Dresden, Chemnitz," on 19 February, stating among other points that Dresden was an important railway center and military supply point and therefore a valuable target. Yet two days later, after reviewing the interim directive from Bottomley, he protested strongly that its emphasis on bombing cities to cause civilian confusion would be ineffective or counterproductive, as it had been in the Balkans, and linked USSTAFF "to indiscriminate homicide and destruction." He argued that if the air forces were to adopt such a strategy, then "it follows as a corollary that our ground forces, similarly, should be directed to kill all civilians and demolish all buildings in the Reich."[34]

Arnold's concern intensified even more when, as the result of a press conference after the Dresden attacks, nationwide headlines appeared such as "Terror Bombing Gets Allied Approval as Step to Speed Victory." Howard Cowan, an AP reporter, based his story on a briefing in Paris by Air Commodore C. M. Grierson of the SHAEF Air Staff. Grierson did not mention morale attacks by name but pointed out that recent heavy-bomber attacks on population centers such as Dresden had caused great need for relief supplies and had strained the economic system. Arnold was appalled at the negative publicity and immediately demanded an explanation from Spaatz. Spaatz was in the Mediterranean, but Anderson replied that the report had exaggerated the briefing officer's statements and had never been cleared by censors. He reiterated that USSTAF's mission remained to destroy Germany's ability to wage war and that the Air Force did not consider attacks on transportation centers terror attacks. "There has been no change in policy, . . . there has been only a change of emphasis in locale." Anderson also wrote to Kuter and told him that because an RAF officer had caused the trouble it had "led some people to say that it was intentional in an effort to tar us with the same brush with which British Bomber Command has been tarred." Anderson disagreed: "I believe it was a shear [sic] case of absolute stupidity by an incompetent officer." Eisenhower confirmed that the briefer had gone beyond his knowledge and authority.[35]

Spaatz's cable to his commanders on the eve of CLARION was probably also inspired by concerns over the adverse publicity following the Dresden raid. Despite AAF fears of U.S. public reaction to the announcements of terror bombing, none came. Arnold was satisfied by 20 February that "the whole matter is now definitely in hand," but on 5 March the secretary of war asked for an investigation of Dresden: "An account of it has come out of Germany which makes the destruction seem on its face terrible and probably unnecessary." He did not want Dresden destroyed since he hoped the capital of Saxony could be "a portion of the country which can be used to be the center of a new Germany which will be less Prussianized and be dedicated to freedom." Typically, Stimson found out about the incident long after the fact and probably not through regular channels. He seems to have read the accounts of Grierson's briefing in the press. Arnold, recuperating in Florida from a heart attack, was perturbed when informed that Stimson was concerned about the raid. Reflecting his exasperation with everyone who questioned AAF bombing policies, Arnold scrawled on a message from his headquarters dealing with Stimson's request, "We must not get soft. War must be destructive and to a certain extent inhuman and ruthless." But the resulting AAF report by Arnold's staff was not so callous and correctly blamed RAF incendiary bombs for most of the damage in Dresden. Trustful of his military advisers, Stimson seemed satisfied, and he let the matter drop. The whole controversy caused Arnold considerable strain and contributed to his declining health and numerous convalescent leaves and trips.[36]

Partly as a result of this controversy and partly because of the accidental bombing of Swiss territory during CLARION, a new bombing policy was issued to USSTAF on 1 March. It emphasized that only military objectives could be attacked and was especially restrictive about attacks in occupied areas. As the number of strategic targets continued to diminish, operations became "more and more of a tactical nature," designed to "help keep the break-throughs rolling." On 9 April Portal sent a message suspending area bombing on "remaining German industrial centres" since the full effects would not be felt before the end of the war and to avoid the destruction of "housing and other facilities which will be needed for the accommodation of our occupying forces." Attacks on built-up areas were still allowed to help ground assaults. When Arnold cabled Spaatz for comment, Anderson wrote a testy reply emphasizing that the U.S. Strategic Air Forces "have not at any time had a policy of making area attacks upon German cities." Anticipating such directives, USSTAF had already cut back operations on 15 March and was concentrating on oil targets, oil-supply routes, and German air fields and training installations. The AAF also assisted ground troops, though the Army continued to request attacks that the airmen considered excessive. Spaatz maintained that a town would be bombed only "when the Army specifically requires the action to secure its advance and specifically requests each town as an individual target in writing." Maj. Gen. David Schlatter, deputy chief of air staff for SHAEF, noted that Spaatz's policy was so restrictive because "he is determined that the American Air Forces will not end this war with a reputation for indiscriminate bombing."[37]

The search for the single aerial deathblow against Germany was unsuccessful. USSTAF's heart was never really in the effort, mainly because of the attitudes of its commander, Lt. General Spaatz. The Americans had resisted getting involved in the attempt to bomb Balkan cities, and Spaatz's Operation CLARION evolved into an attack on transportation and not on morale. He had acquiesced in Eisenhower's desires and permitted THUNDERCLAP, but Doolittle managed to direct that attack at military targets as best he could. The increased emphasis on transportation attacks, especially on marshaling yards in cities, did signify a relaxation of the standards limiting civilian casualties. The larger the target, the more widespread bomb spillover would be. With the diminishing number of good strategic targets, the large number of available bombers, and the constant pressure from the ground forces, such a shift was inevitable. But USSTAF did resist the temptation to attack morale directly and to kill civilians to attain that end.

The lack of *Todestoss* in Europe had important repercussions in the Pacific. The momentum for such an operation continued, and advocates for an independent air force saw their last chance to prove its value against Japan. The Twentieth Air Force had the opportunity to bring about enemy surrender there almost completely on its own. This emphasis on the Pacific was clear to

Spaatz as early as November 1944 when he became disturbed over the increasing diversion of strategic air units to the Pacific to the neglect of Europe. Lovett explained, "It seems to me that we ought to be shot if we don't have more than we can deploy in the Pacific and not try to balance the thing out to the last penny, thereby losing the possibility of exerting such overwhelming air power on the enemy as to give us a chance to find out whether air power can bring a nation to its knees or not. I don't see how we can make a bear rug until we have killed the bear."[38] Many Japanese civilians would be killed as well.

9. TORCHING JAPAN

From the practical standpoint of the soldiers out in the field it doesn't make any difference how you slay an enemy. Everybody worries about their own losses. . . . But to worry about the *morality* of what we were doing—Nuts. A soldier has to fight. We fought. If we accomplished the job in any given battle without exterminating too many of our own folks, we considered that we'd had a pretty good day.

—Gen. Curtis LeMay[1]

What was criminal in Coventry, Rotterdam, Warsaw, and London has now become heroic first in Dresden and now in Tokyo.

—Oswald Garrison Villard[2]

As the air campaign in Europe drew to a close, the focus shifted to the Pacific. The same forces and precedents involved in the assault on Germany influenced the aerial bombardment of Japan, but more than just geographical distance separated the two theaters of operations.

Americans perceived the Japanese and the Germans differently, and many saw "the Japs" as a primitive, cruel race deserving no quarter or compromise. President Roosevelt even approved a project in which bats carrying small incendiary bombs would attack Japan; planners thought this approach would be effective against bamboo houses as well as the superstitious natures of their occupants.[3] As John Dower points out, racism was very evident on both sides in the Pacific. The Japanese were often portrayed as less than human in the American media, and polls showed that 10 to 13 percent of the public favored their annihilation as a people.[4] Roosevelt, who thought the evil of the Japanese might be a result of their less-developed skulls, was convinced that Americans felt much more hatred toward the Japanese than the Germans. He carefully controlled the release of information on Japanese atrocities in order to keep a strong public reaction from threatening the "Germany First" strategy and to prevent retaliation against American POWs.[5] Release of these stories began in late 1943, and they inflamed passions to an even greater degree. The information campaign climaxed in 1944 with the movie *The Purple Heart*, dealing with the execution of captured airmen from the Doolittle Raid. As one character, played by Dana Andrews, is led away to his death, he proclaims:

> It's true we Americans don't know very much about you Japanese, and never did—and now I realize you know even less about us. You can kill us—all of us, or part of us. But, if you think that's going to put the fear of God into the United States of America and stop them from sending other fliers to bomb you, you're wrong—dead wrong. They'll blacken your skies and burn down your cities to the ground and make you get down on your knees and beg for mercy. This is your war—you wanted it—you asked for it. And now you're going to get it—and it won't be finished until your dirty little empire is wiped off the face of the earth.[6]

Fanatical, savage fighting characterized war in the Pacific theater. The Japanese military committed numerous atrocities. Japanese soldiers and civilians usually committed hara-kiri rather than surrender and thought it shameful for their enemies to surrender. Americans retaliated when the Japanese mutilated and killed captives; "not since the French and Indian War had American troops been so brutal." Air commanders such as George Kenney feared that people back at home, including the War Department, were underrating the enemy. He wrote Arnold that the Japanese "national psychology" was "to win or perish"; their soldiers were "undoubtedly a low order of humanity," but they knew how to fight, and being in the army let each soldier "indulge in his Mongol liking for looting, arson, massacre, and rape." They could live on almost nothing and were guaranteed a place in paradise for dying in the service of the emperor. Those who thought the Japanese would be a "pushover as soon as Germany falls" were due "for a rude awakening." Kenney predicted that it would take a "crusading spirit or religious fervor" to win and that there was no time to train gradually for such an effort. "There are no breathers on this schedule. You take on Notre Dame every time you play."[7] Japanese civilians on the home islands were seen to be just as fanatic as their soldiers; everyone supported the war effort. In contrast to commonly held views on Nazi Germany, Japan was not perceived as a police state or as a society containing impressed workers.

The Japanese were also regarded as a direct threat to the continental

United States. Early in the war, Californians feared that San Francisco could be firebombed into a conflagration such as the one caused by the 1906 earthquake, a fate destined for Tokyo instead. Authorities in Washington worried that any actual air raids on the Pacific Coast could bring a public outcry to divert more assets into continental air defense.[8] The Japanese did in fact drop incendiaries on the United States Pacific Northwest as a seaplane launched from a submarine unsuccessfully tried to start forest fires in Oregon in September 1942. Somewhat more dangerous was the A-Go project, balloons carrying small bombs launched into the jet stream from Japan. One killed a family in Oregon, and others exploded as far east as Texas. Arnold expected the Japanese to use the balloons for biological warfare.[9]

Other pressures toward escalation in the Pacific did not exist to the same degree in Europe. American leaders feared that the public could not sustain its war fervor for a long conflict and became particularly apprehensive as V-E Day approached. Adm. Ernest King typified the attitude of the Joint Chiefs of Staff when he told reporters privately that he was afraid "the American people will tire of it quickly, and that pressure at home will force a negotiated peace, before the Japs are really licked."[10] This pressure to do anything to end the war was exacerbated by the confused lines of authority in the theater itself. One critic has argued that the two-pronged advance across the Pacific led by Nimitz and MacArthur was not the "sensible compromise solution" many scholars claim but the result of interservice rivalries that caused much conflict over resources and strategy. The Japanese never did take full advantage of the opportunities this divided command offered, but the AAF did.[11] When Curtis LeMay took command of the XXI Bomber Command of the Twentieth Air Force he generally did as he pleased. Like Spaatz, he dealt directly with Arnold for strategic priorities; unlike Spaatz, LeMay had no close relationship with any other theater commanders. And although competing British strategies forced the Americans in Europe to unite behind a common course of action, the British played a subordinate role to the United States in the Pacific. Because of the long range of the B-29s, the AAF could focus directly on striking at the fortress of Japan and avoid dealing with the incremental island-hopping Nimitz and MacArthur faced.

It is interesting to speculate about the course events might have taken if LeMay had been controlled by MacArthur, who adhered to the most restrictive bombing policy concerning civilians. The prime minister of Australia inquired in 1943 about MacArthur's policies covering the bombing of villages in enemy-occupied Australian territory, and the general assured him that missions were limited strictly to military objectives. When punitive bombing was carried out to ensure the safety of coast watchers, only one or two bombs were used and only with MacArthur's approval. He continued stringent control of air bombardment when he returned to the Philippines. The attack of any target "located within inhabited areas of cities and barrios or sufficiently close thereto to endanger such areas" had to be cleared through MacArthur's headquarters. He sent a message to all air and naval forces under his command explaining his policy, emphasizing that the Filipinos "will not be able to understand liberation if it is accompanied by indiscriminate destruction of their homes, their possessions, their civilization, and their lives." He contended that this position was dictated by "humanity and our moral standing throughout the Far East."[12]

MacArthur maintained his standards even when they hindered his subordinates. He refused Gen. Walter Krueger's request to bomb the Intramuros District during the retaking of Manila even though such air support "would unquestionably hasten the conclusion of the operation." MacArthur maintained that "the use of air on a part of a city occupied by a friendly and allied population is unthinkable." He also respected the laws of war in raids on Japanese targets. When authorities on Rabaul complained that an air raid had destroyed a hospital there, MacArthur ordered a full investigation revealing that planes were attacking an antiaircraft position right next to the hospital. A detailed report with maps was furnished to the Japanese government through the Spanish Embassy.[13]

MacArthur did not have to deal directly with the issue of bombing Japanese civilians during his operations, but in June 1945 one of his key staff aides called the fire raids on Japan "one of the most ruthless and barbaric killings of non-combatants in all history." This judgment probably represented the ethical views of an old soldier like MacArthur, who, in his speech at the formal surrender, emphasized the "spiritual recrudescence and improvement in human character" necessitated by the development of the atomic bomb.[14]

MacArthur's naval counterpart, Adm. Chester Nimitz, commander of the Central Pacific theater, also demonstrated a more restrained view of the role of strategic bombers. He diverted considerable B-29 assets during April and May 1945 to conduct tactical missions against Japanese airfields and kamikazes on Okinawa. When naval and surface forces were in position to strike the enemy homeland in force, Nimitz ordered his units to "attack Japanese naval and air forces, shipping, shipyards and coastal objectives," including shelling iron works at Kamaishi and bombing military targets in Tokyo.[15]

The "planner" and the "operator." Brig. Gen. Haywood Hansell, Jr.
(above), pictured here in Washington shortly before leaving for the Pacific,
helped develop precision doctrine and AWPD/1. When his methods did not
produce effective results, Gen. H. H. Arnold replaced him in January
1945 with the innovative Maj. Gen. Curtis LeMay (opposite), who initiated
mass incendiary raids on Japanese cities in March.

If LeMay had been under MacArthur's or Nimitz's control, the feisty air commander would have been required to work very hard to justify his tactics. But LeMay was not responsible to anyone except Arnold, and even that long link was tenuous, especially after the AAF chief had his fourth heart attack in January 1945. The XXI Bomber Command was headquartered on Guam along with the Central Pacific theater staff, but except for squabbling over resources and the coordinating support for the invasion of Okinawa, LeMay and Nimitz rarely communicated.[16] The Army and the Navy each had a hero, a campaign, and a strategy to pursue the war against Japan; so did the AAF.

LEMAY AND THE FIRE RAIDS

Curtis LeMay was probably the most innovative air commander of World War II. His background was considerably different from that of most AAF leaders, with his commission from Ohio State Reserve Officer Training Corps (ROTC) and his lack of any previous war or barnstorming experience. He had little interest in theory or strategy and did not learn much from his courses at the Air Corps Tactical School. He was suspicious of geniuses because they were "inclined to forget about the rest of the team" and preferred "a group of average individuals who were highly motivated." In addition to his flying instruction, LeMay had received special training as a navigator, and he was always looking for a better way to do things. Like Arnold, he was willing to try new ideas. In Europe he had developed staggered formations to increase defensive firepower, designed the non-evasive-action bomb run to improve bombing accuracy, and trained selected lead crews to specialize on important targets. Known to his men as "Iron Ass," he was tough but fair and insisted upon going on missions to share the risks. He had great respect and admiration for his men and hated to lose them.[17]

Some of his actions in Europe foreshadowed the course he would follow in the Pacific. He pioneered in the use of nonvisual bombing techniques and developed a great interest in the use of incendiary bombs. In October 1943 he led an area raid targeting the center of the city of Münster that destroyed four hospitals, a church, and a museum, along with other targets. His subordinate commanders realized that "the RAF had been doing that sort of thing for a long time," but his superiors and the press took little notice of the Münster raid since it was overshadowed by the epic and costly attacks on ball-bearing plants at Schweinfurt that same week. Whether LeMay was trying to evade effective fighter and antiaircraft defenses that shot down 29 of his 119 bombers or just trying out a new bombing technique is unclear. He may have been experimenting with tactics used by the British in their devastating bombardment of Hamburg. Such area attacks were not repeated by the AAF in Europe, but LeMay would make them commonplace in the fire raids against Japan.[18]

The vulnerability of Japan to firebombing was common knowledge. In 1939 an Air Corps Tactical School course taught that "large sections of the great Japanese cities are built of flimsy and highly inflammable materials. The earthquake disaster of 1924 bears witness to the fearful destruction that may be inflicted by incendiary bombs." In June 1941 the U.S. government agreed to provide the Chinese with some bombers to attack "Japanese industrial areas," and Arnold told Lovett that the Chinese planned to use incendiaries to maximize the damage.[19] Shortly before Pearl Harbor, Gen. George Marshall threatened to send Flying Fortresses "to set the paper cities of Japan on fire," though whether this was actually planned or just a remark to deter Japanese aggression is unclear.[20]

Once the war began, planners in Washington did not take long to focus on targets for incendiaries in Japan. By February 1942 Arnold's staff had prepared target folders on Japanese objectives that included areas of Tokyo ranked in order of "vulnerability to incendiary attack." The AAF chief maintained on file a copy of a 1942 *Harper's* article emphasizing that Japan's main weakness was its concentration of industry in cities vulnerable to "the easiest and cheapest type of bombing—the broad-casting of many small incendiaries over a comparatively wide area." The piece pointed out that ramshackle and combustible buildings sheltering small, dispersed industries would create confla-grations beyond the capacities of fire departments to control. It also conceded that the suffering in some areas that would result from incendiary attacks "is terrible to contemplate," a point that future planners seemed to ignore but that air crews often could not. With Arnold's penchant for new ideas, it is not surprising that he continued to pursue this idea of Japan's vulnerability.[21]

In early August 1943 Kuter called for the convening of a group made up of Seversky and "other avowed civil air power experts" to develop "a purely air plan or plans to defeat Japan without the limitations of practical realities as seen by conventional planners."[22] The problem was also being examined by the Committee of Operations Analysts, a group of military and civilian ex-perts on industrial intelligence and target selection that produced special studies for Arnold, and by planners involved in the B-29 Very Heavy Bomber program. From these efforts, Arnold prepared "An Air Plan for the Defeat of Japan," which he presented at the Quebec Conference later that month. He claimed in a wordy and convoluted passage purposely avoiding any clear ref-erence to killing civilians that a heavy and sustained bombing of concentrat-ed urban industrial areas would produce "the absorption of man-hours in re-pair and relief, the dislocation of labor by casualty, the interruption of public services necessary to production, and above all the destruction of factories engaged in war production."[23] Arnold's statement, with its emphasis on de-stroying industrial targets and its neglect of any consideration for noncomba-tants, foreshadowed the pattern that would be used to develop and evaluate the fire raids.

During 1944 theory began to be put into practice. Arnold had the AAF Board construct some "Little Tokios" at Eglin Field to estimate the effect of incendiaries and fire tactics on Japanese cities. These tests were similar to those carried out by the Chemical Warfare Service at Dugway on simulated German targets, and they demonstrated how potentially destructive fire raids could be. While these tests were being conducted, Arnold sent an outline of his views to the president, which emphasized that "1,700 tons of incendiaries will cause uncontrollable fires in 20 major cities," thus destroying numer-ous war industries.[24] But it is significant that he never made these opinions known to his field commanders and that the real impetus for the incendiary campaign would not come from Washington.

In December 1944 another innovative air commander, Maj. Gen. Claire Chennault, persuaded Gen. Albert Wedemeyer, commanding Ameri-can forces in the China-Burma-India theater, to order an incendiary attack by B-29s on supplies in Hankow. XX Bomber Command (BC) had been operating out of bases in India and China since June 1944. LeMay, commander there since August, reluctantly complied, believing that it was not his mission to attack such a limited objective. The operation was a resounding success, however, and LeMay would not soon forget the results.[25]

The Hankow raid was also notable as one of the few successes of early B-29 operations in the Pacific. The XX Bomber Command's bases in India were too far from Japan to strike targets there, and its bases in China were vulnerable to ground offensives as well as difficult to supply with fuel, which had to be flown over the hump route across the Himalayas. During the ten months it operated in the China-Burma-India theater, XX BC mounted only forty-nine missions.[26] Arnold expected the main strategic attacks on Japan to come from Brig. Gen. Haywood "Possum" Hansell, who took command of the XXI Bomber Command in the Marianas about the same time LeMay arrived in India. Hansell had long been a planner for Arnold and was one of the primary architects of precision doctrine. Hansell's XXI Bomber Command had better logistics, more secure fields, and was closer to Japan than LeMay's XX Bomber Command and could concentrate its firepower against the heart of the enemy home islands. Arnold had high hopes that Hansell could exert decisive air-power against Japan's homeland fortress and prove the worth of an independent air service. The AAF chief had staked a lot on the Very Heavy Bomber program, and it looked as if it was finally going to pay off.

But Hansell faced significant problems, many of them stemming from the haste with which the B-29s had been rushed into combat. The weapons system still had many flaws, and the engines especially were prone to failure, resulting in a high abort rate and many accidents. Training was also a major concern. XX Bomber Command was thought to be too small to fight its way through Japanese defenses in daylight. Since the first elements of XXI Bomber Command had originally been scheduled to go to China as well, crews were supposedly prepared to bomb primarily at night by radar, but operators had received inadequate training in the United States "due to a shortage of equipment and early commitment dates." Most of the strategic targets in Japan assigned to XXI Bomber Command were not suitable for radar bombing anyway. Hansell planned to get around this shortcoming by bombing visually by day in accordance with precision doctrine and Arnold's directives, but the shift in tactics necessitated that all crews be retrained. And no amount of training could prepare the crews for the weather over Japan, which made high-altitude precision bombing almost impossible.[27]

Towering cloud fronts off the Japanese coast broke up formations and increased their vulnerability to fighters. Even if planes arrived safely over the

target, wind speeds exceeding 230 knots at bombing altitude created conditions that surpassed the capabilities of bombardiers and bombsights. Bombing
tables were not designed for the 550-knot ground speeds that tailwinds produced, and B-29s fighting headwinds were sitting ducks for antiaircraft fire.
Wind speeds were highest from December to February but still excessive in
other months, and during those periods with the lowest incidence of high
winds, the cloud cover increased.[28]

As 1945 began, bombing results of XXI Bomber Command remained dismal and abort rates high. B-29 crews were losing faith in their planes and
their tactics. Their precision attacks had little effect on Japanese industry
because of the dispersion of cottage industries as well as the woeful inaccuracy
of high-explosive bombs dropped from high altitude. Hansell seemed unable
to produce timely improvements, and Arnold needed results, not only to
prove the worth of airpower and the B-29s but also to keep from losing control of them to MacArthur or Nimitz or even to Lord Mountbatten in the
China-Burma-India theater. Hansell also did not help matters by admitting in
a lengthy statement published in American newspapers in late December
1944 that his organization still had "much to learn and many operational and
other technical problems to solve." In January Arnold decided to remove XX
Bomber Command from China and India and consolidate all B-29s in the
Marianas under one commander; as part of the reorganization he relieved
Hansell and replaced him with LeMay. Gen. Lauris Norstad, responsible for
B-29 operations as Twentieth Air Force chief of staff under Arnold, was sent
to Guam to supervise the change of command. Norstad later said of the
changeover, "General Arnold—and all of us, including, I think, Possum—
now know that this LeMay is the best man for this particular job, the job of
carrying out what Possum and the rest of us started. LeMay is an operator, the
rest of us are planners." Now it was this operator's job to vindicate AAF planning in the Pacific.[29]

LeMay began with a total shake-up of personnel. The staff was "practically
worthless," and he needed to change some group commanders as well, so he
brought over some of his people from China. Incomplete facilities and bases
significantly hampered training, and he exerted pressure to complete them.
He set new training programs in motion, especially concerning radar. For further assistance in operations and training, Norstad procured some radar lead
crews from Europe. LeMay established a better maintenance program that put
more planes in the air and lowered the abort rate. He even tried breaking the
Russian codes to get their weather reports. The staunchly anti-Communist
LeMay also sent medical supplies to Mao Tze-tung in exchange for the right

B-29s dispersed at one of their bases at Isley Field, Saipan. Incomplete facilities had plagued Brig. Gen. Haywood Hansell's efforts to improve his operations, and one of Maj. Gen. Curtis LeMay's first projects in the Marianas was to finish building adequate airfields.

to establish a radio station in Yenan that provided information on weather and downed airmen. Crew morale rose and performance improved, but the results of daylight precision attacks remained disappointing. LeMay knew that he too could be relieved and began to search for a better way to accomplish his mission.[30]

Some planners on Arnold's staff, wishing to exploit the psychological effects of the loss of the Philippines and further demoralize the Japanese people, recommended that the time was ripe for an incendiary assault on urban industrial centers. But pinpoint attacks on aircraft-engine factories retained first priority in Arnold's directives. Hansell claims he was unaware of General Arnold's "lively interest" in incendiary raids and was prepared to carry out urban area attacks only as a last resort. LeMay also believed that the AAF chief desired a continuation of precision-bombing methods and asked Norstad if Arnold, recuperating from another heart attack, ever went for a gamble. Norstad seemed to imply that being unorthodox was acceptable to the AAF chief but would not "stick his neck out" with anything more definite. With a sense of uncertainty, LeMay decided to switch his tactics without informing Arnold of the details. LeMay claimed that he did not want any of the responsibility for failure laid on Arnold, giving him a free hand to put in a new commander, if necessary, to salvage the B-29 program. LeMay did eventually send Washington notice of his rather radical plans on 8 March, but he knew that both Arnold and Norstad would be out of town that day.[31] There is no evidence that LeMay feared any moral indignation from Washington over the fire-bombing; he never seemed to worry about ethical considerations, anway. He may have been afraid, however, that AAF headquarters would interfere in an attempt to change his tactics if they discovered that he was about to risk such valued aircraft in dangerous attacks at low altitude with reduced defensive armament. Given the dismal results of the air campaign, LeMay probably believed he had nothing to lose by trying something new.

Many tactical reasons supported LeMay's adoption of low-level night incendiary raids. Planes at lower altitudes normally encountered winds of only twenty-five to thirty-five knots and fewer clouds; scope definition on radar was better also. Such attacks took advantage of the lack of effective Japanese night fighters or low-level antiaircraft fire. These factors all improved bombing accuracy. Additionally, low-altitude flying reduced engine strain considerably so that less maintenance was required and there were fewer aborts. With the elimination of the need to climb to high altitudes or to fly in formation, less fuel was needed and a greater bombload could be carried. To increase it further, LeMay also dispensed with all ammunition except that for the tail guns. Selected urban target areas contained numerous industrial objectives. Mission reports emphasized that "it is noteworthy that the object of these attacks was *not* to bomb indiscriminately civilian populations. The object *was* to destroy the *industrial and strategic targets* concentrated in the urban areas."[32] This wording could have been designed to counter any criticisms of the fire raids or perhaps to strengthen the resolve or to ease the troubled consciences of airmen who might have questioned the value of the missions or felt guilty about the stench of charred flesh that lingered in their bomb bays.

RESULTS OF THE FIRE RAIDS

The object of the American bombardment on the night of 9 March 1945 was not clear to people in Tokyo, either, during that first massive fire raid, code-named Operation MEETINGHOUSE. The selected zone of attack covered six important industrial targets and numerous smaller factories, railroad yards, home industries, and cable plants, but it also included one of the most densely populated areas of the world, Asakusa Ku, with a population of more than 135,000 people per square mile.[33]

Before Operation MEETINGHOUSE was over, between 90,000 and 100,000 people had been killed. Most died horribly as intense heat from the firestorm consumed the oxygen, boiled water in canals, and sent liquid glass rolling down the streets. Thousands suffocated in shelters or parks; panicked crowds crushed victims who had fallen in the streets as they surged toward waterways to escape the flames. Perhaps the most terrible incident came when one B-29 dropped seven tons of incendiaries on and around the crowded Kokotoi Bridge. Hundreds of people were turned into fiery torches and "splashed into the river below in sizzling hisses." One writer described the falling bodies as resembling "tent caterpillars that had been burned out of a tree." Tail gunners were sickened by the sight of hundreds of people burning to death in flaming napalm on the surface of the Sumida River. A doctor who observed the carnage there later said, "You couldn't even tell if the objects floating by were arms and legs or pieces of burnt wood." B-29 crews fought superheated updrafts that destroyed at least ten aircraft and wore oxygen masks to avoid vomiting from the stench of burning flesh. By the time the attack had ended, almost sixteen square miles of Tokyo were burned out, and over one million people were homeless.[34]

Newspaper accounts of the incendiary attacks, mirroring Air Force intelligence on bombing results, concentrated on physical damage rather than on civilian deaths. Articles on the Tokyo raid were typical. They noted the heavy population density but emphasized that in the area destroyed, "eight identifiable industrial targets lie in ruins along with hundreds of other industrial plants." One account quoting LeMay mentioned thousands of "home industries" destroyed, and another claimed that the raid's purpose was realized "if the B-29s shortened the war by one day." Accounts did not estimate civilian casualties, but they did proclaim that the many thousands made homeless posed an immense refugee problem for the Japanese government. Deaths were not mentioned, and of course there were no pictures of the destruction, just maps of the destroyed zone.[35] The lack of reference to noncombatant casualties by the press resulted from a similar oversight in AAF accounts of the incendiary attacks. This omission was not an example of AAF censorship since mission reports also neglected such statistics; such figures were difficult to determine even by civil defense authorities on the ground and were not normally included in AAF intelligence assessments that relied primarily on aerial photography.

The resort to fire raids marked another stage in the escalation toward total war and represented the culmination of trends begun in the air war against Germany. Although target selection, especially of transportation objectives, late in the European campaign showed less effort to avoid civilian casualties, LeMay's planning ignored such considerations even more. His intelligence officers and operations analysts advised him that massive fires were essential in order to jump the fire breaks around factories, and residential tinder fed those conflagrations. Precision bombing was no longer more effective than area bombing when applied to combat conditions over Japan; concerns for humanity could not override the desire for efficiency. Noncombatant deaths were unavoidable in order to destroy Japanese industry and forestall an invasion of Japan, which LeMay feared would cost many American lives. The success of the new tactics at producing obvious results also "salvaged the morale and fighting spirit" of LeMay's crews and proved to them that the B-29 was "an efficient and reliable combat aircraft."[36] Although areas of industrial concentrations remained primary targets, the concept of workers as belligerents that had surfaced in European combat once again justified civilian casualties. And all Japanese were perceived as manufacturing for the war effort, often in their homes. LeMay defended burning Tokyo:

We were going after military targets. No point in slaughtering civilians for the mere sake of slaughter. Of course, there is a pretty thin veneer in Japan, but the veneer was there. It was their system of dispersal of industry. All you had to do was visit one of those targets after we'd roasted it, and see the ruins of a multitude of tiny houses, with a drill press sticking up through the wreckage of every home. The entire population got into the act and worked to make those airplanes or munitions of war . . . men, women, children. We knew we were going to kill a lot of women and kids when we burned that town. Had to be done.[37]

LeMay also emphasized that, whenever possible before later incendiary raids, populations were notified to evacuate. As with Doolittle's warnings to Czech workers, aircrews did not like such tactics, fearing defenders would be

likewise forewarned and therefore forearmed.[38] LeMay's intent was to capi-
talize on the fear generated by his fire-bombing to disrupt industry and the
social infrastructure without killing everyone. Refugees clogged the roads and
caused the Japanese government immense relocation problems. The leaflet
design was carefully chosen. "Objectionable" pictures that demeaned the Japanese were rejected by the AAF; instead, their leaflet depicted a B-29 dropping incendiaries with the names of eleven cities printed around the plane.
The text emphasized that air attacks were aimed only at military installations,
"to destroy all the tools of the military clique which they are using to prolong
this useless war. . . . But, unfortunately, bombs have no eyes. So, in accordance with America's well-known humanitarian principles, the American
Air Force, which does not wish to injure innocent people, now gives you
warning to evacuate the cities named and save your lives." The leaflet proclaimed that America was not fighting the Japanese people, only the military
group that had enslaved them, and encouraged the populace to demand "new
and good leaders who will end the war." It concluded with the promise that
at least four of the named cities would be attacked but also noted that un-
named others could be hit as well. This psychological-warfare campaign was
quite successful, and at its height more than six-and-one-half-million Japanese were leaving their cities. The government had been trying to get people
to disperse from the hard-to-defend cities, but the fire raids actually convinced one-seventh of the Japanese population eventually to flee to the
country.[39]

This campaign to exploit civilian morale incorporated a plan that had
been proposed and rejected in Europe, another sign of the intensification of
the war in the Pacific.[40] Indeed, this use of psychological warfare made the
generation of terror a formal objective of the fire raids. Though no American
leader would publicly admit it, the AAF was now engaged in area attacks
against Japan similar to those raids that RAF Bomber Command had conducted against Germany. Moreover, LeMay's XXI Bomber Command was
more efficient than the RAF and Japanese cities were much more vulnerable
than German cities. While he was destroying the enemy's industrial and military infrastructure in accordance with precision objectives, LeMay was also
mounting mass assaults on civilian morale.

AAF headquarters in Washington was ecstatic about the incendiary attacks, and planners quickly constructed a new list of industrial sectors within
cities for priority targets. LeMay received congratulatory letters from Arnold,
Norstad, and Giles. Among leaders there, only Stimson seemed troubled.
Typically, he apparently learned the details of the raids later and then from

An area of Tokyo in flames near the Imperial Palace, bombed on the night of 26 May 1945. Information from this raid finally prompted a troubled Henry Stimson to question Gen. H. H. Arnold about the justification for the mass incendiary attacks on Japanese cities.

press accounts. He told Arnold that Lovett had promised that only precision bombing would be used against Japan. Arnold explained that because of Japanese dispersal of their industry "it was practically impossible to destroy the war output of Japan without doing more damage to civilians connected with the output than in Europe." Arnold did promise that "they were trying to keep it down as far as possible." Having no other information, Stimson seems to have believed Arnold. In a later meeting with President Truman, the secretary of war repeated Arnold's arguments. Stimson was anxious because he did not want his country to "get the reputation of outdoing Hitler in atrocities." Paradoxically, he also was afraid that the AAF would leave Japan "so thoroughly bombed out" that no suitable target would remain to demonstrate the atomic bomb.[41]

PLANS TO END THE WAR

Stimson may have had misgivings about the moral implications of the fire raids, but he was even more concerned with the war-weariness of the American people. Military leaders feared that victory in Europe would bring "a general let-down in this country" and that perhaps public opinion would demand the return home of forces from Europe instead of allowing them to be deployed in the Pacific. The JCS was alarmed by reports of unrest, irritability, and ignorance about the continuation of the war, fears shared by President Truman. In Europe it had been fairly obvious when the end of the war approached and targets disappeared, but air attacks on Japan had to continue in preparation for the invasion of the home islands. The Japanese had never been forced to surrender to a foreign power, and planners had no way to predict their behavior. Resistance seemed fanatic; the Japanese people appeared to be prepared to die for their emperor. When the Japanese organized a People's Volunteer Corps, making all men from fifteen to sixty and all women from seventeen to forty liable for defense duties, the Fifth Air Force intelligence officer declared, "There are no civilians in Japan," a policy that contributed to two cases of fighters strafing civilians. American battle casualties in the Pacific increased dramatically as the average monthly rate of losses quadrupled to nearly 13,000. The desperate fighting on Okinawa during the spring and early summer foreshadowed the consequences of invasion and increased doubts as to whether the American people had the stamina and will to achieve unconditional surrender.[42] Grim G-2 estimates predicted that 200,000 regular troops and 575,000 reservists would defend Kyushu, and Japanese reinforcements might be able to overcome planned American local superiority. Intelligence experts expected 350,000 regulars and up to 600,000 reservists to resist subsequent operations on the Kwanto Plain of Honshu.[43]

In this atmosphere leaders pursued any idea that held hope of speeding victory and reducing losses and believed that the public expected them to do so. The tortured ethical calculus involved in deciding the conduct of the war and leading to the use of the atomic bomb could also be applied to enemy casualties. A successful siege could avoid the costs of assault for the Japanese as well as for the Americans, though considerations of friendly losses were far more important to decision makers and bomber crews. LeMay wrote in April

1945 that he believed he had the resources to destroy the enemy's ability to wage war within six months. When Arnold visited Guam in June, LeMay's staff presented a briefing describing how their bombers could bring Japan to the brink of defeat by destroying all industrial facilities by 1 October. Arnold was skeptical but wrote in his journal, "We did it in Germany with much more difficult targets and much more intense antiaircraft. Why not in Japan? We will see." Arnold had already received a message that President Truman wanted to meet with the JCS to discuss the invasion of Japan and whether the AAF could really win the war by bombing; and the AAF chief decided to send LeMay back to Washington to assist Eaker, now Arnold's deputy, in presenting the Air Force's position. Arnold saw this effort as "another opportunity to make military history." LeMay's staff went with their commander and repeated the briefing they had just given Arnold to the JCS. General Marshall slept through most of the presentation, and LeMay came away convinced that leaders in Washington were fully committed to invading Japan just as they had invaded Europe.[44]

Among the points that Arnold had wanted his staff to emphasize to the president and the JCS were the increased use of psychological warfare and the employment of poison gas. Arnold had ordered the preparation of AAF plans for the retaliatory use of poison gas against Japan as early as 1943, and he was not alone in his advocacy of first use of the weapon in 1945;[45] Joseph Stilwell and Douglas MacArthur both favored the gassing of enemy troops to assist the invasion of the home islands.[46] So did Marshall, in keeping with his tendency to favor more drastic measures to end the war as the conflict dragged on. He emphasized that the gas did not have to be the most potent, just enough to sicken and weaken enemy soldiers. The weapon would not be used "against dense populations or civilians," but the matter of public opinion would still have to be considered.[47] In June Marshall presented a study to Adm. Ernest King proposing that the JCS issue instructions to build up stockpiles of gas for the invasion of Japan and that "the question of the acceptance of the principle of initiating gas warfare against the Japanese . . . be informally discussed with the President." If Truman approved, he could then take up the matter with Stalin and Churchill. Marshall believed that if faced with the possible costs of continuation of the war, the American people would approve the use of gas. After all, he argued, that weapon was not as terrible as others such as the flame thrower or the "petroleum bomb" that had set so many fires in Japan.[48]

There is no evidence that the JCS decided to pursue the use of poison gas against Japan, perhaps because of strong resistance from Leahy. They did consider in some detail the application of biological or chemical agents to destroy the Japanese rice crop, however. In January 1945 Stimson's staff had requested a legal opinion on the use of "LN Agents" to destroy crops. The judge advocate general concluded that the use of such chemicals was legal as long as they were not toxic to humans. He added, "The proposed target of destruction, enemy crop cultivations, is a legitimate one, inasmuch as a belligerent is entitled to deprive the enemy of food and water, and to destroy his sources of supply." The National Academy of Sciences and the U.S. Biological Warfare Committee urged Stimson to approve the use of LN chemicals,[49] and the JCS seriously considered the option. King pushed for a decision by 1 August so that shipping could be arranged in time to ensure the destruction of Japanese crops in June 1946.[50]

In May 1945 Arnold received the suggestion for a similar plan to attack Japanese food supplies and to use medium bombers to destroy schools of fish. Norstad claimed that the AAF had been working on such a project already, but Eaker asked for further study. By August experiments in Terre Haute, Indiana, had demonstrated that an agent known as VKA was effective in destroying cereal crops such as rice when raw crystals were dropped into paddies from the air.[51]

Arnold's staff continued to search for better ways to achieve victory through airpower over Japan. One of the obvious sources for new ideas was the experience of the USSTAF in the European theater, and many officers were transferred to the Pacific. Anderson warned, "These officers should be selected both for their experience and their flexibility of thought, for those tactics which are sound in the European theater may not be the best for the Japanese theater."[52] Nonetheless, AAF headquarters expected to gain valuable lessons from the air campaign against Germany, especially from the work of the U.S. Strategic Bombing Survey (USSBS).

During June and July Norstad chaired meetings in Washington between the Joint Target Group (JTG) and the USSBS staff, which had studied bombing results in Europe. Roosevelt's directive, the inspiration for the creation of the survey, recommended that the focus include the "indirect" results of attacks on industries, especially the impact of refugees on transportation, food, medical attention, and morale. Norstad was interested in these aspects in relation to RAF area bombing. He was astonished, however, by reports that workers' morale was affected very little by the attacks. In fact, impressed workers actually worked harder after air raids, "joined in as a common herd against a common enemy." Absenteeism was a problem after major raids as people relocated their families, but otherwise the efficiency of German workers did not decrease materially. The USSBS gave Norstad a detailed study of Hamburg, tracing its recuperation from the firestorm, and Norstad predicted the information would be helpful in plotting the war against Japan.[53]

In final reports to the secretary of war, both the USSBS and the JTG agreed that a large gap existed between the most important target system, Japanese transportation, and any other objective. Second in priority for the USSBS was ammunition reserves, followed by precision industrial targets and chemical attacks on rice production. Attacks on urban industrial targets were last, and they were to be hit only if there was less than a one-third chance of hitting more precise objectives. The JTG was in general agreement except that they placed no emphasis on most precision targets or on the rice crop and more on incendiary attacks on cities. Both groups briefed Spaatz, the newly designated commander of the recently created U.S. Army Strategic Air Forces (USASTAF), which included the Eighth and Twentieth Air Forces. He was being sent to the Pacific to take over the direction of most strategic air operations there. Typical of the convoluted command structure in the theater, MacArthur and Kenney retained control over their own heavy bombers. In accordance with his record of adherence to precision bombing, Spaatz agreed with the USSBS's recommendations for his forces. He went to Guam with a directive from Eaker to concentrate on Japanese railway targets, aircraft production, ammunition supplies, and industrial concentrations and stores, in that order of priority.[54]

Spaatz could do little to change the course of the air war in the Pacific, however; there was too much momentum behind the fire raids. Ammunition dumps were stocked with incendiary clusters, and operations and training for the strategic-bomber crews were geared for low-level, night area attacks. Statistics covering the number of bombs dropped and the number of factories destroyed were being used to demonstrate the power of the AAF, and data on civilian bombing casualties was ignored. Predictions of potential losses of American lives received much attention, however, and the devastating raids were linked to preparations for the impending invasion. The Twentieth Air Force was fully committed to the firebombing of Japanese cities.

So was General Arnold. While Spaatz was trying to reshuffle priorities, the AAF chief was telling his staff at the Potsdam Conference, "The war with Japan is over as far as creative work is concerned. The die is cast. There is very little we can do other than see the planes and personnel with supplies get over there." Arnold passed out books of photographs showing the destruction of Japanese cities, and when Stalin proposed a toast to a meeting in Tokyo, Arnold boasted, "If our B-29s continue their present tempo there [will] be nothing left of Tokyo in which to have a meeting." His attitude was well received by those assembled. Hatred for the Japanese was evident, typified by Lord Mountbatten's remarks that the Japanese royal family were "morons" and should be liquidated. Arnold was optimistic about his air forces' ability to end the war, betting Portal that it would be over "nearer Christmas 1945 than Valentine's Day 1946."[55]

Arnold would win his bet handily. When Spaatz arrived in the Pacific, an examination of the situation convinced him "that unless Japan desires to commit national suicide, they should quit immediately." The dropping of the atomic bombs helped bring some Japanese leaders to the same conclusion. Appalled by the destruction being wrought on Japan, Spaatz wrote in his diary about the new weapon and the fire raids: "When the atomic bomb was first discussed with me in Washington I was not in favor of it just as I have never favored the destruction of cities as such with all inhabitants being killed." According to the recollections of Spaatz's family, he had been reluctant to take the USASTAF command because of his revulsion over the destruction dealt German cities and his expectations of a worse fate for the Japanese. Directed to continue bombing until arrangements for surrender were completed, Spaatz canceled one raid because of bad weather and tried to limit other attacks to military targets. When the press interpreted Spaatz's cancellation as a cease-fire, Truman ordered him to halt the bombing to avoid a misperception that its resumption indicated a breakdown in negotiations. When the Japanese delayed, Truman ordered more strategic attacks, and Arnold demanded a peak effort to show the importance and power of the AAF. Despite Spaatz's anxious queries, no cancellation was ordered, and more than 1,000 planes hit Japan on 14 August, some even after Japanese radio announced acceptance of the terms of surrender.[56]

Although AAF officers quibbled over the number of American lives saved by bombing, they agreed with Prince Konoye's claim: "Fundamentally, the thing that brought about the determination to make peace was the prolonged fire bombing by the B-29s." The AAF was worried, however, that the Japanese "were conducting an intensive propaganda campaign concerning the bombing of their cities with the view to getting sympathy out of Americans."[57] But little sympathy was available, even though the B-29s had burned out 180 square miles of sixty-seven cities, killed over 300,000 people, and wounded another 400,000. Twentieth Air Force losses were remarkably light, a tribute to the effectiveness of American tactics as well as to the weakness of Japanese defenses. Only 437 of the Very Heavy Bombers were lost in combat operations, mostly because of technical failures. In contrast, over 3,000

B-17s and 1,000 B-24s had been lost by the Eighth Air Force against Germany.[58]

Hansell, who remains notably objective in his memoirs, makes a strong case that precision attacks on the Japanese electrical industry, using low-altitude attacks at night with new radars and tactics finally perfected by the 315th Wing, would have destroyed Japan's ability to make war and brought it to the peace table "at less cost with fewer undesirable side effects." This alternative strategy would have taken fewer sorties and saved many civilian lives, though it would have taken more time (and perhaps cost more American lives) because of the wait for the arrival of new equipment. Another possibility might have been to expand the B-29 aerial-mining program, but that also probably would have required more time to produce decisive results. In four and one-half months, LeMay's 313th Wing sowed over 12,000 mines in ports and waterways, sinking almost a million tons of Japanese shipping. Along with submarines and tactical air attacks, the strategic-mining campaign had almost completely halted Japanese seaborne traffic of raw materials and foodstuffs by mid-August 1945. One can only wonder what would have happened if another leader, such as Spaatz, had commanded the B-29s, someone more committed to precision doctrine and perhaps more experienced and secure in his position. Would he have been more inclined to take the time and effort to explore alternatives before resorting to the extreme of the fire raids? Such a course would have been difficult, especially after Hansell's experience. And if Prince Konoye is to be believed, different tactics or a delay in resorting to the incendiary attacks might have had serious consequences in forcing a Japanese capitulation. The massive destruction, social dislocation, and psychological impact of the B-29 campaign against Japanese cities perhaps made it key in the series of shocks that produced a surrender. Even Hansell concedes that the chosen strategy of the fire raids was "decisively effective" and a "sound military decision," especially with the time pressures that existed in the Pacific.[59]

Leaders could not wait for XXI Bomber Command to experiment and train; the invasion was too close and looked too costly and the will of the home front appeared to be on the wane. With the air resources available, the fire raids seemed to be the easiest and the quickest method for destroying the ability of Japan to wage war. Military and industrial targets were the primary objectives, but just as in Europe, as the war dragged on, civilian casualties from strategic attacks clearly were less of a consideration. Perhaps the culmination of this trend is best exemplified by the message Norstad sent to Spaatz on 8 August: "It is understood that the Secretary of War in his press conference tomorrow will release a map or photostat of Hiroshima showing the aiming point and the general area of greatest damage. . . . It is believed here that the accuracy with which this bomb was placed may counter a thought that the CENTERBOARD [A-bomb] project involves wanton, indiscriminate bombing."[60] If an atomic bomb dropped on a city could be construed as a method of precision bombing, then that doctrine had evolved to the point where civilian casualties were no longer taken into consideration at all.

10. STRATEGIC AIRPOWER
IN LIMITED WARS

I regret the necessities of war have compelled us to bomb North Vietnam. We have carefully limited those raids. They have been directed at concrete and steel and not at human life.

—*President Lyndon Johnson*[1]

For the men who dropped bombs on Japan, there was little difference between destroying cities with incendiary bombs and with atomic ones. Spaatz abhorred both means, and LeMay wrote of the new weapons, "Nothing new about death, nothing new about deaths caused militarily. We scorched and boiled and baked to death more people in Tokyo on that night of 9–10 March than went up in vapor at Hiroshima and Nagasaki combined." The attack on Hiroshima was followed by the same psychological campaign that had been used for the fire raids. Leaflets emphasized that the new bomb was to be used "to destroy every resource of the military by which they are prolonging this useless war" and ended with the demand, "Evacuate Your Cities!"[2] The atomic bomb would be used as its predecessors had been, to destroy urban industrial and military centers and to terrorize city dwellers into fleeing to the countryside. From the perspective of those airmen dropping bombs on the Japanese, the decision to use an atomic weapon was much easier than the choice to resort to the fire raids, but for Secretary of War Henry L. Stimson, it was a difficult course of action to adopt. Devoted to morality and to keeping the war "within the bounds of humanity," he viewed using such a terrible weapon to destroy a city as contrary to everything he stood for. Yet after confronting weary troops headed for the Pacific and upon contemplating the costs of more war, he approved "the least abhorrent choice" for the destruction of Hiroshima and Nagasaki, to some extent because "it stopped the fire raids."[3]

The violent precedent established by LeMay's incendiary campaign helps explain the civilian authorities' acceptance of the use of atomic warfare against Japanese cities. Although this new policy troubled Stimson, most of the other leaders in Washington strongly endorsed it, an attitude transmitted through Arnold to the rest of the AAF leadership. Even Spaatz made plans to use a third atomic bomb, proposing that it be dropped on Tokyo to exert "psychological effect on the government officials."[4] Knowing that more nuclear weapons would be employed if they were available and never one to disobey direct orders, Spaatz probably hoped that this final raid on the enemy capital would end the war and conclude the deadly air campaign against Japanese cities.

Despite the extravagant claims by airmen during the war, the true destructive capacity of airpower was not clear to leaders until they visited conquered enemy cities. When LeMay landed in Yokohama to help arrange the final surrender, he was amazed at the "unpopulated wilderness" his bombers had created. He was proud of his accomplishments; in contrast, Stimson, after seeing the destruction of Berlin, had written, "I felt as though I had done a distasteful duty." Other observers with similar misgivings about the bombing of German cities had their doubts dispelled by the revelations of the barbarism in the concentration camps. USSTAF historian Bruce Hopper noted after visiting Buchenwald in April, "Stench everywhere: piles of human bone remnants at the furnace. Here is the antidote for qualms about strategic bombing."[5]

ANALYZING RESULTS OF STRATEGIC BOMBING

Hopper was on a jeep trip with Anderson when he saw Buchenwald, collecting data for a book on USSTAF operations against Germany. He never published the manuscript. Disillusioned and frustrated by the lack of cooperation from airmen, he found he was considered a "nuisance," and he himself felt he had no role or function. His experience seems indicative of a general mistrust of historians by the image-conscious Air Force. Unlike the ground forces, the AAF had no real combat historians. Teams directed by Col. S. L. A. Marshall conducted interviews and examined documents for the Army as its units came out of action; officers and especially the enlisted military personnel who were historians had an advantage over civilians in dealing with troops. But the Army also accepted the historians' role more readily than did the AAF, apparent if one compares the massive "Green Book" series on World War II supported by the Department of the Army's Office of Military History with

Aerial view of Mannheim, Germany, taken 19 April 1945, showing the devastation caused by Allied planes and artillery. Scenes such as this prompted Henry Stimson to feel that he had carried out "a distasteful duty." (Special Collections Division, U.S. Military Academy Library, West Point, N.Y.)

the seven-volume AAF history, designed more to assist the AAF in justifying independence. Moreover, the historians involved in AAF work admitted that they did not have access to all necessary documents, especially those papers involving controversial issues.[6]

Instead of relying upon historians for lessons, the AAF looked to technical experts. The Committee of Operations Analysts appraised target systems for Arnold, Operational Research Sections examined tactical problems with air support in Europe, and the Operations Analysis Section of XXI Bomber Command advised LeMay about dealing with the weather problems affecting strategic attacks on Japan. These experts focused on technical problems without giving much, if any, consideration to ethical or human factors.[7] Air operations are more conducive to objective analysis than are comparatively subjective land operations, but the AAF approach soon influenced other services. In the postwar period, American military doctrine as a whole began to shift its focus to quantifiable firepower at the expense of more subjective maneuver considerations and to Douhetian formulas on the amount of fire support needed to defeat an enemy. The characteristics of atomic warfare also influenced this trend.[8]

With the postwar focus on firepower formulas and the use of nuclear weapons, neither historians nor analysts systematically examined the ethical aspects of conventional bombing. The Air Force concentrated primarily on precise data that could be applied to future target selection. To AAF leaders, the main lessons of the U.S. Strategic Bombing Survey, prepared mostly by economists and scientists, apparently were that better analysis of target systems and an earlier focus on key industrial objectives such as oil would have collapsed enemy economies much sooner. Applying these lessons to the future, Anderson and Maxwell believed that the best way to prevent Germany from ever waging war again was to ensure that the country was rebuilt with an economic system and predesignated strategic targets "in a permanently vulnerable position" to air attack.[9]

The use of the atomic bombs on Japan and the relatively short strategic air campaign there tended to obscure any lessons about conventional bombing in the Pacific theater. As a result, those seeking justification for precision-bombing doctrine focused on the European theater. This orientation was reinforced because Arnold's next three successors as chief of the air force—Spaatz, Vandenberg, and Twining—had gained their primary wartime experiences commanding major units in Europe. A good indication of their attitudes was revealed by the findings of a board Arnold convened in late 1945 to determine the implications of the atomic bomb for the future air force. The group, headed by Spaatz and including Vandenberg, concluded that since atomic bombs would be few and expensive, conventional pinpoint bombing would still be necessary to strike most strategic targets. "Notwithstanding the fire bombing of Tokyo and other Japanese cities, there was little indication in the report that area bombing had gained favor among its writers."[10]

Spaatz maintained his devotion to precision-bombing doctrine and worked for a large air force to carry out both conventional and atomic missions, but a few dissenters led by LeMay were pushing for a "small striking force capable of exploiting the atomic bomb." As the new deputy chief of staff to the commander of the AAF, LeMay continued to demonstrate his penchant for innovative tactics and his commitment to obliteration bombing; he was joined in his campaign by Eaker. With public acceptance of atomic bombs and the growing realization that an independent air force would be needed to employ nuclear weapons properly, Eaker apparently decided that "throwing the strategic bomber at the man in the street" was a good idea.[11]

Most American air leaders came out of the war believing that their doctrine had been vindicated. Conventional bombing could be effective in defeating enemy nations, and adequate accuracy could be achieved. The USSBS also looked to some extent at the psychological effects of aerial bombardment on enemy civilians. In Germany, "the power of a police state over its people" kept them working efficiently even when their will to fight declined. The effects of bombing on civilian morale in Japan were more important although "the interrelation of military, economic, and morale factors" that produced the surrender was "complex." The ethical implications of conventional air attack could not be measured and were not systematically studied, nor was there any motivation to do so. The AAF encountered none of the postwar criticism over city bombing that RAF Bomber Command experienced.[12] The victorious American public and its warriors were just glad to have the war in the Pacific concluded. Their relief was heightened as postwar reports revealed the extent of strong Japanese defenses against invasion that would have caused many casualties.[13] American decision makers, who had been deluged with glowing reports and carefully selected photographs of AAF bombing results (similar to the optimistic bomb-damage assessments and impressive bombsight videotapes offered at press briefings during DESERT STORM), believed that the AAF could now exert decisive airpower in any conflict, even without atomic weapons, and with pinpoint accuracy.[14] A more effective analysis of nonquantifiable factors probably would not have changed formal doctrine, but it would have made leaders more aware of the actual effectiveness and the political implications of conventional bombing in urban areas. Such an analysis also might have suggested that different enemy economies and national characters or changing international relations could limit the effectiveness of future strategic air campaigns.

DISAPPOINTING RESULTS IN KOREA

The war in Korea presented the United States Air Force with a different set of challenges from those of World War II and should have provided astute observers with some disturbing lessons about the future efficacy of strategic bombing in limited wars. Political constraints restricted the area and nature of operations, and the simple nature of the North Korean economy along with the inviolable sanctuary of Chinese bases made strategic bombing unproductive. American air units entered combat shortly after the June 1950 invasion, and air superiority over the North Koreans was achieved quickly. World War II–vintage B-26s and B-29s destroyed the eighteen major enemy strategic targets by 25 September 1950. By 24 October the Far Eastern Air Forces' (FEAF) Bomber Command B-29s had to stand down because of a lack of suitable targets south of the Yalu River. Even this relatively small strategic campaign brought accusations of indiscriminate and barbarous attacks against peaceful civilians, not only from the Russian delegation at the United Nations but also from American, British, and Indian newspapers. This response was a sign of things to come; such international reactions to USAF air strikes in or near urban areas have become commonplace since World War II. After the Chinese intervention, strategic bombers concentrated on interdiction of enemy lines of communication. Although this campaign achieved some notable successes, it could not prevent the war from dragging on.[15]

As frustration with stalemate and enemy intransigence mounted, the FEAF mounted a campaign to pressure Communist negotiators into an armistice. The tactics and goals had much in common with the HURRICANE-style operations proposed late in World War II in the European theater. Operation PRESSURE PUMP on 11 July involved a concentrated attack on thirty military objectives in Pyongyang, though Brig. Gen. Jacob Smart, FEAF deputy for operations, also intended to exploit the psychological effects of airpower. In a statement reminiscent of the early concept for Operation CLARION, he directed, "Whenever possible, attacks will be scheduled against targets of military significance so situated that their destruction will have a deleterious effect upon the morale of the civil population actively engaged in the support of enemy forces." As with the emphasis on bombing Berlin in World War II, mass raids on the North Korean capital had the highest priority and included attacks in August designed "to cause a noise in Moscow" by destroying all public offices. By 1 September no worthwhile precision targets were left in Pyongyang. The campaign caused much damage and dislocated many civilians, but the resolve of enemy leaders was unshaken.[16]

FEAF planners did not rely only on European precedents from World War II. In a move that resembled LeMay's psychological operations, Fifth Air Force Commander Lt. Gen. Glenn Barcus announced to press and radio the names of seventy-eight North Korean towns containing targets to be bombed. Although the USAF considered these warnings "humanitarian and utilitarian" and Radio Seoul warned residents to evacuate, the State Department complained that the American campaign would be exploited intensely

Some examples of USAF targets in North Korea, the central marshaling yard in Pyongyang (top) and the Chasan Dam near Sunchon (bottom). Following many precedents from World War II, American airpower strategy included pummeling the enemy capital and causing a rice shortage by destroying irrigation dams.

by Communist propaganda. Many villagers fled, and the air attacks did highlight enemy defenselessness. Some international outcry occurred, especially
in Britain over attacks on power installations. As an additional part of these
raids, FEAF bombers destroyed an important chemical plant on the Yalu that
was the "last of the marginal strategic-type targets in Korea." Yet the pressure
of the air campaign failed to bring about progress in negotiations.[17]

The official Air Force history claims that a combination of aerial pounding
of Chinese ground offensives and new strategic attacks against hydroelectric
plants and irrigation dams in May 1953 was instrumental in finally persuading
the Communists to accept armistice terms. One of the reasons for bombing
the dams was to destroy North Korean food crops and cause a "rice famine,"
a tactic that had never been used even in LeMay's total air war against Japan.
Fears of American war-weariness and the frustrations of dealing with a stubborn Asian enemy again contributed to an escalation of bombing operations
although this time there were no direct attacks on civilians and no urban
incendiary raids. According to the official history, "Whether the Reds yielded
because they feared an expanding air war, or whether they quit because of the
pounding pressure of air attacks against their forces in North Korea, one thing
was certain: airpower was triumphant in the Korean War."[18] While appreciat-
ing the contributions of American air forces in the war, few objective observers could make such a positive conclusion after three years of such a bloody
and disappointing conflict. USAF doctrine and practice had really not been
effective in Korea, including the policies involving nuclear weapons. Perceptions of public opinion and diplomatic reality again worked to limit bombing
operations. Although President Truman and his advisers had discussed plans
to destroy Russian Far East bases with A-bombs and despite MacArthur's suggestions, Truman's misstatements, and Eisenhower's hints, American leaders
never seriously considered the use of nuclear weapons.[19] Yet Air Force doctrine after the Korean War still emphasized the use of strategic bombing with
nuclear weapons in a total war against the war-making capacity of a modern
industrialized nation; the 1964 doctrinal manuals had no provision for strategic bombardment using nonnuclear weapons.[20] The USAF did not appreciate
that fears of the possibility of Russian retaliation or international condemna-
tion as well as more restricted political goals might require them to work with
conventional munitions and to avoid total war. The next conflict, in Vietnam, would again highlight the inability of the USAF to act decisively in a
limited war and would center attention on the increasing military, public, and
diplomatic demands for accuracy in bombing operations in urban areas.

MORE FRUSTRATION IN SOUTHEAST ASIA

By the time the United States was deeply embroiled in the war in Southeast Asia, the use of operations research and systems analysis (ORSA) that the AAF had pioneered during World War II had become almost a religion in the Department of Defense headed by Secretary Robert S. McNamara. Instead of supplementing strategic and tactical objectives as in World War II, the process was now to define these objectives. This rationalistic approach was characterized by "the pretension to universality of solutions, . . . quantification, simplification, and lack of flexibility." The process proved useful to structure forces for a war but not to fight it. Human and political factors and the inconsistencies of actual war were incompatible with ORSA, and plans and strategies developed through the process were too inflexible to deal with alternatives.[21] Yet this process had influenced the development of USAF doctrine in the 1960s as well as the plans developed for "Victory through Airpower" over North Vietnam.

Even before major United States forces were committed to South Vietnam, the USAF had already developed a scheme to shock Hanoi quickly and decisively with American firepower and resolve. Chairman of the JCS Gen. Earle Wheeler presented McNamara with a plan to strike ninety-four key targets in sixteen days, an operation designed to convince North Vietnam to abandon its support of the insurgency in the South. Primarily for political reasons, President Johnson decided to apply pressure gradually, in the campaign ROLLING THUNDER. Target lists grew to 240 and then 427 fixed objectives, and priorities ranking interdiction, oil, industry, and electrical power fluctuated. Johnson prohibited attacks on many targets near cities, and Wheeler was sensitive about the prospect of civilian casualties. Military advisers repeatedly tried to expand and accelerate air attacks on North Vietnam throughout Johnson's presidency, including asking for permission to destroy rice crops, but with little success.[22]

American fighter-bombers roamed the skies over Vietnam, but any bombing near urban areas was strictly controlled. Enemy tactics and propaganda forced extraordinary measures. Rules of engagement required air strikes to be preceded by warnings with leaflets or loudspeakers; pilots could not fly over friendly populated areas when armed. Despite precautions, friendly troops or villages were hit, mostly through technical failures or poor communication. Eventually pilots were ordered not to deliver ordnance unless they were completely sure of their target and equipment. By 1967 only 1 in 6,000 sorties

New Army Chief of Staff William Westmoreland confers on strategy with President Lyndon Johnson and Walt W. Rostow in 1968. Rostow, perhaps Johnson's most hawkish adviser on the Vietnam War, had analyzed bombing targets during World War II with the Enemy Objectives Unit of the Economic Warfare Division of the U.S. Embassy in London. The economy of North Vietnam presented different problems for strategic bombing from those encountered in Germany, however. (Westmoreland Collection, Special Collections Division, U.S. Military Academy Library, West Point, N.Y.)

involved accidental bombing of friendly units or towns, a circumstance reflecting sound training, "smart bombs," and strict control.[23] Much of this precision can be attributed to technical advances pioneered during World War II.

But improved accuracy alone was not enough to ensure a successful air war. As in Korea, a resolute enemy with a simple economy thwarted superior technology in weapons. Operations such as ROLLING THUNDER (referred to by some Air Force officers in hindsight as "Rolling Blunder") drew directly on precision-bombing doctrine to target North Vietnam's vital economic and military centers and to destroy its capacity to wage war. A combination of political restrictions, gradualist tactics in the application of force, and the nature of the enemy's will and infrastructure frustrated these grandiose plans. Perhaps because of an exaggerated opinion of American success with air interdiction in Korea, the USAF concentrated heavy bombing on enemy supply lines and sources in North and South Vietnam. In 1967 Gen. Matthew Ridgway wrote, "There were those who felt, at the time of the Korean War, that air power might accomplish miracles of interdiction. . . . The fact that it could not accomplish these miracles has not yet been accepted as widely as it should have been." He believed that "some in high position" still failed to appreciate the "limitations" of airpower. These limitations were evident in ineffective campaigns against precision target systems such as oil and electric power. As McNamara came to realize that the agrarian economy and guerrilla forces of the North Vietnamese would never collapse from bombing, USAF leaders chafed to be free of political restrictions to strike harder at key targets in Hanoi and Haiphong.[24]

A new president, Richard Nixon, gave the Air Force its chance with Operations LINEBACKER I and LINEBACKER II, which included sending strategic bombers against objectives in North Vietnamese cities. Earlier attempts to destroy small factories with B-52 bombers had just highlighted their "inability . . . to hit a small target without damage to the surrounding civilian population," a result that brought a halt to such missions. Nixon allowed even more extensive targeting of urban storage and transportation facilities. Once again, American aircraft pounded an enemy capital. Accuracy was relatively good and evacuations helped keep casualties low. Though 730 B-52 sorties attacking urban targets during LINEBACKER II in December 1972 caused only 1,318 civilian deaths, considerable public outcry arose against the operation, and world opinion quickly compared the attacks with area bombing raids such as those against Dresden. The operations did fulfill the commander-in-chief's goal to bring the North Vietnamese back to the peace talks, however, and helped persuade them to accept a cease-fire in January 1973. Nixon may also have intended LINEBACKER II to impress the South Vietnamese and to gain their support for the results of the negotiations as well.[25]

Five months of LINEBACKER I had crippled North Vietnam's military capability, and the eleven days of LINEBACKER II had unsettled its urban populace. Despite harsh criticisms in the American press, Nixon had continued attacks on Hanoi and Haiphong until the North Vietnamese agreed to return to the peace table. The aerial operations against cities that had to be defended had depleted North Vietnam's supply of surface-to-air missiles as well as military and civilian food stocks; thus leaders decided to negotiate to stop further bombing. Air Force proponents used the results of LINEBACKER II to claim that political constraints had prevented them from winning the war, and retired generals Curtis LeMay and William M. Momyer echoed that sentiment by asserting that unrestrained airpower could win any war. Yet as Mark Clodfelter has pointed out, "Most air commanders fail to understand that the 'Eleven-Day War' was a unique campaign for very limited ends." It did not cause the North Vietnamese army or nation to surrender; it simply furthered Nixon's political goal for a negotiated settlement and delayed final victory for his enemies. LINEBACKER did not vindicate precision tactics or the selection of urban targets.[26] But another limited conflict involving air raids on cities, this time in Southwest Asia, would produce more USAF arguments for the decisiveness of airpower.

SUCCESS IN SOUTHWEST ASIA

For most of us, the arrival of DESERT STORM was heralded by televised American air raids on another enemy capital. We remember the vivid images of Tomahawk cruise missiles and Stealth fighters over Baghdad and broken Iraqi troops in Kuwait. The systematic development of war-weary bombers, radar bombing, and Azon bombs had evolved into an impressive array of high-technology weapons, constantly displayed in briefings that emphasized the precision and the destructive might of American airpower. Conventional bombing of pinpoint objectives was the rule, with a repeatedly announced goal of avoiding harm to civilians. Theory, practice, and ethics seemed to merge in a clean and decisive air campaign to eject a tyrant at a minimum cost in friendly casualties. Though many operational details are yet to be revealed, some conclusions can be made from available data about the use and accomplishments of American airpower against Iraq.

From the beginning, limited war aims and concerns about maintaining the fragile Allied coalition influenced the execution of the air offensive. This does not mean that extensive bombing of targets in Iraqi cities did not occur. American air strikes destroyed water, power, and transportation facilities in Baghdad in attacks suggesting Seversky's idea of an aerial blockade. Strategic targets pinpointing electricity, oil, communications, supply depots, and transportation nodes were hit throughout Iraq. From the beginning of the war, administration officials and military leaders emphasized that commanders in the field would be allowed to fight the war free of interference from Washington, and there were few limitations on targeting of military and economic objectives. In one notable exception, Secretary of Defense Richard Cheney ordered the JCS to review all missions over Baghdad after the bombing of the Amiriya bunker that killed many civilians.[27] Otherwise, the USAF exercised proper restraint regarding sacred sites and residential areas though some collateral damage resulted from near misses or downed cruise missiles. Learning their lesson from Vietnam, leaders in Southwest Asia and Washington responded quickly to counter any claims of indiscriminate bombing with explanations and photographs.

Though the bombing of Iraqi cities disrupted civilian life, it did not break the Iraqi will to fight. But the air campaign had a different goal: to cripple the Iraqi army in Kuwait through interdiction of its lines of communication and by tactical strikes on its troops and positions so that a ground war might prove unnecessary. The results were impressive. Total air supremacy ensured the success of the efforts to hide the massing of forces on the western flank. Frontline enemy conscripts were demoralized by the bombing and were starving from lack of supplies. Farther to the rear, Republican Guard units were better protected and provisioned, but the degraded Iraqi command-and-control system prevented them from reacting effectively to the coalition's enveloping attacks. Contrary to initial reports, some strong enemy ground resistance occurred as coalition forces drove deeper into Iraq, but superior troops, equipment, and training were decisive in those engagements. Though weakened by air attacks, the Republican Guard did maneuver units to try to stop VII Corps. Although newscasts implied that the USAF had been the main destroyer of enemy armored vehicles, figures from Gen. Norman Schwarzkopf's Central Command show that ground forces destroyed 2,162 tanks out of total Iraqi losses of 3,847, and these figures may actually be too low. Lt. Gen. Frederick Franks claims that his VII Corps troops, carrying out Schwarzkopf's main attack, destroyed over 1,300 tanks on their four-day sweep into Iraq and 600 more in mopping-up operations. U.S. Marine forces alone claimed about 1,000 tanks.[28] One of the most widely circulated stories among Army officers returning from the war concerns an Iraqi regimental commander in the Republican Guard who admitted to his captors from the Second Armored Cavalry Regiment that after losing only 7 of his 39 tanks during a month of bombing, he decided it was time to quit when he lost the other 32 tanks after only thirty minutes of combat against VII Corps forces.

Apparently, the most significant effects of the air campaign were to break the morale of the second-rate troops in frontline defenses and to seriously damage Iraqi command, control, communications, and intelligence systems. The ground war was still necessary but was miraculously easy, helped in part because the land offensive possessed combat power designed to defeat a much larger enemy force, which had been projected by faulty intelligence.[29] But military-budget talks were in full swing, and the Air Force was quick to claim sole credit for victory over Iraq. The USAF spokesman, Gen. Merrill McPeak, in words echoing statements made after the surrender of Pantelleria, announced, "My private conviction is that this is the first time in history that a field army has been defeated by air power." Air Force historians have already begun to garner evidence to support McPeak's assertion. For example, in *Storm over Iraq*, Richard Hallion provides a detailed analysis of the air campaign that is noteworthy for its discussions of the impact of technology in the Gulf War and how the versatility of modern airpower has blurred the traditional distinction between tactical and strategic roles. Among the lessons that Hallion draws from the conflict is that airpower demonstrated that it can now seize and hold ground without ground forces, and in future wars it will not only be "decisive," but also "the determinant of victory."[30]

Until all reports from DESERT STORM are analyzed in detail, final judgment on McPeak's conviction must wait, and even then major disagreements will probably remain between proponents of ground and air power. But the USAF claim hardly vindicates theories of strategic bombing designed to defeat an enemy nation by destroying its total war-making capability or by breaking its national will. Precision doctrine and technology did receive deserved praise for their contribution to DESERT STORM, though some of McPeak's disclosures at the press conference also tarnished the image of the pinpoint accuracy of USAF weaponry displayed in so many videotapes at war briefings. Iraq absorbed half again as many so-called "smart bombs" in forty-three days as Vietnam did in eight years, but precision munitions made up only 6,250 of 88,500 tons of bombs dropped on Iraq and occupied Kuwait. And although 90 percent of the smart weapons hit their targets, the accuracy rate for unguided bombs was only 25 percent. McPeak admitted that over 62,000 tons of bombs had missed their targets, reflecting a rather disappointing level of precision.[31]

These figures should not detract from the impressive successes of the air campaign. Careful targeting ensured that few misses caused collateral damage in urban areas, and one must realize that the psychological effects of misses can be as devastating as a hit. Many vital targets were destroyed by the 26,000 tons of accurate bombs, but the most important result of the air campaign may have been to destroy the morale of the Iraqi troops manning the defenses of the "Saddam line" in southern Kuwait. Iraqi prisoners reported that B-52 saturation raids on their positions had especially devastating psychological effects, and intelligence sources estimate that from 20 percent to 40 percent of frontline troops had deserted prior to the ground campaign.[32] Contrary to McPeak's claim, some precedent does exist for such a result, and it comes from an earlier conflict in the same region.

Interestingly, some commentators have looked at the relative casualties between the coalition forces and Iraq and compared DESERT STORM with examples of colonial warfare, such as Omdurman, where technologically superior armies devastated ill-equipped local contingents. These pundits are more correct than they probably realize. During the 1920s, as part of its search for missions to justify its independence, the RAF developed a doctrine of air control for British colonial mandates in the Middle East. Principles and tactics were perfected in countering an Iraqi insurgency that involved at least 131,000 armed rebels. As in DESERT STORM, bombing and psychological warfare were used to generate a sense of helplessness and to induce many desertions and surrenders. In actions foreshadowing occurrences in DESERT STORM, rebels often gave up at the mere sound of aircraft approaching. In 1920 Britain needed 135,000 troops to maintain order in Iraq; by 1930 it had only four RAF squadrons and one armored-car company there.[33]

The British ground operations in Iraq in the 1920s were of course much different from the armored onlaught of DESERT STORM, but the results of the associated air campaigns were similar.[34] A poorly led Third World force in open country was broken by a technologically superior air force. DESERT STORM gave the USAF a unique opportunity to fight a fast-paced conventional war against a vulnerable enemy on a battlefield with few political restrictions, though it was a limited conflict aimed at dislodging an army rather than at subduing a whole nation. This optimum situation allowed American airmen to demonstrate the full range of their capabilities and the evolution of modern airpower. Traditional strategic bombing by mass raids of B-52s was not a factor in the coalition victory; instead, attacks by individual aircraft using precision tactics and technology were highly effective against key targets in enemy urban areas. Pictures of broken bridges and destroyed factories in Baghdad and a widespread recognition of the sincere and generally successful attempt to avoid civilian casualties in Iraqi cities demonstrated that American airmen had continued their adherence to precision-bombing doctrine and had made significant progress toward achieving the ideal capabilities first envisioned at the Air Corps Tactical School almost sixty years earlier.

11. LEGACIES

It was an illusion of the historian to assume that the participants would help prepare history current with operations. It is likewise an illusion of warriors to assume they will do it after hostilities.

—*Bruce Hopper, USSTAF historian*[1]

Some observers of the Gulf War against Iraq disagreed with the prevailing view that coalition air forces were consciously and effectively avoiding indiscriminate bombing of civilians. Yasuo Kurata, a political commentator for *Tokyo Shimbun*, was highly critical of Americans and the USAF after the bombing of the air-raid shelter in Amiriya that "slaughtered more than 400 people, including about 100 infants and young children." Discounting official insistence that the underground bunker was a communications center, Kurata claimed that Americans are insensitive to civilian casualties because they have never been bombed themselves, a charge that brings to mind Vera Brittain's writings during World War II. He invoked images of Dresden and Tokyo, describing his own memories of the latter raid in graphic detail, and accused the U.S. military of a tendency to dismiss the loss of life as "collateral damage," an "inevitable byproduct of aerial warfare. . . . Carpet bombing by B-52s is the U.S. Air Force's stock in trade. The huge aircraft can destroy entire cities from 30,000 feet; the collateral damage can well be imagined." He also condemned the use of fuel-air explosives against Iraqi troops as well as the entire American strategy of air superiority and bombing. He implied that Asians and Europeans, sensitized by their own experiences of being bombed, were opposed to the air war against Iraqi cities but that Americans remained ignorant of the costs of such aerial bombardment and did not seem to care.[2]

It is easy to criticize Kurata's position. Americans did not ignore the tragedy in Amiriya. It received extensive media coverage, and command authorities from the president on down took action to ensure that such incidents did not recur. The experience of being bombed did not stop British or German raids during World War II, nor did it affect European support for the effort to dislodge Iraq from Kuwait. B-52s have never carpet-bombed cities, though Kurata seems to imply that Americans are uniquely preoccupied with urban area attacks. Obviously this is a distortion of history; he could be reminded that Japanese aircraft conducted the first air war against population centers when they bombed China in the 1930s. Yet one should not completely discount Kurata's perceptions. Fears of massive retaliatory American air raids on Baghdad may have deterred Saddam Hussein from using chemical or biological weapons in the Gulf War. The idea that the American way of war tends toward an overall technological onslaught against an enemy society is a legacy of American strategic bombing in World War II and is echoed in many recent books on the subject.

Despite the controversy over Amiriya, the USAF demonstrated during DESERT STORM that it apparently has learned to apply precision tactics and technology to achieve military objectives effectively without extensive collateral damage in urban areas and the resulting political and diplomatic complications. The achievement of this goal was delayed partly because of the AAF's hasty and insufficient historical assessment of its operations during World War II. Ethical and practical implications of air attacks on urban areas were not adequately examined, and the lessons of victory through airpower gleaned from World War II did not apply to the conflicts in Korea and Vietnam. The industry and infrastructures in those Asian countries were unlike the systems in Germany, Japan, or Italy, and the international climate during those limited wars was far different from that of the 1940s. Yet a thorough AAF analysis of the total effects of urban bombing in World War II would have prepared the USAF for a better use of airpower in Korea or Vietnam.

Another result of this incomplete assessment by the AAF has been the recent criticism questioning the reality of World War II precision bombing. Beginning after the war and sometimes based on distorted facts, isolated criticisms of individual missions such as the attacks on Dresden and Tokyo have now grown into general doubts about the ethics and practices of the entire strategic air campaign. Hopper's prophecy has come true, and the initiative in discussions of AAF performance has passed from participants to critical historians who are not always as knowledgeable or as sympathetic. Although the ideal of pinpoint air attacks that could send bombs down industrial smokestacks was never achieved in World War II, the claim that adherence to precision-bombing doctrine was a myth ignores the operational record.

The devastation caused by Maj. Gen. Curtis LeMay's fire raids on Tokyo. Images such as this have inspired critics to question American sensitivity to civilian casualties.

In Europe, despite many pressures to do otherwise, American airmen consistently followed their doctrine. Precision advocates like Spaatz and Hughes at USSTAF headquarters, Cabell at MAAF, and Doolittle at Eighth Air Force seemed motivated at least partly by concerns for morality; other leaders in the European theater, such as Anderson and Eaker, were more concerned with bombing effectiveness or public relations. The result, however, was the same. Although theory did exceed technology, American airmen in Europe did the best they could with what they had. Air operations during DESERT STORM again demonstrated the difficulty of achieving accuracy with "dumb bombs" of the kind used by the Eighth and Fifteenth Air Forces against Germany, and their practices must be seen as an attempt to halt or at least to slow the rush to unlimited warfare. Although it is difficult to separate efficiency from ethics in AAF doctrine and practice, a limitation on the "uncurbed bestial instincts" of war did emerge. Objective observers can still perceive a definite difference between AAF strategic bombing in Europe and the British area raids on cities or the German Blitz on London.

The moral tenets of World War II AAF doctrine are still present in current

American military manuals on the law of war. Military necessity for aerial bombardment is defined in terms of precision bombing. One case study explains that the destruction of a city is not justified because of warehouses or transportation routes; only recognized military targets can be attacked. Another emphasizes that the rules of war prohibit attacks that cause "unnecessary suffering and destruction" or attacks against "the civilian population or against cultural, historical, religious, or other protected objects." A third study, inspired by Cassino, asserts that cultural protection can be forfeited if the structure is used for military purposes. The emphasis throughout focuses on the military or economic justification for targets and the protection of civilians as much as possible. The issue of workers as belligerents is not directly addressed, however.[3]

The devotion of men such as Spaatz and Doolittle to precision doctrine during World War II established an important precedent for later American air operations. Arnold's drive to develop new technology also had important implications. American prototypes for cruise missiles, precision munitions, and radar bombing aids that were so impressive for their pinpoint accuracy during DESERT STORM were first tested in combat during World War II. Precision doctrine has influenced the development of technology to the extent that the motivation for recent cuts in American nuclear weapons has come in part from the realization that conventional "smart bombs" can remove many targets more effectively, especially at the tactical and operational levels of war.

On the other hand, the legacy of the fire raids can be seen in the acceptance of urban targeting policies involving strategic nuclear weapons.[4] Sanctions restricting the bombing of civilians eroded as World War II entered its complex final phases, and pressure increased for the Allies to achieve their stated aim of winning the war "as decisively and speedily as possible."[5] Once Hansell had left the Pacific, no real advocate of precision bombing remained there, and LeMay and his superiors saw the area incendiary attacks as the best method for ending the war quickly, saving American lives, demonstrating a true victory through airpower, and securing a strong position to bargain for postwar status as an independent service. The fire raids and the exploitation of the accompanying terror marked the culmination of the American escalation to total war. Once that course of destroying cities was adopted, with its complete disregard for any restraint against killing civilians, the use of the atomic bomb was logical. Most Americans and their leaders considered the new weapon simply as a more powerful version of conventional ordnance; recognized restrictions limiting chemical and biological warfare did not appear to apply to nuclear weapons in 1945. The *Chicago Sun* echoed popular sentiment: "There is no scale of values which makes a TNT explosion right and an uranium explosion wrong." Once the fire raids became accepted policy, any form of warfare against Japan seemed permissible. If the invasion of Kyushu in November had been a bloodbath, poison gas and crop destroyers probably would also have been used to support the invasion of Japan's main island in March 1946. As Marshall had noted, those weapons were not as terrible as the incendiary bombs being used to incinerate Japanese urban areas.[6]

Yet we should not make hasty moral judgments about the men who firebombed Tokyo or dropped the atomic bombs. Michael Howard reminds us that "the overwhelming majority of the people concerned, not simply the decision makers but the public that supported them, did not see this as a moral problem at all." He has also observed that when statesmen and their generals deal with the ethical issues of a war threatening their people and nation, "the options open to them are likely to be far more limited than is generally realized."[7] And the problems of leaders are much more complex in an era of total war and nuclear weapons. The issues of law, technology, and airpower ethics that every AAF commander faced are part of the problem that Bill Moyers has called "the great unresolved dilemma of our age: Will we go on doing what our weapons make possible?"[8]

APPENDIX. SUGGESTED REPLY TO LETTERS QUESTIONING HUMANITARIAN ASPECTS OF AIR FORCE

The most fundamental difference between beast and man is in the fact that the beast is a realist, taking life at its face value, while man attempts by his emotions to camouflage, and thereby to make more bearable, unpleasant prospects which he faces.

War, no matter how glorious the cause, is horrible by every civilized standard. Clothing it in shining armor does not hide the blood and suffering except from him who would be blind; neither does changing the vehicle of destruction alter the fact that death and destruction form the inevitable body and face of war.

By drawing aside the curtain, we see air warfare as being different only in the range of its potential destruction. The air gives uncurbed bestial instincts a wider field of expression, leaving only humanity and common sense to dictate limitations. Law cannot limit what physics makes possible. We can depend for moderation only upon reason and humane instincts when we exercise such a power.

We believe that we are using those curbs to the proper extent in our application of Air Power, but I can well understand your confusion in the light of propaganda and misguided reports of air operations. The fact that no adequate explanation has ever been offered has likewise confused others in a much better position to understand.

All of us have seen the result of air power as used by the beast. To one such as he, any horror is justified so long as his end is accomplished, but he fails to realize that even his purpose could be better accomplished if he used methods which are more efficient and which happen, at the same time, to be most humane.

This can best be illustrated by our own concept of the proper role of air power in war. It works on the principle of the old adage to the effect that for the lack of a nail the house fell down. We take away the nail.

It has always been recognized that armies can be defeated through the killing of men; but are not modern armies as futile without weapons and equipment? The armored force is nothing without a tank, and we can take the tank by killing its occupants and, at the same time, suffering casualties on our part. But we can also take the tank away, in effect, "before it is born," thereby saving the casualties on both sides. We can hit the factory where it is built, the steel plant where the armor is made, or the refinery from which it gets its fuel. We do not mean the cities containing the factories, but by exercising the precision which is the keynote of America, we mean that we carefully select and, to the best of our ability, hit the precise spot which is most vital to the enemy. We hold no brief for terror bombing. True, that will cause casualties on both sides, and there will still be ground fighting, but the final score in blood will be much less.

Those are the factors of reason and humanity which we allow to curb the awful weapon at our disposal. Those are the factors which the brute mind of the beast cannot conceive. With the understanding cooperation of you and thousands of others like you, we will prove to the beast that humanity pays and that Air Power is the most powerful urge for peace.

—From "Humanitarian Aspects of Airpower" binder,
Papers of Frederick L. Anderson,
Hoover Institution on War, Revolution and Peace,
Stanford University, Stanford, California.

NOTES

AFHRA	Air Force Historical Research Agency	FDR	Franklin D. Roosevelt
		GC	Group Commander
AFPAC AG	U.S. Army Forces, Pacific Adjutant General	HQ	headquarters
		JTG	Joint Target Group
A-2	Intelligence Staff (designation)	LC	Library of Congress
		NA	National Archives
CCW	Committee on Chemical Warfare	PIO	Public Information Office
CINC SWPA	Commander in Chief, Southwest Pacific Area	RG	Record Group
		USAMHI	U.S. Army Military History Institute
COPC	Combined Operational Planning Committee	WAR	War Department

CHAPTER 1. INTRODUCTION

1. Carl A. Spaatz to H. H. Arnold, 27 August 1944, diary (personal), August 1944, Box 15, Papers of Carl A. Spaatz, Library of Congress (LC).

2. Larry J. Bidinian, *The Combined Allied Bombing Offensive against the German Civilian, 1942–1945* (Lawrence, Kans.: Coronado Press, 1976), 160.

3. Russell F. Weigley, *The American Way of War* (Bloomington: Indiana University Press, 1977), 354–358.

4. Wesley Frank Craven and James Lea Cate, eds., *The Army Air Forces in World War II*, 7 vols. (Chicago: University of Chicago Press, 1948–1953), 1: 78, 95.

5. Ibid., 3: 638, 733. These include Kent Roberts Greenfield, *American Strategy in World War II: A Reconsideration* (1963; reprint, Westport, Conn.: Greenwood Press, 1979).

6. F. M. Sallagar, *The Road to Total War* (New York: Van Nostrand Reinhold, 1975), 127. John Keegan has also emphasized the superior "moral scruple" of AAF policies in "We Wanted Beady-eyed Guys Just Absolutely Holding the Course," *Smithsonian* 14 (August 1983): 34–43.

7. Max Hastings, *Bomber Command* (New York: Dial Press, 1979), 124.

8. Ronald Schaffer, "American Military Ethics in World War II: The Bombing of German Civilians," *Journal of American History* 67 (September 1980): 319, and Schaffer, *Wings of Judgment: American Bombing in World War II* (New York: Oxford, 1985), xii.

9. Michael S. Sherry, *The Rise of American Air Power: The Creation of Armageddon* (New Haven, Conn.: Yale University Press, 1987), 362–363; see also Sherry, "The Slide to Total Air War," *New Republic* 137 (16 December 1981): 24–25.

10. Sherry, *American Air Power*, 52.

11. For a summary of some of the problems with the York, see "After a Big Gun Comes up a Dud," *US News and World Report* 99 (9 September 1985): 11.

12. Kevin A. Dougherty, "R&D Strategy in WWII," *Army Research, Development, and Acquisition Bulletin* (March–April 1990): 44.

13. Maj. Robert A. Doughty, *The Evolution of U.S. Army Tactical Doctrine, 1946–1976* (Fort Leavenworth, Kans.: Combat Studies Institute, 1979), 2.

14. Robert Frank Futrell, *Ideas, Concepts, Doctrine: A History of Basic Thinking in the United States Air Force, 1907–1964* (Maxwell AFB, Ala.: Air University Aerospace Studies Institute, 1971), 1: 168.

15. On results and technology of the Libya raid, see William R. Doerner, "In the Dead of Night," *Time* 127 (28 April 1986): 28–31; see also chapter 10 of this book on DESERT STORM.

16. Doughty, *Evolution of U.S. Army Tactical Doctrine*, 1.

17. Fred Reed, "NATO Is in the Business of Projecting Uncertainty," *El Paso Times*, 1 October 1989, 8B.

18. Craven and Cate, *Army Air Forces in World War II*, 3: 721.

19. Sherry, *American Air Power*, 222.

20. Sallagar, *Road to Total War*, 156–157.

21. W. W. Rostow, *Pre-Invasion Bombing Strategy* (Austin: University of Texas Press, 1981), 40–42.

22. Operational-level commanders are those who manage campaigns in a theater of war; tactical commanders fight battles and engagements.

23. This goal is from a U.S. Chiefs of Staff memorandum, adopted at a meeting of Combined Chiefs of Staff (CCS) at Quebec on 13 May 1943, U.S. State Department, *Foreign Relations of the United States: The Conferences at Washington and Quebec, 1943* (Washington, D.C.: GPO, 1970), 222.

24. Paul Fussell, *Wartime: Understanding and Behavior in the Second World War* (New York: Oxford, 1989), 14. He has admitted that his impressions are those of a "pissed-off" infantryman, and he has no adequate documentation for his view of American airmen.

25. Schaffer does analyze isolated individual operations in some detail, but I believe his focus, especially on European operations, is too narrow. He does not completely examine operational and tactical aspects of operations or the rest of the air war around them.

26. Martin Middlebrook, *The Battle of Hamburg* (New York: Charles Scribner's Sons, 1980), 340.

27. Grace Person Hayes, *The History of the Joint Chiefs of Staff in World War II: The War against Japan* (Annapolis, Md.: Naval Institute Press, 1982), 728.

28. Thomas M. Coffey, *Iron Eagle* (New York: Crown, 1986), 139, 243.

CHAPTER 2. DEVELOPING DOCTRINE

1. From a draft text for an Air Corps Tactical School (ACTS) course, *Air Force*, 1 December 1935, para. 28, File 248.101–1, Air Force Historical Research Agency (AFHRA), Maxwell Air Force Base (AFB), Ala.

2. I. B. Holley, Jr., *Ideas and Weapons* (Hamden, Conn.: Archon Books, 1971), 140.

3. Ibid., 140–146, 157–172.

4. Maurer Maurer, ed., *The U.S. Air Service in World War I*, 4 vols. (Washington, D.C.: Office of Air Force History, 1978), 1: v, 2: 141, 161–163.

5. Thomas H. Greer, *The Development of Air Doctrine in the Army Air Arm, 1917–1941* (Maxwell AFB, Ala.: Air University Research Studies Institute, 1955), 11. Edgar Gorrell first used the metaphor that a nation's army is the point of a drill and the nation the shank that must support it.

6. Maurer, *U.S. Air Service*, 2: 141–151.

7. Ibid., 253.

8. Ibid., 4: 363–499.

9. Ibid., 497.

10. Raymond H. Fredette, *The Sky on Fire* (New York: Harcourt Brace Jovanovich, 1976), 30, 262. The Germans also planned devastating incendiary raids on Paris and London in late summer 1918, but the attacks were canceled out of fear they would harm peace negotiations.

11. Maurer, *U.S. Air Service*, 4: 500–503.

12. Alfred F. Hurley, *Billy Mitchell, Crusader for Air Power* (Bloomington: Indiana University Press, 1975), 25–26.

13. Ibid., 142–145.

14. Maj. Gen. Haywood S. Hansell, Jr., *Strategic Air War against Japan* (Maxwell AFB, Ala.: Airpower Research Institute, 1980), 1. Smuts may have been influenced by his South African perspective on the ravages of the Boer War.

15. Edward Warner, "Douhet, Mitchell, Seversky: Theories of Air Warfare," in *Makers of Modern Strategy*, ed. Edward Mead Earle, Princeton, N.J.: Princeton University Press, 1941), 489–491.

16. Hurley, *Billy Mitchell*, 75–76.

17. Warner, "Douhet, Mitchell, Seversky," 487–491; Giulio Douhet, *The Command of the Air*, trans. Dino Ferrari (1942; reprint, New York: Arno Press, 1972), 10.

18. Lee Kennett, *A History of Strategic Bombing* (New York: Charles Scribner's Sons, 1982), 50–53.

19. Douhet, *Command of the Air*, 57–61, 69, 188; Michael Howard, *Studies in War and Peace* (New York: Viking, 1971), 143; Kennett, *History of Strategic Bombing*, 56.

20. Warner, "Douhet, Mitchell, Seversky," 498–500; Perry M. Smith, "Douhet and Mitchell: Some Reappraisals," *Air University Review* 18 (September–October 1967): 98–99.

21. Hurley, *Billy Mitchell*, 6, 146–147; John F. Shiner, *Foulois and the U.S. Army Air Corps, 1931–1935* (Washington, D.C.: Office of Air Force History, 1983), 48.

22. Robert Frank Futrell, *Ideas, Concepts, Doctrine* (Maxwell AFB, Ala.: Air University Aerospace Studies Institute, 1971), 1:38–39; Douhet, *Command of the Air*, 1; Hurley, *Billy Mitchell*, 146–147.

23. John M. Collins, *Grand Strategy: Principles and Practices* (Annapolis, Md.: Naval Institute Press, 1973), 17–18.

24. On the development of British bombing policy, see Max Hastings, *Bomber Command* (New York: Dial Press, 1979), and John Terraine, *A Time for Courage* (New York: Macmillan, 1985). The former is rather critical of British policy, the latter more sympathetic.

25. Shiner, *Foulois*, 44–45.

26. Donald M. Snow and Dennis M. Drew, *Introduction to Strategy* (Maxwell AFB, Ala.: Air Command and Staff College, 1982), 64–69.

27. Hansell, *Strategic Air War*, 3.

28. Shiner, *Foulois*, 47–48; Greer, *Development of Air Doctrine*, 57; Haywood S. Hansell, Jr., "Harold L. George: Apostle of Air Power," in *Makers of the United States Air Force*, ed. John L. Frisbee (Washington, D.C.: Office of Air Force History, 1987), 77.

29. Russell F. Weigley, *The American Way of War* (Bloomington: Indiana University Press, 1977), 516.

30. Futrell, *Ideas, Concepts, Doctrine*, 33; Greer, *Development of Air Doctrine*, 57–58.

31. Greer, *Development of Air Doctrine*, 57.

32. Ibid., 58; Hansell, "Harold L. George," 78.

33. Greer, *Development of Air Doctrine*, 58; Hansell, "Harold L. George," 78.

34. Ronald Schaffer, *Wings of Judgment* (New York: Oxford, 1985), 27; Michael S. Sherry, *The Rise of American Air Power* (New Haven, Conn.: Yale University Press, 1987), 55.

35. From a 1931 ACTS text, *The Air Force*, pp. 54–55, File 248.101-1, AFHRA.

36. Shiner, *Foulois*, 47–48; a copy of the article is in Box 245 of the Papers of Henry H. Arnold, Library of Congress (LC); instructor text for 1934–1935 *Air Force* course, p. 3, File 248.101-1, AFHRA.

37. From draft text for *Air Force* course, 1 December 1935, para. 28, File 248.101-1, and from lesson plan for "Conference on Air Operations against National Structures," 11 April 1939, p. 14, File 248.2020A-25, AFHRA.

38. For an example of the influence on Command and General Staff School (CGSS), see Maj. William C. Sherman, *Air Warfare* (New York: Ronald Press, 1926). Sherman was an instructor in air tactics at Fort Leavenworth; his writings follow ACTS doctrine of the time and deviate from official policy.

39. M. Hamlin Cannon, *Flying Training at West Point* (Colorado Springs: U.S. Air Force Academy, 1970), 30–32.

40. Cannon, *Flying Training*, 27; memorandum from the Dept. of Tactics to the superintendent, "Analysis of Cadet Military Training and Recommended Changes," 19 January 1939, United States Military Academy (USMA) Archives, West Point, N.Y.

41. See Tactical Course File 351.051 and Dept. of Civil and Military Engineering Organizational History/Program of Instruction Files, USMA Archives.

42. Student handouts, "The Sino-Japanese War" and "The Civil War in Spain," Dept. of Civil and Military Engineering Organizational History/Program of Instruction Files, Academic Year 1938–1939, Box 2, USMA Archives.

43. Hilton P. Goss, *Civilian Morale under Aerial Bombardment, 1914–1939* (Maxwell AFB, Ala.: Air University, 1948), 253; "Franco Exhibits Himself," *New Republic* 94 (30 March 1938): 205.

44. Dallas D. Irvine, "The Misuse of Air Power," *Infantry Journal* 44 (May–June 1937): 255–256.

45. P. W. Wilson, "Are Laws of War Scraps of Paper?" *New York Times*, 3 October 1937, sec. 4E, p. 1.

46. Col. Byron Q. Jones, "Air Forces in War" File, Command Course No. 6, 1939, and Capt. Carter W. Clarke, memorandum for the asst. commandant, 28 February 1940, File 7-1940-87, Army War College Curricular Archives, U.S. Army Military History Institute (USA MHI), Carlisle Barracks, Pa.

47. Robert Frank Futrell, "Commentary," in *Command and Commanders in Modern Warfare*, ed. Lt. Col. William Geffen (Colorado Springs: U.S. Air Force Academy, 1969), 313; Maj. Alexander P. de Seversky, *Victory through Airpower* (Garden City, N.Y.: Garden City Publishing, 1942), 145–147.

48. Seversky to Maj. Gen. Frederick L. Anderson, 7 September 1943, Box 9A, Anderson Papers, Hoover Institution on War, Revolution and Peace, Stanford Univer-

sity, Stanford, Calif. The film was "designed to educate people on new concepts of air power."

49. Hansell, "Harold L. George," 79.

50. Wesley Frank Craven and James Lea Cate, eds., *The Army Air Forces in World War II*, 7 vols. (Chicago: University of Chicago Press, 1948–1953), 1: 114–116, 146.

51. Memorandum for the chief of air staff, "Notes on Preparation of AWPD/1," 19 November 1941, Box 7, Carl A. Spaatz Papers, LC; Hansell, *Strategic Air War*, 5; David R. Mets, *Master of Airpower* (Novato, Calif.: Presidio Press, 1988), 112–113.

52. "Notes on AWPD/1," Spaatz Papers; Hansell, *Strategic Air War*, 5; Mets, *Master of Airpower*, 112–113; Hansell, "Harold L. George," 86–87; quote from James C. Gaston, *Planning the American Air War: Four Men and Nine Days in 1941* (Washington, D.C.; National Defense University Press, 1982), 103.

53. "Army and Navy Estimate of United States Overall Production Requirements," 11 September 1941, AWPD/1, tab 2, sec. 2, pt. 3, app. 2, Joint Army–Navy Board File 355, Serial 707, Record Group (RG) 225, National Archives (NA), Washington, D.C.; F. M. Sallagar, *The Road to Total War* (New York: Van Nostrand Reinhold, 1975), 187, 233.

54. "Notes on Preparation of AWPD/1", Spaatz Papers; Craven and Cate, *Army Air Forces*, 1: 146–147; for AWPD/1's long-range impact, see Haywood S. Hansell, Jr., *The Air Plan That Defeated Hitler* (Atlanta: Higgins-MacArthur, 1972).

CHAPTER 3. ATTITUDES OF LEADERS AND THE PUBLIC

1. Mrs. Katharine A. Hooper to H. H. Arnold, 3 May 1943, "Humanitarian Aspects of Airpower" Binder, Box 9A, Papers of Frederick L. Anderson, Hoover Institution on War, Revolution and Peace, Stanford University, Stanford, Calif. Many materials originally in that box may have been spread back out through the collection by archivists.

2. Wesley Frank Craven and James Lea Cate, eds., *The Army Air Forces in World War II*, 7 vols. (Chicago: University of Chicago Press, 1948–1953), 2: 238–241.

3. For American dreams about the airplane, see Joseph J. Corn, *The Winged Gospel: America's Romance with Aviation, 1900–1950* (New York: Oxford, 1983).

4. James Parton, *"Air Force Spoken Here": General Ira Eaker and the Command of the Air* (Bethesda, Md.: Adler & Adler, 1986), 140.

5. Hadley Cantril and Mildred Strunk, eds., *Public Opinion, 1935–1946* (Princeton, N.J.: Princeton University Press, 1951), 1067.

6. F. M. Sallagar, *The Road to Total War* (New York: Van Nostrand Reinhold, 1975), 187, 233.

7. Cantril and Strunk, *Public Opinion*, 1067–1069.

8. Vera Brittain, *Seeds of Chaos* (London: New Vision Publishing, 1944). This is a British version of her pamphlet.

9. Lawrence S. Wittner, *Rebels against War: The American Peace Movement, 1941–1960* (New York: Columbia University Press, 1969), 59; "Obliteration Raids on German Cities Protested in U.S.," *New York Times*, 6 March 1944, 1.

10. "Letters to the Times," *New York Times*, 9 March 1944, 16; William J Fili, *Passage to Valhalla* (Media, Pa.: Filcon Publishers, 1991), 26.

11. George E. Hopkins, "Bombing and the American Conscience during World War II," *Historian* 28 (May 1966): 467–471.

12. John C. Ford, "The Morality of Obliteration Bombing," *Theological Studies* 5 (September 1944): 271; for an example of support for Britain, see "Massacre by Bombing," *Politics* 1 (April 1944): 67–68.

13. "City Bombing Backed by Cousins and Elliot," *New York Times*, 31 March 1944, 3.

14. Lyle Evans Mahan to Arnold, 2 July 1945, File 091.412, Box 61, Papers of H. H. Arnold, Library of Congress (LC); Hopkins, "Bombing," 464–466; R. Alfred Hassler, "Slaughter of the Innocent," *Fellowship* (February 1944): 58–62.

15. Ford, "Morality," 286, 304.

16. Robert C. Batchelder, *The Irreversible Decision, 1939–1950* (Boston: Houghton Mifflin, 1962), 180–181.

17. See Hopkins, "Bombing," 467–471; he argues that the average American would have denied acquiescence in any attacks on women and children.

18. Michael Howard, *The Causes of War and Other Essays*, 2d ed. (Cambridge, Mass.: Harvard University Press, 1984), 104.

19. U.S. Department of State, *Foreign Relations of the United States, Diplomatic Papers 1939*, 5 vols. (Washington: GPO, 1955–1957), 1: 541–542.

20. Cordell Hull, *The Memoirs of Cordell Hull*, 2 vols. (New York: Macmillan, 1948), 1: 671–672.

21. *Foreign Relations 1939*, 1: 542–553.

22. Henry Morgenthau, *The Presidential Diaries of Henry Morgenthau, 1938–1945*, microfilm ed. 7 vols. (Frederick, Md.: University Publications of America, 1981), 4: 952.

23. Michael S. Sherry, *The Rise of American Airpower* (New Haven, Conn.: Yale University Press, 1987), 78–79.

24. Batchelder, *Irreversible Decision*, 176–177; Ford, "Morality," 271.

25. Memo, Franklin D. Roosevelt to Henry Stimson, 26 August 1944, President's Secretary File, File 1944–1945, Box 104, FDR Library, Hyde Park, N.Y.

26. Lawrence Kuter to F. L. Anderson, 8 August 1944, file 145.161-7, April 1944–May 1945, misc. correspondence of Anderson and Kuter, Air Force Historical Research Agency (AFHRA), Maxwell AFB, Ala.

27. Maj. Gen. H. H. Arnold and Col. Ira C. Eaker, *Winged Warfare* (New York: Harper, 1941), 133–134.

28. H. H. Arnold, *Global Mission* (New York: Harper, 1949), 227; diary of trip to England, April 1941, Box 271, Arnold Papers, LC.

29. H. H. Arnold, "Precision Blows for Victory: A Report to the Nation," text of planned speech scheduled for Soldiers Field, Chicago, on 16 May 1943, Box 9A, Anderson Papers. This wording was typical of Arnold's rhetoric.

30. T. J. Hanley, Jr., to asst. chiefs of air staff, personnel et al., 30 April 1943, File 385, Box 114, Arnold Papers; War Dept. transcript of extemporaneous remarks by Arnold at a Pentagon news conference, 18 October 1943, Box 14, Papers of Carl A. Spaatz, LC.

31. Thomas M. Coffey, *Hap: The Story of the U.S. Air Force and the Man Who Built It* (New York: Viking, 1982), 358–375.

32. Arnold to Spaatz, 15 September 1942, Box 8, Spaatz Papers; Arnold to Eaker, 29 June 1943, Box 16, Papers of Ira C. Eaker, LC (Arnold's italics).

33. Eaker to Lt. Gen. Barney Giles, 29 September 1943, Eaker Papers; Arnold to Spaatz, 26 September 1944, and Giles to Spaatz, 11 November 1944, Box 16, Spaatz Papers; Giles to Curtis LeMay, 11 November 1944, Box B11, Papers of Curtis LeMay, LC.

34. Arnold to Eaker, 26 November 1944, File 000.7, Box 57, Arnold Papers.

35. Memo from Arnold to all Air Force commanders in combat zones, "Evaluation of Bombing Methods and Purposes," Box 121, Papers of Nathan F. Twining, LC; Michael S. Sherry, *Preparing for the Next War* (New Haven, Conn.: Yale University Press, 1977), 19.

36. Memo, Arnold to each Air Force commander throughout the world, "Employment of Air Forces," 29 October 1942, Directive File, Box 42, Arnold Papers.

37. Ronald Schaffer, *Wings of Judgment* (New York: Oxford, 1985), 16; "Report on Suggestion for Bombing Japanese Volcanoes," 21 May 1942, President Folder, Box 45;

and Maj. Gen. V. E. Bertrandias to Arnold, with documents, 4 June 1945, File 385, Japan, Box 115, Arnold Papers.

38. Record sheets reference "Booby Traps," File 400.112, Box 117; Col. E. W. Hill to Vannever Bush, with documents, 28 May 1942, File 452.3, Box 132, Arnold Papers.

39. "Evaluation of Bombing Methods," Twining Papers.

40. Dwight Macdonald, *Memoirs of a Revolutionist* (New York: Farrar, Straus, and Cudahy, 1957), 76–77.

41. Diary of Henry L. Stimson, 5 September 1944, Yale University Library (microfilm).

42. Ibid., 3 January 1945, 2 July 1945, 6 May 1945.

43. Ibid., 6 June 1945; Noam Chomsky, *American Power and the New Mandarins* (New York: Pantheon, 1969), 167; Len Giovannitti and Fred Freed, *The Decision to Drop the Bomb* (New York: Coward-McCann, 1965), 36.

44. Schaffer, *Wings*, 180.

45. Stimson to Arnold, with reply by Eaker, 11 June 1945, Sec. of War File, Box 46, Arnold Papers; on Kyoto, see Schaffer, *Wings*, 143–146; Stimson to sec. of state, 11 January 1944, Box 114, Arnold Papers; Stimson diary, 11 October 1944.

46. Russell F. Weigley, *Eisenhower's Lieutenants* (Bloomington: Indiana University Press, 1981), 104; Spaatz to Arnold, 19 November 1944, Box 16, Spaatz Papers.

47. Statement by Spaatz to public relations officers, 8 April 1944, Box 14, Spaatz Papers.

48. Weigley, *Eisenhower's Lieutenants*, 59.

49. Personal diary, 11 August 1945, Box 21, Spaatz Papers; Spaatz, interview with Noel Parrish and Alfred Goldberg, 21 February 1962, USAF Oral History Program K239.0512–754, Office of Air Force History, Bolling AFB, Washington, D.C.

50. Spaatz to Maj. Gen. George Stratemeyer, 14 September 1942, Box 8, Spaatz Papers.

51. Carl Mann, *Lightning in the Sky* (New York: Robert H. McBride, 1943), 244–245, 252–255; Lowell Thomas and Edward Jablonski, *Doolittle, a Biography* (New York: Da Capo, 1976), 173–174, 245–246, 294; Craven and Cate, *Army Air Forces*, 3: 638–639, 725.

52. Gen. James H. Doolittle, with Carol Glines, *I Could Never Be So Lucky Again* (New York: Bantam, 1991), 376.

53. Material on Anderson's early career is in Boxes 3 and 4 of his papers; "Memorandum to Mr. Murphy," Box 13, Anderson Papers; Anderson to Fulton Lewis, Jr., 18 April 1945, File 519.1611, 1945, AFHRA.

54. Ronald Schaffer, "American Military Ethics in World War II," 324; *Journal of American History* 67 (September 1980): Eaker to Arnold, 5 January 1945, Box 22, Eaker Papers.

55. Parton, "Air Force Spoken Here," 24–25, 41–42, 46–47, 216–228; minutes of meeting of Joint Chiefs of Staff (JCS), 29 March 1943, Record Group (RG) 218, National Archives (NA), Washington, D.C.; "General Eaker Explains Strategy of 24-Hour Bombing of Germany," 18 February 1943 release, War Dept., Bureau of Public Relations, Box 9A, Anderson Papers.

56. Memo, Eaker to Arnold, 25 August 1939, Box 3, Arnold Papers; Eaker, interview with Joe Green, 1972, Ira C. Eaker Papers, U.S. Army Military History Institute (USAMHI), Carlisle Barracks, Pa. In 1972 he did believe, however, that without daylight bombing the Luftwaffe would not have been defeated and the invasion would have failed.

57. Minutes of U.S. Strategic Air Forces (USSTAF) Air Commander's Conference, 15 October 1944, Box 16, and Eaker to Spaatz, 1 January 1945, Box 20, Spaatz Papers.

58. See attaché reports in G-2 Regional File, Great Britain, 1933–1944, 9600–9670, Box 1620, War Dept. General and Special Staffs, RG 165, Modern Military Field Branch, NA, Suitland, Md.

59. Report by Anderson, 5 January 1942, Box 2, Anderson Papers; memo, Eaker to Spaatz, "Night Bombing," 8 October 1942, Box 10, Spaatz Papers.

60. Memo, George Stratemeyer to Robert Lovett, 6 February 1943, File 385, Box 114, Arnold Papers.

61. William D. Leahy, I Was There (New York: McGraw-Hill, 1950), 82–83; "Radio Message from American GHQ to Occupied France," 6 October 1942, Box 10, and personal diary, 20 October 1942, Box 9, Spaatz Papers.

62. Craven and Cate, Army Air Forces, 2: 240; memo on bombardment policy from Air Vice Marshal J. C. Slessor, 29 October 1942, File 519.318–1, 1942–1945, Combined Bomber Offensive (CBO) Policy Directives, AFHRA.

63. Bruce Hopper, memo on USSTAF history preparation, 22 September 1944, Box 287, Spaatz Papers.

64. Memo, Lovett to Judge Robert Patterson, 18 March 1943, with supporting documents, File 385, Box 114, Arnold Papers.

65. Craven and Cate, Army Air Forces, 2: 320; Eaker to Air Vice Marshal Norman Bottomley, 9 April 1943, Box 19, Eaker Papers, LC; Sir Charles Portal to Eaker, 21 April 1943, Box 41, Arnold Papers; draft of letter, Arnold to Portal, "Humanitarian Aspects of Airpower" Binder, Box 9A, Anderson Papers.

66. Weigley, Eisenhower's Lieutenants, 58–64; "Review of Oil and Transportation Target Systems," 6 June 1944, File 168.7026–6, January–June 1944, Papers of Gen. Charles P. Cabell, AFHRA.

67. Weigley, Eisenhower's Lieutenants, 58–64; "Review of Target Systems," AFHRA.

68. Cabell interview with Hopper, 9 July 1944, Box 135; memo to Eisenhower with cable to JCS, "Loss of Civilian Lives during Overlord Preparatory Phase," from Overlord Air Support Advisory Committee, 11 April 1944, Box 17; minutes of meeting in Gen. Sir H. M. Wilson's HQ, 30 April 1944, Box 14, Spaatz Papers.

69. "Humanitarian Aspects of Airpower," Binder, Box 9A, Anderson Papers.

70. Michael Howard, Studies in War and Peace (New York: Viking, 1971), 238–241.

CHAPTER 4. ATTITUDES AND PERCEPTIONS
OF AMERICAN AIRMEN

1. Herman Melville, "A Utilitarian View of the Monitor's Fight," Collected Poems of Herman Melville, ed. H. P. Vincent (Chicago: Packard, 1947), 40.

2. Maj. Gen. J. F. C. Fuller, Generalship: Its Diseases and Their Cure (1936; reprint, Fort Leavenworth, Kans.: Combat Studies Institute, 1987), 13.

3. S. L. A. Marshall, Men against Fire: The Problem of Battle Command in Future War (1947; reprint, Gloucester, Mass.: Peter Smith, 1978), 204. Despite recent controversy about his methods, Marshall still offers many valuable insights.

4. Michael S. Sherry, The Rise of American Air Power (New Haven, Conn.: Yale University Press, 1987), 204–218; Schaffer, Wings of Judgment (New York: Oxford, 1985), 17–18.

5. W. F. Craven and J. L. Cate, eds., The Army Air Forces in World War II, 7 vols. (Chicago: University of Chicago Press, 1948–1953), 6: 538–556; Marshall, Men against Fire, 15–17; Roy R. Grinker and John P. Spiegel, Men under Stress (Philadelphia: Blakiston, 1945), 8; Samuel A. Stouffer et al., The American Soldier, 2 vols. (Princeton, N.J.: Princeton University Press, 1949), 2: 326–327.

6. See, for instance, Charles B. MacDonald, *Company Commander* (New York: Bantam, 1978), preface, 293; Charles P. Roland, military historian and former WWII infantryman, interview with author, West Point, N.Y., 30 January 1986; Wilbur H. Morrison, *Point of No Return* (New York: Times Books, 1979), 241.

7. Philip Kaplan and Rex Alan Smith, *One Last Look* (New York: Abbeville Press, 1983), 20–21; Martin Caidin, *Black Thursday* (New York: Bantam, 1981), 77–79.

8. "Flak versus Heavy Bombers," *Coast Artillery Journal* 89 (March–April 1946): 24; Elmer T. Lian, *POW*, 1–10, manuscript, Lian Papers, U.S. Army Military History Institute (USAMHI), Carlisle Barracks, Pa. Flak suits were fifteen-pound aprons with small steel discs sewn in to provide some protection from low-velocity shrapnel.

9. Bernard Nalty and Carl Berger, *The Men Who Bombed the Reich* (New York: E. P. Dutton, 1978), 25–26; letter 197, Letters of Robert E. O'Donnell, USAMHI; Grinker and Spiegel, *Men Under Stress*, 33–34.

10. Memo, Eaker to Spaatz, "Lessons Learned from Operations to Date," 25 August 1942, Box 38, Papers of H. H. Arnold, Library of Congress (LC); minutes of U.S. Strategic Air Forces (USSTAF) staff meeting, 28 October 1944, Box 19, Papers of Carl Spaatz, LC; survey is in Box 14, Spaatz Papers; Stouffer, *American Soldier*, 2: 407; Lian, *POW*, 1–25; Martin E. Kestenbaum, World War II veteran and president of the New Jersey Chapter of the Eighth Air Force Historical Society, interview with author, West Point, N.Y., 23 May 1992.

11. Research Division, Special Service Division, HQ, European Theater of Operations, June 1944, "Survey of Combat Crews in Heavy Bombardment Groups in ETO," 11, Box 18, Spaatz Papers.

12. Lowell Thomas and Edward Jablonski, *Doolittle, a Biography* (New York: Da Capo Press, 1976), 301.

13. Roger Freeman, *The U.S. Strategic Bomber* (London: McDonald and Jane's, 1975), 87–100; David A. Anderton, *B-29 Superfortress at War* (New York: Charles Scribner's Sons, 1978), 19, 23, 35, 123.

14. For a good example, see Philip Ardery, *Bomber Pilot* (Lexington: University Press of Kentucky, 1978), 214–219.

15. E. Bartlett Kerr, *Flames over Tokyo: The U.S. Army Air Forces' Incendiary Campaign against Japan, 1944–1945* (New York: Donald J. Fine, 1991), 35, 128; Morrison, *Point of No Return*, 257.

16. See, for instance, foreword to XXI Bomber Command Tactical Mission Report, Mission No. 40, Urban Area of Tokyo, 10 March 1945, dated 15 April 1945, Box 26, Papers of Curtis Lemay, LC.

17. Craven and Cate, *Army Air Forces*, 6: 566–589; see Anderson's September 1941 curriculum, Box 3, Papers of F. L. Anderson, Hoover Institution on War, Revolution and Peace, Stanford University.

18. O'Donnell letters, USAMHI; Leroy W. Newby, *Target Ploesti: View from a Bombsight* (Novato, Calif.: Presidio Press, 1983), 93–98; Ardery, *Bomber Pilot*, 171–174. The O'Donnell letters present a vivid picture of the intense pressure for accurate bombing placed on bombardiers.

19. Lord Moran, *The Anatomy of Courage* (1945; reprint, Garden City Park, N.Y.: Avery Publishing Group, 1987), 102.

20. John Muirhead, *Those Who Fall* (New York: Random House, 1986), 174; Grinker and Spiegel, *Men under Stress*, 34–35; Cleveland Amory, "The Man Even Hollywood Likes," *Parade Magazine* (21 October 1984): 9; Ardery, *Bomber Pilot*, 2–3, 180–181.

21. Grinker and Spiegel, *Men under Stress*, 29; Lian, *POW*, 1–15.

22. Bert Stiles, *Serenade to the Big Bird* (New York: Bantam, 1984), 21, 77–78, 84, 122. This unique book, a combination of philosophical musings and brutal depictions of aeri-

al combat, like the war Stiles describes, "never stays the same for any length of time."

23. Lian, POW, 1–9; Elmer Bendiner, The Fall of Fortresses (New York: G. P. Putnam's Sons, 1980), 148–149, 154–155, 211, 238–239.

24. Collected Letters of Earle C. Cheek, U.S. Military Academy (USMA) Manuscript Collection, Special Collections, West Point, N.Y.; his death is described in a letter from Sergeant Keenan to Cheek's mother, 25 June 1945, in the collection.

25. Quotes are from Cheek's letters of 29 March 1944, 6 August 1944, 22 October 1944, 8 February 1945, 28 February 1945.

26. Grinker and Spiegel, Men under Stress, 24–25, 35–36; Donald W. Hastings et al., Psychiatric Experiences in the Eighth Air Force (New York: Josiah Macy, Jr., Foundation, 1944), 21–22; Roger Spiller, interview with author, Combat Studies Institute (CSI), Fort Leavenworth, Kans., 28 February 1991.

27. "The Aims and Accomplishments of Strategic Bombing," lecture, Maj. Russell Post to the 2d Bombardment Division, File 526.716E, 3–29 August 1944, Air Force Historical Research Agency (AFHRA), Maxwell AFB, Ala.; 25,000 men heard this particular lecture.

28. Dubois to Smith, "Flying Stress and Lack of Moral Fibre," War Dept. File for 1943, Box 104, President's Secretary Files, FDR Library, Hyde Park, N.Y.; "Survey of Combat Crews," 22, and Col. Leroy A. Rainey, "Strategical Pattern Bombing," Box 81, Spaatz Papers; Stiles, Serenade, 122.

29. Hastings, Psychiatric Experiences, 137–138.

30. Diary of Henry L. Stimson, 31 December 1944, Yale University Library (microfilm); Richard Polenberg, War and Society: The United States, 1941–1945 (New York: J. B. Lippincott, 1972), 41–43, 135; Stouffer, American Soldier, 2: 157–159; Kaplan and Smith, One Last Look, 156–184.

31. Impact: The Army Air Forces' Confidential Picture History of World War II, 8 books. (1943–1945 periodicals; reprint, Harrisburg, Pa.: Historical Times, 1982), 1: vi–viii; April 1943, inside cover.

32. Impact, April 1943, 2; September 1943, 42–43; June 1943, 18–19; July 1945, 4, 51.

33. Ibid., May 1945, 34; March 1945, 19–21; May 1944, 41; April 1944, 42; "Leaflet Bombing—The Appeal to Reason," lecture, Maj. Russell Post to 2d Bombardment Division, File 526.716E, 3–29 August 1944, AFHRA.

34. Impact, April 1945, 2–23; June 1945, 24–37; August 1945, 19, 34–37.

35. Minutes of USSTAF Commanders Meeting, 20 July 1944, Box 18, Spaatz Papers.

36. Quentin Reynolds, The Amazing Mr. Doolittle (New York: Appleton-Century-Crofts, 1953), 263. Doolittle also received unexpected support from his Catholic chaplains, who appreciated the importance of Rome as a communications and supply center.

37. Lt. Sawyer, 5th Bomb Wing asst. A–2 (Intelligence Staff), to Lt. Col. Arthur Clark, 5th Wing A–2, 18 February 1944, Box 17, Twining Papers.

CHAPTER 5. BOMBING AIDS

1. Carl Spaatz to Lt. Gen. Barney Giles, chief of Air Staff, 15 December 1944, Box 16, Papers of Carl A. Spaatz, Library of Congress (LC).

2. Spaatz to H. H. Arnold, 19 November 1944, Box 16, Spaatz Papers; Arnold to all Air Force commanders in combat zones, 10 June 1943, Box 121, Papers of Nathan F. Twining, LC.

3. Secret report by Major Anderson, 5 January 1942, Box 3, Papers of F. L. Anderson, Hoover Institution on War, Revolution, and Peace, Stanford University; notes on accu-

racy of bombing, A-2 (Intelligence Staff) Report, 6 October 1942, Box 10, Spaatz Papers. The Norden was supposedly accurate within 5 mils at any altitude versus 30–40 mils for the Mark XIV.

4. Philip Kaplan and Rex Alan Smith, *One Last Look* (New York: Abbeville Press, 1983), 193–197; Wesley Frank Craven and James Lea Cate, eds., *The Army Air Forces in World War II*, 7 vols. (Chicago: University of Chicago Press, 1948–1953), 2: 343–346.

5. Dale O. Smith, *Screaming Eagle* (New York: Dell, 1990), 144; letter from Milt Groban, *Commentary* 66 (July 1978): 10; letter from Charles M. Bachman, *Commentary* 66 (November 1978): 20.

6. Arnold to all Air Force commanders in combat zones, 10 June 1943, Box 121, Twining Papers; Spaatz to Arnold, 20 October 1942, Box 9, Spaatz Papers.

7. John Terraine, *A Time for Courage* (New York: Macmillan, 1985), 473–474, 514–515.

8. Craven and Cate, *Army Air Forces*, 2: 690–693; 3: 13–18; minutes, Joint Chiefs of Staff (JCS) Special Meeting, 29 April 1943, Combined Chiefs of Staff (CCS) 334, meetings 71–86, Record Group (RG) 218, National Archives (NA), Washington, D.C.: Military Attaché Reports, Files 9600–9670, Boxes 1621 and 1622, RG 165, NA, Suitland, Md.; Ronald Schaffer, "American Military Ethics in World War II," *Journal of American History* 67 (September 1980): 322.

9. Headquarters, European Theater of Operations, U.S. Army Release No. 8231, 28 December 1943, Box 9A, Anderson Papers.

10. Memo, H. M. McClelland to chief of Air Staff, 24 November 1943, Box 114, Papers of Henry H. Arnold, LC; Arnold to Spaatz, 5 January 1944, Box 14, Spaatz Papers; Office of Chief Press Censor, U.S. Army, London, Edition 7, 13 December 1943, Box 1593, RG 165, NA, Suitland, Md.; memo, Brooks to Curtis Lemay, 3 December 1943, Box B9, Papers of Curtis E. LeMay, LC.

11. Ira Eaker to Barney Giles, 13 December 1943, and Eaker to Col. George Brownell, Robert Lovett's executive officer, 22 December 1943, Box 17, Papers of Ira C. Eaker, LC.

12. Craven and Cate, *Army Air Forces*, 3: 17.

13. David R. Mets, *Master of Airpower* (Novato, Calif.: Presidio Press, 1988), 180–181; Spaatz to Arnold, 14 January 1944, Box 17, and January 1944 Files and Minutes of Press Conference, 13 March 1944, Box 14, Spaatz Papers.

14. Spaatz to Arnold, 4 April 1944, and James Doolittle to Spaatz, 22 March 1944, Box 17, Spaatz Papers; Glenn Infield, *Big Week* (Los Angeles: Pinnacle Books, 1974), 89–90.

15. Intelligence summaries in Box 6 and daily diary, Anderson Papers; on Schaffhausen, see File 519.5991-2, 1944, Indiscriminate Bombing, Air Force Historical Research Agency (AFHRA), Maxwell Air Force Base, Ala.; Collected Letters of Earle C. Cheek, 16 March 1944, U.S. Military Academy (USMA) Manuscript Collection, Special Collections, West Point, N.Y.

16. *Impact*, 8 books (1943–1945 periodicals; reprint, Harrisburg, Pa.: Historical Times, 1982), January 1944, 12–14; *The Official World War II Guide to the Army Air Forces* (1944; reprint, New York: Bonanza Books, 1988), 264.

17. Subject File: Bombing Overcast (H2X), Box 82, Spaatz Papers; Craven and Cate, *Army Air Forces*, 3: 190–193. Figures are from Doolittle's remarks in the file; they differ slightly from Craven and Cate.

18. Gordon A. Harrison, *Cross-Channel Attack* (Washington, D.C.: Office of the Chief of Military History, 1951), 300–302.

19. *Impact*, March 1945, 28–31, and May 1945, 34–38; Col. William B. Reed, ed.,

Condensed Analysis of the Ninth Air Force in the European Theater of Operations (1946; reprint, Washington, D.C.: Office of Air Force History, 1984), 34.

20. Minutes of 20 July 1944 U.S. Strategic Air Forces (USSTAF) Commanders Meeting, Box 18, Spaatz Papers.

21. Spaatz to Advisory Specialist Group, 30 September 1944, Box 18; Dr. E. L. Bowles to Spaatz, 9 November 1944, Box 19; Spaatz to Doolittle, 18 November 1944, Box 16, Spaatz Papers.

22. Craven and Cate, *Army Air Forces*, 3: 649; Eighth Air Force memo no. 55–24, "Attack of Secondary and Last Resort Targets," 29 October 1944, File 519.318–1, 1942–1945, Combined Bomber Offensive (CBO) Policy Directives, AFHRA.

23. Craven and Cate, *Army Air Forces*, 3: 667; U.S. Strategic Bombing Survey Military Analysis Division, "Daylight Bombing Accuracy of the 8th, 9th, and 15th Air Forces," 27–28, File 137.306.6, 24 August 1945, AFHRA.

24. Minutes, USSTAF Staff meeting, 14 November 1944, Anderson diary, Anderson Papers; Doolittle to Spaatz, 19 December 1944, and Spaatz to Giles, 15 December 1944, Box 16, Spaatz Papers.

25. Craven and Cate, *Army Air Forces*, 3: 666–667; Fifteenth Air Force monograph, "Operational Employment of Lone Wolf Tactics," 18 January 1945, Box 82, Spaatz Papers; message, 15th Air Force to USSTAF, 14 November 1944, Anderson diary, Anderson Papers.

26. Message CS–533–1IE, Eaker to Spaatz, 2 January 1945, Box 17, Twining Papers; Eaker to Giles, 4 January 1945, Box 106, Arnold Papers; Craven and Cate, *Army Air Forces*, 3: 667.

27. Mets, *Master of Airpower*, 258–259; entry for 26 January 1945, David Schlatter daily diary, File 168–7052–5, AFHRA; memo, McClelland to Giles, 22 January 1945, File 370.2, England, Box 105, Arnold Papers.

28. Memo, McClelland to Giles, 22 January 1945, Arnold Papers; Giles to Spaatz, 6 January 1945, Box 20, Spaatz Papers.

29. Spaatz to Giles, 23 February 1945, Box 9A, Anderson Papers; "Daylight Bombing Accuracy of the 8th, 9th, and 15th Air Forces," AFHRA, 24; Lauris Norstad to Spaatz, 3 March 1945, File 519.9701–15, 44–45, General Correspondence, AFHRA.

30. Donald W. Hastings et al., *Psychiatric Experiences in the Eighth Air Force* (New York: Josiah Macy, Jr., Foundation, 1944), 117, 327; memo, McClelland to Giles, Arnold Papers; Craven and Cate, *Army Air Forces*, 3: 738–743.

31. Hugh Odishaw, *Radar Bombing in the Eighth Air Force* (Cambridge, Mass.: Overseas Office, Radiation Laboratory, MIT, 1946), 124–126; Adolf Galland, *The First and the Last: The Rise and Fall of the German Fighter Forces, 1938–1939*, trans. Mervyn Savill (1957; reprint, New York: Ballantine, 1973), 190; Richard G. Davis, "Bombing Strategy Shifts, 1944–45," *Air Power History* 36 (Winter 1989): 44; Wilbur Morrison, *Point of No Return* (New York: Times Books, 1979), 267–268.

32. Craven and Cate, *Army Air Forces*, 5: 567.

CHAPTER 6. BETTER BOMBS

1. Jack Olsen, *Aphrodite: Desperate Mission* (New York: Pyramid Books, 1972), 196.

2. Ronald Schaffer, *Wings of Judgment* (New York: Oxford, 1985), 85–86.

3. W. F. Craven and J. L. Cate, eds., *The Army Air Forces in World War II*, 7 vols. (Chicago: University of Chicago Press, 1948–1953), 3: 727.

4. Kenneth P. Werrell, *The Evolution of the Cruise Missile* (Maxwell AFB, Ala.: Air University Press, 1985), 15–16.

5. H. H. Arnold, *Global Mission* (New York: Harper, 1949), 74–76, 227, 260–261. For a more detailed discussion on these "Bugs," officially termed the GMA-1, see Craven and Cate, *Army Air Forces*, 6: 253–254; Werrell, *Evolution of the Cruise Missile*, 26–30.

6. Cable, Spaatz to War Department (WAR), 20 June 1944, official diary, Box 18, Papers of Carl A. Spaatz, Library of Congress (LC).

7. Russell Weigley, *Eisenhower's Lieutenants*, (Bloomington: Indiana University Press, 1981), 258–259.

8. Olsen, *Aphrodite*, 175–176.

9. Telephone conversation, Lawrence Kuter and F. L. Anderson, 22 June 1944, personal diary, Box 15, and cable, Mediterranean Allied AF (MAAF) to WAR, 7 July 1944, official diary, Box 18, Spaatz Papers.

10. Cable WX58750, Washington to Commander in Chief, Southwest Pacific Area (CINC SWPA), 2 July 1944, Box 11079/22, and cable, George Kenney to Arnold, 3 July 1944, Box 11061/42, 373 files, U.S. Army Forces, Pacific Adjutant General (AF-PAC AG) Correspondence Files, Records of U.S. Army Commands, Record Group (RG) 338, National Archives (NA), Suitland, Md.

11. "Report of Aphrodite Mission, 4 August 1944," 6 August 1944, official diary, Box 18, Spaatz Papers; "Report on Aphrodite Project," 20 January 1945, file 527.431A–1, January 1945, Air Force Historical Research Agency (AFHRA), Maxwell AFB, Ala.; Olsen, *Aphrodite*, 123–126, 165–167, 173, 189–196.

12. "Report on Aphrodite Project," AFHRA; cable UG6379, Spaatz to Arnold, 13 August 1944, and cables UG7658 and UX67648, Spaatz to Arnold, 6 September 1944, Anderson's diary, Papers of F. L. Anderson, Hoover Institution on War, Revolution and Peace, Stanford University; Olsen, *Aphrodite*, 232, 280–288, 298, 302–321.

13. "Report on Aphrodite Project," AFHRA; cable 1E1000CS, Spaatz to Ira Eaker, 13 August 1944, and cable, Spaatz to James Doolittle, 7 September 1944, Anderson's diary, Anderson Papers; Olsen, *Aphrodite*, 327, 360–361.

14. Alfred Maxwell to Anderson, "Plan, Willie Orphan—Phase B," 14 November 1944; cable W61260, Arnold to Spaatz, 11 November 1944; cable, Spaatz to Arnold, 21 November 1944, Anderson's diary, Anderson Papers; "Report on Aphrodite Project," AFHRA.

15. Cable UX70102, Hoyt Vandenberg to Spaatz, 22 November 1944, and cable S71437, Dwight Eisenhower to Arnold, 18 December 1944, Anderson's diary, Anderson Papers.

16. Joint Chiefs of Staff (JCS) 1150, Combined Chiefs of Staff (CCS) 729, CCS 729/1, CCS 729/2, CCS 729/4, File 373.11 Germany (4 November 1944), Records of the United States Joint Chiefs of Staff, RG 218, NA, Washington, D.C.

17. "Newest Attempts of the Luftwaffe," *Impact*, 8 books (1943–1945 periodicals; reprint, Harrisburg, Pa.: Historical Times, 1982), October 1944, 42–43; Kuter to Arnold, 5 February 1945, Box 38, Papers of H. H. Arnold, LC.

18. Arnold to Spaatz, 23 November 1944, and Spaatz to Arnold, 10 December 1944, personal diary, Box 16, Spaatz Papers.

19. Grandison Gardner to Spaatz, 6 February 1945, official diary, Box 20, Spaatz Papers.

20. Minutes, JCS 190th meeting; memo from Adm. William Leahy to the president, 26 March 1945, CCS 373.11 Germany (4 November 1944), RG 218, NA, Washington, D.C.

21. Minutes, JCS 190th meeting; Francis L. Loewenheim et al., eds., *Roosevelt and Churchill: Their Secret Wartime Correspondence* (New York: E. P. Dutton, 1975), 688–689; Giles to Spaatz, 27 April 1945, File 519.9701-15, AFHRA.

22. Donald Hutchinson, chief of Far Eastern Air Forces (FEAF) Air Staff, to S. J.

Chamberlin, G-3 SWPA 16 June 1945, Box 11061/42, and cable WX-44043, Washington to Guam, 5 August 1945, Box 11079/22, 373 Files AFPAC, RG 338, NA, Suitland, Md.

23. See September to November 1942 correspondence on glide bombs between Arnold, Eaker, and Spaatz in Box 9, and Kuter to Anderson, 10 September 1943, Box 80, Spaatz Papers; Dale O. Smith, *Screaming Eagle* (New York: Dell, 1990), 156–157.

24. John Muirhead, *Those Who Fall* (New York: Random House, 1986), 172–175; *Impact*, March 1945, 33–35; Kenneth P. Werrell, *"Who Fears?" The 301st in War and Peace 1942–1979* (Dallas: Taylor Publishing, 1991), 90–92.

25. Entry for 16 June 1944, journal, trip to England, 8 June 1944–21 June 1944, Box 272, Arnold Papers.

26. Werrell, *Evolution of the Cruise Missile,* 62–63, 68–70.

27. See correspondence in File 452.11, Rockets, Box 131, Arnold Papers; *Impact*, January 1945, 5–7.

28. Message WARX 44137, Arnold to Spaatz and Eaker, 10 October 1944, File 519.8671–8, 1943–1944, AFHRA; memo, "Stoppage of Flying Bomb Production," Col. W. F. McKee to Col. Dean, 29 November 1944, File 471.6, Box 137, Arnold Papers; minutes, U.S. Strategic Air Forces (USSTAF) Staff meeting, 23 December 1944, Box 16, Spaatz Papers.

29. Cable W78828, George C. Marshall to Eisenhower, 18 December 1944, Anderson's diary, Anderson Papers; memo, McKee to Barney Giles, "Subject: Buzz Bomb (JB-2)," 19 January 1945, Box 131, and memo, "Buzz Bomb Program," deputy chief of Air Staff to Staff, 12 June 1945, File 471.6, Buzz Bombs, Box 138, Arnold Papers.

30. Giles to Vannever Bush, 13 February 1945, File 471.6, Buzz Bombs, Box 138, Arnold Papers.

31. Some truly strange ideas on missile guidance were being tested; one, Project ORCON with psychologist B. F. Skinner, involved using pigeons pecking at a target image. Irving Wallace, "Significa," *Parade Magazine* (31 July 1983): 19.

32. Memo, D. T. Griggs to Spaatz, "The Role of Controlled Buzz Bombs in the German War," 5 February 1945, Box 23, Spaatz Papers; Griggs to Robert Lovett, 17 February 1945, and memo, Lt. Gen. W. B. Smith to Spaatz, 27 February 1945, Box 41, Arnold Papers.

33. Memo, "Buzz Bomb Program," Brig. Gen. P. W. Timberlake, deputy chief of Air Staff, to Staff, 12 June 1945, and Eaker to Kenney, 5 June 1945, File 471.6, Buzz Bombs, Box 138, Arnold Papers.

34. See Barton J. Bernstein, "America's Biological Warfare Program in the Second World War," *Journal of Strategic Studies* 11 (September 1988): 292–317.

35. Barton J. Bernstein, "Why We Didn't Use Poison Gas in World War II," *American Heritage* 36 (August–September 1985): 40–45; War Cabinet, Inter Service Committee on Chemical Warfare, CCW (44) 2, 23 January 1944, File 519.8085–3, 1943–1945, Chemical Warfare, AFHRA.

36. Arnold to Spaatz, 2 February 1944, Box 14, Spaatz Papers; memo, "Retaliatory Use of Chemical Warfare against the Japanese," Haywood Hansell to Arnold, 20 March 1944, File 385, Japan, Box 115, Arnold Papers. Arnold ordered plans prepared on 7 December 1943.

37. Spaatz to undersecretary of state, Air Ministry, undated, Box 16, and memo, "Gas Attack by Air Forces," Spaatz to Eisenhower, 20 May 1944, Box 17, Spaatz Papers; Bernstein, "Poison Gas," 43.

38. John W. Mountcastle, "Trial by Fire: U.S. Incendiary Weapons 1918–1945" (Ph.D. diss., Duke University, 1979), 136–138.

39. Ibid., 138–140; memo, "BDRC Report on Incendiary Bomb Requirements," Maj.

Gen. George Stratemeyer, chief of air staff, to deputy chief of staff, War Dept., 24 October 1942, File 385, Box 114, Arnold Papers.

40. Memo, "Incendiary Bombs," Arnold to asst. chief of air staff, Material, Maintenance and Distribution, 26 April 1943, Box 38, Arnold Papers; Mountcastle, "Trial by Fire," 141, 146–150; translation of article on Braddocks, 19 February 1945, File 520.464, 16 March 1943–18 July 1945, AFHRA.

41. Mountcastle, "Trial by Fire," 146, 151–154, 163; Supreme Headquarters, Allied Expeditionary Forces (SHAEF), Bedell-Smith to Spaatz, 16 October 1944, Anderson's diary, Anderson Papers; Roger Freeman, The U.S. Strategic Bomber (London: McDonald and Jane's, 1975), 154–155, 160.

CHAPTER 7. THE LURE OF THE DEATHBLOW IN EUROPE

1. "Army and Navy Estimate of United States Overall Production Requirements," 11 September 1941, AWPD/1, tab 2, sec. 2, pt. 3, app. 2, p. 6, Joint Army-Navy Board File 355, Serial 707, RG 225, National Archives, Washington, D.C.

2. W. F. Craven and J. L. Cate, eds., The Army Air Forces in World War II, 7 vols. (Chicago: University of Chicago Press, 1948–1953), 2: 415–433; Impact, 8 books (1943–1945 periodicals; reprint, Harrisburg, Pa.: Historical Times, 1982), August 1943, 40–41; George Patton to Carl Spaatz, 19 November 1944, Box 16, Papers of Carl Spaatz, Library of Congress (LC).

3. Craven and Cate, Army Air Forces, 2: 463; Quentin Reynolds, The Amazing Mr. Doolittle (New York: Appleton-Century-Crofts, 1953), 262–263; File MR 303, Bombing of Rome, Box 33, Map Room Files, Franklin D. Roosevelt (FDR) Library, Hyde Park, N.Y.; memo, Winston Churchill to Joint Chiefs of Staff (JCS), 10 June 1943, and H. H. Arnold's written comments on JCS memo for George Marshall, Ernest King, and Arnold, 3 July 1943, Box 39, Papers of H. H. Arnold, LC.

4. Memo, Churchill to JCS, and Combined Chiefs of Staff (CCS) memo, "Bombing of Rome," 22 June 1943, Box 39, Arnold Papers; Craven and Cate, Army Air Force, 2: 464; Col. Leroy A. Rainey, "Strategical Pattern Bombing," Box 81, Spaatz Papers.

5. Craven and Cate, Army Air Forces, 2: 464–465; File MR 303, FDR Library; Rainey, "Strategical Pattern Bombing"; Ernest R. May, Lessons of the Past (New York: Oxford, 1973), 128.

6. Memo, Maj. D. Dalziel to Brig. Gen. E. P. Curtis, "Surrender of Bulgaria," 24 October 1943, Box 13, Spaatz Papers.

7. J.P.(43)346, 15 October 1943, "Air Attack on the Balkans," File 512.3171-1, Air Force Historical Research Agency (AFHRA), Maxwell AFB, Ala.

8. Ronald Schaffer, Wings of Judgment (New York: Oxford, 1985), 54–59.

9. Memo, F. L. Anderson to director of intelligence, 18 January 1944, and memo, Spaatz to Ira Eaker, 3 February 1944, File 519.318-1, AFHRA; Schaffer, Wings, 57.

10. Air Ministry msgs. to Joint Intelligence Committee, 16 February 1944, and to Britman Washington, 10 March 1944, File 621.609-4, AFHRA.

11. Msg. AX779, Air Ministry to U.S. Strategic Air Forces (USSTAF), 25 March 1944, Box 14, and msg. W13745, Arnold to Spaatz, 24 March 1944, Box 17, Spaatz Papers; Schaffer, Wings, 57.

12. Msg., Spaatz to Arnold, 6 March 1944, Box 14, and statement, Col. Richard Hughes to Bruce Hopper, 13 June 1944, Box 135, Spaatz Papers.

13. CCS 626, 20 July 1944, U.S. Chiefs of Staff, "Integration of Political Considerations with Military Decisions in Bombing Europe," enclosures include paraphrase of 23 April 1944 note from John Winant to FDR, ABC 384.5 (25 May 1944), Record Group

(RG) 165, National Archives (NA), Washington, D.C.; Schaffer, *Wings*, 58; Craven and Cate, *Army Air Forces*, 3: 411, 652, 748–749.

14. Eaker to Arnold, 17 September 1944, President Folder, Box 45, and sec. of war to sec. of state, 11 November 1944, Box 106, Arnold Papers.

15. Memorandum for personal file, 12 October 1944, Box 38. Papers of General of the Army Omar N. Bradley, U.S. Military Academy (USMA) Special Collections, West Point, N.Y.

16. Henry Morgenthau, *The Presidential Diaries of Henry Morgenthau*, 7 vols. (microfilm ed.) (Frederick, Md.: University Publications of America, 1981), 4: 952; Robert Dallek, *Franklin Roosevelt and American Foreign Policy, 1932–1945* (New York: Oxford, 1979), 290; coordinator of information, Monograph No. 3, "The German Military and Economic Position," 21, Box 101, Arnold Papers.

17. Office of the Asst. Chief of Air Staff, Intelligence, "The Strategic Aerial Bombardment of Europe: Accomplishments and Potentialities," 10 December 1943, 3: 39–41, Box 248, Arnold Papers.

18. Craven and Cate, *Army Air Forces*, 3: 76; "Plan for the Completion of the Combined Bomber Offensive," 5 March 1944, pt. 1, suppl., File 519.318–1, AFHRA.

19. E. Frey to Spaatz, 21 August 1942, Box 8, and memo, Spaatz to CGs 15th and 8th Air Forces, "Exploitation of Air Supremacy," 4 March 1944, Box 14, Spaatz Papers.

20. Memo, Capt. John Harris to Brig. Gen. George McDonald, "Operation SHATTER," 27 June 1944, File 519.322–1, AFHRA; memo, Charles Cabell to Anderson, "Attacks for Demoralization of the German People," 26 June 1944, THUNDERCLAP File, Box 153, Spaatz Papers.

21. W. W. Rostow, *Pre-Invasion Bombing Strategy* (Austin: University of Texas Press, 1981), 17; Richard Hughes, memo, 5 July 1944, POINTBLANK Folder, File 519.4511–14, AFHRA.

22. Memo, Lowell Weicker to McDonald, 6 July 1944; memo, McDonald to Charles Williamson, 5 July 1944; undated memo, Charles Taylor to Williamson; Taylor comments on proposed memo, Anderson to Sir Arthur Tedder, 8 July 1944; draft, Psychological Warfare Plan with handwritten note from Taylor to Williamson, 16 July 1944, POINTBLANK Folder, AFHRA.

23. Laurence Kuter to Anderson, 20 July 1944, and Anderson to Kuter, 27 July 1944, Anderson's diary, Papers of F. L. Anderson, Hoover Institution on War, Revolution and Peace, Stanford University.

24. Memo, Kuter to Arnold, "Attack on German Civilian Morale," 9 August 1944, THUNDERCLAP File, Box 153, Spaatz Papers; Martin Middlebrook, *The Battle of Hamburg* (New York: Charles Scribner's, 1980), 270–272, 327–328.

25. Craven and Cate, *Army Air Forces*, 2: 677, 707–719; Eaker to Robert Lovett, 9 August 1943, Box 17, Eaker Papers; Anderson to Eaker, 13 August 1943, Box 143, Spaatz Papers; Schaffer, *Wings*, 66. Hamburg may have influenced Curtis LeMay; see chapter 9 of this book.

26. Kuter to Anderson, 15 August 1944, THUNDERCLAP File, Box 153, Spaatz Papers.

27. Memo, Williamson to Kuter, 4 September 1944, with 6 September Kuter endorsement; memo, Williamson to Anderson, 12 September 1944, THUNDERCLAP File, Box 153, Spaatz Papers.

CHAPTER 8. DELIVERING THE DEATHBLOW TO GERMANY

1. Ira Eaker to Carl Spaatz, 1 January 1945, Box 20, Papers of Carl A. Spaatz, Library of Congress (LC).

2. Msg. CS93JD, James Doolittle to Spaatz, 30 January 1945, File 520.422, THUNDER-CLAP, Air Force Historical Research Agency (AFHRA), Maxwell AFB, Ala.

3. Spaatz to H. H. Arnold, 5 February 1945, Box 20, Spaatz Papers.

4. Combined Operational Planning Committee (COPC) 2111, "Tactical Plan for the Air Attack of Targets in and in the Neighborhood of the Ruhr," and memo, F. L. Anderson to COPC, 6 October 1944, HURRICANE File, Box 150, Spaatz Papers.

5. Operation THUNDERCLAP, 20 August 1944, File 519.321, and Charles Cabell to Richard Hughes, 8 September 1944, File 168.7026–9, AFHRA; Spaatz to Arnold, 27 August 1944, Box 15, Spaatz Papers.

6. Memo, Spaatz to D. D. Eisenhower, 24 August 1944, with 28 August endorsement from Eisenhower, Box 18, and diary entry, 9 September 1944, Box 16, Spaatz Papers; Russell Weigley, Eisenhower's Lieutenants (Bloomington: Indiana University Press, 1981), 268–273; Charles B. MacDonald, The Mighty Endeavor (New York: William Morrow, 1986), 361–362.

7. Eaker to Robert Lovett, 9 August 1943, Box 17, Papers of Ira C. Eaker, LC; memo, Brig. Gen. Thomas White to Arnold, "Morale and Human Effects of Berlin Bombings," 2 February 1944, Germany File, Box 50, Papers of Henry H. Arnold, LC.

8. W. F. Craven and J. L. Cate, eds., The Army Air Forces in World War II, 7 vols. (Chicago: University of Chicago Press, 1948–1953), 3: 284–285; interview, Lt. Col. Cecil Hahn with Brig. Gen. Orville Anderson, 10 November 1944, Box 135, Spaatz Papers.

9. Minutes, Joint Chiefs of Staff (JCS) 176th meeting, 14 September 1944, Combined Chiefs of Staff (CCS) Decimal File, Box 179, Record Group (RG) 218, National Archives (NA), Washington, D.C.

10. Arnold to Spaatz, 30 December 1944, Box 20, and msg., Anderson to Spaatz, 1 February 1945, CLARION File, Box 170, Spaatz Papers; diary entry, 29 January 1945, Box 1, Papers of Hoyt Vandenberg, LC.

11. Craven and Cate, Army Air Forces, 3: 725–726; minutes, U.S. Strategic Air Forces (USSTAF) Staff meeting, 2 February 1945, Box 20, Spaatz Papers.

12. Msg. CS93JD, Doolittle to Spaatz, 30 January 1945; msg. JD104CS, Spaatz to Doolittle, 30 January 1945; msg. UA53649, Spaatz to Doolittle, 2 February 1945, File 520.422, AFHRA.

13. Msg. CS96JD with Spaatz note, Doolittle to Spaatz, 2 February 1945, Box 23, Spaatz Papers; Craven and Cate, Army Air Forces, 3: 725–726; USSTAF Air Intelligence summaries 66, 67, and 68, AF spec. safe, Box 126, records of interservice agencies, RG 334, NA, Suitland, Md.

14. Spaatz to Lovett, and msg. U68773, Spaatz to Arnold, 1 October 1944, Anderson diary, Papers of Frederick L. Anderson, Hoover Institution on War, Revolution and Peace, Stanford University.

15. Msg. CS139EC, Anderson to Spaatz, 30 September 1944; msg. CS150EC, Anderson to Spaatz, 1 October 1944; memo, Anderson to COPC, "Operation HURRICANE," 6 October 1944; msg. W40454, Arnold to Spaatz, 3 October 1944, HURRICANE File, Box 150, Spaatz Papers; Craven and Cate, Army Air Forces, 3: 319–322.

16. Memo, Alfred Maxwell to Spaatz, "Comments on RAF version of Plan HURRICANE," 3 October 1944, HURRICANE FILE, Spaatz Papers.

17. Target Section, USSTAF working papers, on "Plan for Operation HURRICANE," 2 October 1944, and untitled, undated work on Transportation Attack Plan, File 519.321, AFHRA.

18. Notes from Allied Air Commanders Conference, 15 December 1944, Anderson diary; Bowles to H. L. Stimson with extracts from Griggs letter, 21 November 1944, Box 2, E. L. Bowles's File, Office of the Secretary of War, RG 107, NA, Washington, D.C.: Arnold to Spaatz, 14 January 1945, Box 20, Spaatz Papers.

19. "General Plan for Maximum Effort Attack against Transportation Objectives," 17 December 1944, File 168.7026–9, AFHRA.

20. Ibid., includes Cabell's handwritten comments, and memo, "The German Transport System as a Strategic Bombing Target," by Capt. W. A. Salant, 12 October 1944, and N. F. Twining to Eaker, 4 January 1945; Eaker to Spaatz, 1 January 1945, Box 20, Spaatz Papers.

21. Doolittle to Spaatz, 27 December 1944; Maxwell to Anderson, 5 January 1945; msg. AX991, Sir Norman Bottomley to Spaatz, 26 December 1944, File 519.430A, AFHRA.

22. Spaatz to Arnold, 7 January 1945, Box 49, Arnold Papers; Spaatz to Arnold, 5 February 1945, Box 20, Spaatz Papers; msg. UAX 53778, Spaatz to all units, 5 February 1945, File 519.430A, and msg. UAX 64613, Spaatz to all units, 21 February 1945, File 520.3233–40, AFHRA.

23. Schaffer, Wings, 86–95; memo, F. L. Anderson to O. Anderson, "Press Conference in US," 2 March 1945, Anderson diary, Anderson Papers.

24. Forty-second Bomb Wing Plan for CLARION, File 549.322H, and msg. F6055A1, 28 February 1945, File 519.318–1, AFHRA; msgs. UAX 64905, D1933, D61872, and M47480, 1 March 1945, Anderson diary, Anderson Papers; situation maps, 22–23 February 1945, MR 300, sec. 18, Box 148, Map Room Files, Franklin D. Roosevelt (FDR) Library, Hyde Park, N.Y.

25. Alfred C. Mierzejewski, The Collapse of the German War Economy, 1944–1945 (Chapel Hill: University of North Carolina Press, 1988), 170.

26. Msg. MSW 305, 6 March 1945, and msg. FWD 17651, 8 March 1945, Anderson diary, Anderson Papers; CLARION summary, Box 20, Spaatz Papers; Doolittle to Barney Giles, 20 March 1945, Box 61, Arnold Papers; Craven and Cate, Army Air Forces, 3: 732–735; entry for 3 March 1945, Vandenberg diary, Vandenberg Papers.

27. Mierzejewski, Collapse of German War Economy, 184.

28. See maps in Gotz Bergander, Dresden im Luftkrieg (Cologne: Bohlan Verlag, 1977).

29. David Irving, The Destruction of Dresden (New York: Ballantine, 1965), 151, 177, 186–191. Irving, who gave wide publicity to the higher figure, accepted the lower in 1966. See letter from Max Rosenberg, Air Force Magazine (April 1973): 4.

30. Melden E. Smith, Jr., "The Bombing of Dresden Reconsidered: A Study in Wartime Decision Making" (Ph.D. diss., Boston University, 1971), 208–209, 237–247; Joseph W. Angell, "Historical Analysis of the 14–15 February 1945 Bombing of Dresden," 11–15, File K239.046–38, AFHRA.

31. USSTAF Air Intelligence summary 68, RG 334, NA, Suitland, Md.; see articles, New York Times, 15 February 1945, 1; notes from Allied Air Commanders Conference, 15 February 1945, File K239.046–38, AFHRA.

32. Craven and Cate, Army Air Forces, 3: 640, 653, 724–725.

33. Memo, Bottomley to Sir Charles Portal, 31 January 1945, and msg. W37181, Giles to Eaker, 14 February 1944, File 519.318–1, AFHRA; msg. Cricket 38, Lawrence Kuter to Giles, 1 February 1945, Box 316; msg., Giles to Spaatz, 17 February 1945, and msg. UA64462, Spaatz to Arnold, 18 February 1945, Box 20, Spaatz Papers.

34. Memo, George McDonald to Anderson, 19 February 1945, File 519.523–6, AFHRA; memo, 21 February 1945, Anderson's diary, Anderson Papers.

35. M. Smith, "Bombing of Dresden," 70–78; memo, Anderson to Spaatz, 19 February 1945, with msgs. UA64462, W39222, UA64470, W39730, UA64471, W39722, File K239.046–38; Anderson to Kuter, 27 February 1945, File 519.1611, AFHRA.

36. Msg. UA 64555, Spaatz to Eaker, 20 February 1945, Box 23, Spaatz Papers; Diary of H. L. Stimson, 5 March 1945, Yale University Library (microfilm); Schaffer, Wings, 99–103; "Report of Air Attacks on Targets in Dresden," File 519.523–6, AFHRA.

37. 1 March 1945 Bombardment Policy with Anderson memo, Box 118, Papers of Nathan F. Twining, LC; Anderson to Kuter, 26 March 1945, File 519.1611, AFHRA; Msg. WAR 65558, 9 April 1945, with Anderson response, 10 April 1945, Box 21, Spaatz Papers; David Schlatter, diary, 15 March 1945, File 168.7052–5, AFHRA.

38. Lovett to Spaatz, 27 November 1944, Box 16, Spaatz Papers.

CHAPTER 9. TORCHING JAPAN

1. Gen. Curtis LeMay, with MacKinley Kantor, *Mission with LeMay* (Garden City, N.Y.: Doubleday, 1965), 382.

2. Lawrence Cortesi, *Target: Tokyo* (New York: Kensington Publishing, 1983), 276.

3. Joe Michael Feist, "Bats Away," *American Heritage* 33 (April–May 1982): 93–94.

4. John Dower, *War without Mercy* (New York: Pantheon, 1986), 53–54, 77–93.

5. Christopher Thorne, *Allies of a Kind: The United States, Britain, and the War against Japan* (New York: Oxford, 1978), 158–159, 168; Diary of Henry L. Stimson, 31 December 1944, Yale University Library (microfilm); memos, Stimson to FDR, 17 September 1943, and Joint Chiefs of Staff (JCS) to FDR, 22 September 1943, Box 104, Personal Secretary File, Franklin D. Roosevelt (FDR) Library, Hyde Park, N.Y.

6. Dower, *War without Mercy*, 49–50.

7. William Manchester, *The Glory and the Dream* (New York: Bantam, 1975), 268–269; George Kenney to H. H. Arnold, 1 January 1943, Box 121, Papers of Nathan F. Twining, Library of Congress (LC).

8. Air Raids File, Box 313, Papers of Harry Hopkins, FDR Library.

9. *Retaliation: Japanese Attacks and Allied Countermeasures on the Pacific Coast in World War II* (Corvallis: Oregon State University Press, 1975), 69–77, 142–143; memo, Arnold to George Marshall, 26 May 1945, Box 117, Papers of H. H. Arnold, LC.

10. Charles F. Brower IV, "The Joint Chiefs Of Staff and National Policy: American Strategy and the War with Japan, 1943–1945," (Ph.D. diss., University of Pennsylvania, 1987), 209–210.

11. Ronald H. Spector, *Eagle against the Sun* (New York: Vintage Books, 1985), xiii.

12. Prime Minister John Curtin to Douglas MacArthur, 7 April 1943, with 10 April reply, 11061/43; memo, Brig. Gen. B. M. Fitch to Allied Commanders, "Air Attack of Objectives within the Philippine Archipelago," 1 November 1944; and msg. to same from MacArthur, 2 September 1944, 11061/41, Record Group (RG) 338, National Archives (NA), Suitland, Md.

13. Correspondence on Intramuros incident, 16–17 February 1945 in File 373.21, 11061/44, and on Rabaul hospital, 23–24 May 1944 in File 373.11, 11061/41, Records of U.S. Army Commands, RG 338, NA, Suitland, Md.

14. Dower, *War without Mercy*, 41; Douglas MacArthur, *Reminiscences* (New York: McGraw-Hill, 1964), 276.

15. W. F. Craven and J. L. Cate, eds., *The Army Air Forces in World War II*, 7 vols. (Chicago: University of Chicago Press, 1948–1953), 5: 628–635; Samuel Eliot Morison, *The Two-Ocean War* (New York: Ballantine Books, 1972), 477–478.

16. LeMay with Kantor, *Mission*, 340–341, 370–372.

17. Thomas M. Coffey, *Iron Eagle* (New York: Crown, 1986), 4, 34–38, 50, 56, 69, 139, 243.

18. Craven and Cate, *Army Air Forces*, 2: 698–699; Ronald Schaffer, *Wings of Judgment* (New York: Oxford, 1985), 66–67; U.S. Strategic Air Forces (USSTAF) Air intelligence summary No. 50, RG 334, NA, Suitland, Md.; minutes of 3rd Bombardment

Group Commanders Meeting, 15 October 1943, Box B8, Papers of Curtis LeMay, LC; Coffey, *Iron Eagle*, 99.

19. Lesson plan for Conference on Air Operations against National Structures, 11 April 1939, File 248.202A–25, Air Force Historical Research Agency (AFHRA), Maxwell AFB, Ala.; plan, "Aircraft Requirements for the Chinese Government," Serial 691, and memo, Arnold to Robert Lovett, 11 June 1941, Joint Army-Navy Board No. 355, RG 225, NA, Washington, D.C.

20. For both sides of this issue, see Forrest Pogue, *George C. Marshall, Ordeal and Hope, 1939–1942* (New York: Viking Press, 1966), 201–203; and Michael S. Sherry, *The Rise of American Air Power* (New Haven, Conn.: Yale University Press, 1987), 109–110.

21. Memo, Brig. Gen. Martin Scanlon to Barney Giles, "Priorities: Japanese Objective Folder Material," 19 February 1942, File 360.02, Box 101, and Voucher No. 40971, "One Way to Cripple Japan," File 452.3, Box 132, Arnold Papers.

22. Memo, Lawrence Kuter to Arnold, "Radical Air Plans to Defeat Japan," 3 August 1943, Box 113, Arnold Papers.

23. Craven and Cate, *Army Air Forces*, 2: 354–355; Schaffer, *Wings*, 110–111; Herman S. Wolk, "The B-29, the A-Bomb, and the Japanese Surrender," *Air Force* (February 1975): 55; "Air Plan for the Defeat of Japan," ABC 381 Japan (27 August 1943), File ABC 384.5, Boxes 477–478, Army Staff, RG 319, NA, Washington, D.C.

24. Memo, Brig. Gen. Mervin Gross to Giles, "Test of Incendiaries," 5 May 1944, File 400.112, Box 117, Arnold Papers; "Outline of Presentation of Views of Commanding General, AAF, on the Role of the Air Forces in the Defeat of Japan," 22 February 1944, Naval Aide's Files, Map Room, Box 167, FDR Library.

25. Coffey, *Iron Eagle*, 127–128.

26. Craven and Cate, *Army Air Forces*, 5: 58–175.

27. Coffey, *Iron Eagle*, 121; Haywood S. Hansell, Jr., *The Strategic Air War against Germany and Japan* (Washington, D.C.: GPO, 1986), 167; Pasco to Arnold, 18 December 1944, Box 41, Arnold Papers; Schaffer, *Wings*, 124.

28. Schaffer, *Wings*, 124; msg., Hansell to Arnold, 16 January 1945; memo, H. E. Lanasberg to Robert Stearns, "Estimate of Possibilities of Visual Bombardment of Primary Targets," 28 February 1945; memo, J. T. Seaver to Donald Loughridge, "Ballistic Winds over Japan," 1 March 1945, File 762.912–1, AFHRA.

29. Craven and Cate, *Army Air Forces*, 5: 551–567; Coffey, *Iron Eagle*, 129–132, 144–145; E. Bartlett Kerr, *Flames over Tokyo* (New York: Donald I. Fine, 1991), 119; Hansell, *Strategic Air War against Germany and Japan*, 208–215; H. H. Arnold, *Global Mission* (New York: Harper, 1949), 541.

30. LeMay to Lauris Norstad, 31 January 1945, Box B11, LeMay Papers; LeMay with Kantor, *Mission*, 344–345, 368; Norstad to Carl Spaatz, 3 March 1945, File 519.9701–15, AFHRA; Coffey, *Iron Eagle*, 125–126.

31. Craven and Cate, *Army Air Forces*, 5: 568–576, 611; Haywood S. Hansell, Jr., *Strategic Air War against Japan* (Maxwell AFB, Ala., Airpower Research Institute: 1980), 51; Coffey, *Iron Eagle*, 147–157; Kerr, *Flames over Tokyo*, 156.

32. Foreword to XXI Bomber Command Tactical Mission Report, Mission No. 40, Urban Area of Tokyo, 10 March 1945, prepared 15 April 1945, Box 26, LeMay Papers.

33. "Pacific Report #90," in *The United States Strategic Bombing Survey*, 10 vols. (New York: Garland, 1976), 10: 70–73.

34. Wilbur H. Morrison, *Point of No Return* (New York: Times Books, 1979), 224; Cortesi, *Target: Tokyo*, 233–274; Thomas R. Havens, *Valley of Darkness* (New York: W. W. Norton, 1978), 178–181.

35. *New York Times*, 11 March 1945, 1, 13.

36. LeMay with Kantor, *Mission*, 351–352; Morrison, *Point of No Return*, 225; XXI

Bomber Command, "Analysis of Incendiary Phase of Operations against Japanese Urban Areas," 39–40, Box 37, LeMay Papers.

37. LeMay with Kantor, Mission, 384. This description matches the AAF conception of Japanese home industry described in Impact, 8 books (1943–1945 periodicals; reprint, Harrisburg, Pa.: Historical Times, 1982), April 1945, 10–11.

38. Wilbur Morrison, Hellbirds: The Story of the B-29s in Combat (New York: Duell, Sloan and Pearce, 1960), 156–157.

39. Robert L. Gleason, "Psychological Operations and Air Power," Air University Review 22 (March–April 1971): 36–37; C. C. Chauncey to Giles, 16 July 1945, File 091.412, Box 61, Arnold Papers; Twentieth AF Mission Reports 297–302, 28–29 June 1945, File 760.331, AFHRA; Havens, Valley of Darkness, 167.

40. Kuter to Anderson, 15 August 1944, Anderson diary, Papers of F. L. Anderson, Hoover Institution on War, Revolution and Peace, Stanford University.

41. Craven and Cate, Army Air Forces, 5: 624–625; Arnold to LeMay, 21 March 1945, and Norstad to LeMay, 3 April 1945, Box B11, LeMay Papers; Giles to LeMay, 20 April 1945, Box 106, Arnold Papers; Stimson diary, 1 June and 6 June 1945.

42. Brower, "Joint Chiefs of Staff," 273–281; Craven and Cate, Army Air Forces, 5: 696–697; George C. Marshall, H. H. Arnold, and Earnest J. King, The War Reports (New York: J. B. Lippincott, 1947), 275.

43. "Amendment No. 1 to G–2 Estimate of the Enemy Situation with Respect to Kyushu," 29 July 1945, and "G–2 Estimate of the Enemy Situation with Respect to an Operation against the Tokyo (Kwanto) Plain of Honshu," 31 May 1945, Quintin S. Lander Papers, U.S. Army Military History Institute (USAMHI), Carlisle Barracks, Pa.

44. LeMay with Kantor, Mission, 373; journal, "Trip to Pacific June 6, 1945 to June 24, 1945," 13 June entry, Box 272, and msg., Arnold to Ira C. Eaker, Anderson, and Norstad, undated, Truman File, Box 45, Arnold Papers; Coffey, Iron Eagle, 174–175.

45. Msg., Arnold to Eaker, Anderson, and Norstad; memo, Hansell to Arnold, "Retaliatory Use of Chemical Warfare against the Japanese," 20 March 1944, File 385 Japan, Box 115, Arnold Papers.

46. Memo, Arnold to Marshall, "Comments on Air Aspects of General Stilwell's Memorandum Relative to the Invasion of Japan," 30 May 1945, Box 115, and journal, "Trip to Pacific," 17 June entry, Arnold Papers.

47. David E. Lilienthal, The Journals of David E. Lilienthal, The Atomic Energy Years, 1945–1950 (New York: Harper and Row, 1964), 199–200; J. J. McCloy, memorandum of conversation with General Marshall, 29 May 1945, 11:45 a.m., RG 107, NA, Washington, D.C.

48. Memo, Marshall to Ernest King, "U.S. Chemical Warfare Policy," 15 June 1945, Box 75, Folder 35, George C. Marshall Papers, George C. Marshall Research Library, Lexington, Va.

49. Barton J. Bernstein, "Why We Didn't Use Poison Gas in World War II," American Heritage 36 (August–September 1985): 45; memo, Myron Cramer to George Merck, "Destruction of Crops by Chemicals," 5 March 1945, and memo, Merck to Stimson, "Destruction of Crops by LN Chemicals," 25 April 1945, Box 84, Folder 27, Marshall Papers.

50. JCS 1371, "Destruction of 1946 Crops in Japan," 30 May 1945, ABC 475.92 (25 February 1944), RG 165, NA, Washington, D.C.

51. V. E. Bertrandias to Arnold, 29 May 1945, with attached memo to Arnold from R. P. Proctor; memo, Eaker to Hoyt S. Vandenberg, "Experiment in Destruction of Crops by Air," 3 August 1945, with 10 August reply from Vandenberg, File 385, Japan, Box 115, Arnold Papers.

52. Anderson to Brig. Gen. Joe Loutzenheiser, chief, AAF Operational Plans Division, 20 March 1945, File 519.1611, AFHRA.

53. FDR to Stimson, 9 September 1944, Box 277, Arnold Papers; transcript of meeting of Joint Target Group (JTG) and U.S. Strategic Bombing Survey (USSBS), entry 1, File .001, U.S. Strategic Bombing Survey, RG 243, NA, Washington, D.C.

54. Memo, Lovett to Stimson, 31 July 1945, with accompanying "Report on USSBS and JTG Conferences," File Aircraft, Air Corps General, RG 107, NA, Washington, D.C.; David Mets, *Master of Airpower* (Novato, Calif.: Presidio Press, 1988), 298–299; directive, Eaker to Commanding General, U.S. Army Strategic Air Forces, 26 July 1945, Box 13, LeMay Papers.

55. Diary of Terminal Conference, 10 July 1945–30 July 1945, entries for 13, 15, 17, 23, and 24 July, Box 249, Arnold Papers.

56. Msg., Spaatz to Eaker, 2 August 1945, and diary entry, 11 August 1945, Box 21, Papers of Carl A. Spaatz, LC; Mets, *Master of Airpower*, 302–303; Barton J. Bernstein, "The Perils and Politics of Surrender: Ending the War with Japan and Avoiding the Third Atomic Bomb," *Pacific Historical Review* 46 (1977): 16–17.

57. Craven and Cate, *Army Air Forces*, 5: 756; memo, J. E. Hull to Eaker, 13 September 1945, File 091.412, Box 61, Arnold Papers.

58. Wartime History, 20th Air Force (Public Information Office [PIO] version), File 760.01, AFHRA; U.S. Army Strategic Air Forces Communique No. 12, 17 August 1945, Box 121, Twining Papers; Philip Kaplan and Rex Alan Smith, *One Last Look* (New York: Abbeville Press, 1983), 213.

59. Craven and Cate, *Army Air Forces*, 5: 662–674; Hansell, *Strategic Air War against Japan*, 74–93. Other important shocks included Russian entry into the war, the American submarine and B-29 mining campaigns against Japanese shipping, and the atomic bombs.

60. Msg. 082328Z, Norstad to Spaatz, 8 August 1945, Box 21, Spaatz Papers.

CHAPTER 10. STRATEGIC AIRPOWER IN LIMITED WARS

1. Michael Maclear, *The Ten Thousand Day War: Vietnam, 1945–1975* (New York: Avon Books, 1981), 124.

2. Curtis LeMay with MacKinley Kantor, *Mission with LeMay* (Garden City, N.Y.: Doubleday, 1965), 387; Tactical Mission Report, 509th Composite Group, 20th AF, 60, File 760.331, Air Force Historical Research Agency (AFHRA), Maxwell AFB, Ala. LeMay's calculations seem inaccurate; the two atomic bombs together were probably more deadly. See Michael S. Sherry, *The Rise of American Air Power* (New Haven, Conn.: Yale University Press, 1987), 406n.

3. Henry L. Stimson and McGeorge Bundy, *On Active Service in Peace and War* (New York: Harper and Brothers, 1948), 632–633.

4. Barton J. Bernstein, "The Perils and Politics of Surrender," *Pacific Historical Review* 46 (1977): 13–14.

5. LeMay with Kantor, *Mission*, 387; Diary of Henry L. Stimson, 17 July 1945, Yale University Library, microfilm; Folder, Bruce C. Hopper, "Jeeping the Targets in the Country That Was," 17 April 1945 entry, Box 5, Papers of F. L. Anderson, Hoover Institution on War, Revolution and Peace, Stanford University.

6. Hopper documents, Box 5, Anderson Papers, and Boxes 286 and 287, Papers of Carl A. Spaatz; James McGregor Burns interview with author, 11 April 1986, West Point, N.Y.; Ronald Schaffer, *Wings of Judgment* (New York: Oxford, 1985), 252–253.

7. *Operational Research in North West Europe*, text for course OA 3655, Naval Post-

graduate School, Monterey, Calif.; see Operations Analysis Section reports in File 762.912–1, AFHRA; Schaffer, *Wings*, 162–163.

8. Maj. Robert A. Doughty, *The Evolution of U.S. Army Tactical Doctrine, 1946–1976* (Fort Leavenworth, Kans.: Combat Studies Institute, 1979), 12–13.

9. *United States Strategic Bombing Survey: Summary Reports* (1945–1946; reprint, Maxwell AFB, Ala.: Air University Press, 1987), 37–39, 110–113; memo, Alfred Maxwell to Anderson, "Creation of Strategic Targets during Reconstruction of Germany," 20 April 1945, File 519.318–1, AFHRA.

10. David Mets, *Master of Airpower* (Novato, Calif.: Presidio Press, 1988), 314–315.

11. Gregg Herken, *The Winning Weapon* (New York: Alfred A. Knopf, 1980), 212; Eaker, quote, to Spaatz, 1 January 1945 on Operation CLARION, Box 20, Spaatz Papers.

12. *Bombing Surveys: Summary Reports*, 34–39, 92–96; Donald W. Hastings et al., *Psychiatric Experiences in the Eighth Air Force* (New York: Josiah Macy, Jr., Foundation, 1944), 403–404.

13. See, for example, "Defenses of Southern Kyushu," a 3 June 1946 speech by Edmund J. Winslett, Winslett Papers, U.S. Army Military History Institute (USAMHI), Carlisle Barracks, Pa. Some British citizens had similar sentiments: see Stephen Harper, *Miracle of Deliverance: The Case for the Bombing of Hiroshima and Nagasaki* (London: Sidgwick and Jackson, 1985).

14. Good examples of the bombing assessments furnished key leaders are in Box 6 of the Anderson Papers. These highly selective reports concentrating on target destruction may have led to an exaggerated belief in capabilities for precision.

15. James T. Stewart, ed., *Airpower: The Decisive Force in Korea* (New York: D. Van Nostrand, 1957), 76–82; Robert F. Futrell, *The United States Air Force in Korea 1950–1953* (New York: Duell, Sloan and Pearce, 1961), 186, 285–313.

16. Futrell, *USAF in Korea*, 480–490. In fairness to the USAF, it must be noted that Pyongyang had also been damaged by severe ground fighting during 1950.

17. Ibid., 483–493; Dean Acheson, *The Korean War* (New York: W. W. Norton, 1971), 135–136.

18. Futrell, *USAF in Korea*, 605–643; Stewart, *Airpower: Korea*, 166–188. Japanese rice probably would have been a target for American bombers if the Pacific War had gone into 1946 (see chapter 9 of this book).

19. U.S. Department of State, *Foreign Relations of the United States, 1950*, 7 vols. (Washington, D.C.: GPO, 1977–1980), 7: 159; Clay Blair, *The Forgotten War: America in Korea 1950–1953* (New York: Doubleday, 1989), 124, 522–523, 971.

20. Col. Dennis M. Drew, *ROLLING THUNDER 1965: Anatomy of a Failure* (Maxwell AFB, Ala.: Air University Press, 1986), 24–27.

21. Harry G. Summers, Jr., *On Strategy: The Vietnam War in Context* (Carlisle, Pa.: U.S. Army War College, 1982), 28–30.

22. Mark Clodfelter, *The Limits of Airpower: The American Bombing of North Vietnam* (New York: Free Press, 1989), 39–146.

23. John Schlight, *The War in South Vietnam: The Years of the Offensive, 1965–1968* (Washington, D.C.: Office of Air Force History, 1988), 258–261.

24. Clodfelter, *Limits of Airpower*, 39–146; Matthew B. Ridgway, *The Korean War* (New York: Popular Library, 1967), 238.

25. John F. Kreis, *Air Warfare and Air Base Air Defense* (Washington, D.C.: Office of Air Force History, 1988), 293–296; editorial, *Air Force Magazine* (April 1973): 3; Karl J. Eschmann, *Linebacker: The Untold Story of the Air Raids over North Vietnam* (New York: Ivy Books, 1989), 202–203.

26. Clodfelter, *Limits of Airpower*, 194–210; for a USAF view on the effects of political

restrictions, see Gen. William M. Momyer, *Air Power in Three Wars* (Washington, D.C.: GPO, 1978).

27. U.S. Dept. of the Air Force, *White Paper: Air Force Performance in Desert Storm* (Washington, D.C.: GPO, April 1991), 1–2; Tom Mathews, "The Secret History of the War," *Newsweek* 117 (18 March 1991): 36.

28. Charts accompanying transcript of Gen. Norman Schwarzkopf's Central Command Briefing, 27 February 1991, *Military Review* 71 (September 1991): 100; Lt. Gen. Frederick Franks, CG, VII Corps, interview with author, 30 May 1991, Fort Leavenworth, Kans.

29. Mathews, "Secret History," 38. Planners expected 540,000 Iraqi troops in the Kuwait theater, with more than half in Kuwait itself; instead, the actual total was about 250,000, with about 150,000 in Kuwait.

30. Barton Gellman, "70% of U.S. Bombs Missed Their Targets, Figures Show," *Kansas City Star*, 16 March 1991, A–15; Richard P. Hallion, *Storm over Iraq* (Washington, D.C.: Smithsonian, 1992).

31. Ibid.

32. USAF, *Air Force Performance in Desert Storm*, 5.

33. Lt. Col. David Dean, *Airpower in Small Wars: The British Air Control Experience* (Maxwell AFB, Ala.: Air University Press, 1985); Henry Foster, *The Making of Modern Iraq* (Norman: University of Oklahoma Press, 1935), 236–237; Lt. Gen. Charles A. Horner, "The Air Campaign," *Military Review* 71 (September 1991): 25–27.

34. Most British actions were against relatively small parties, often raiding from northern Saudi Arabia. See John Bagot Glubb, *War in the Desert* (New York: Norton, 1961).

CHAPTER 11. LEGACIES

1. Bruce Hopper, U.S. Strategic Air Forces (USSTAF) historian, memo on USSTAF history preparation, 22 September 1944, Box 286, Papers of Carl A. Spaatz, Library of Congress (LC).

2. Yasuo Kurata, "Americans Are Insensitive to Casualties Because Their Country Hasn't Been Bombed," *Kansas City Star*, 5 May 1991, sec. K, p. 2.

3. U.S. Department of the Army, *Training Circular 27-10-1, Selected Problems in the Law of War* (Washington, D.C.: GPO, 1979), 44, 52–54. Similar examples are presented in U.S. Department of the Army, *Field Manual 27–2, Your Conduct in Combat under the Law of War* (Washington, D.C.: GPO, 1984).

4. Ronald Schaffer notes, however, that counterforce nuclear strategies are often presented as a relatively humane form of warfare, like conventional precision bombing, and rely on pinpoint techniques; see *Wings of Judgment* (New York: Oxford, 1985), 213.

5. U.S. Joint Chiefs of Staff (JCS) memorandum, read at a meeting of the Combined Chiefs of Staff (CCS) on 13 May 1945, U.S. State Department, *Foreign Relations of the United States: The Conferences at Washington and Quebec, 1943* (Washington, D.C.: GPO, 1970), 222.

6. Michael J. Yavenditti, "The American People and the Use of Atomic Bombs on Japan: The 1940s," *Historian* 36 (February 1974): 231; memo, George Marshall to Ernest King, "U.S. Chemical Warfare Policy," 15 June 1945, Box 73, Folder 35, Papers of George C. Marshall, Marshall Research Library, Lexington, Va.

7. Richard H. Kohn, "The Scholarship on World War II: Its Present Condition and Future Possibilities," *Journal of Military History* 55 (July 1991): 376; Michael Howard, *Studies in War and Peace* (New York: Viking, 1971), 239.

8. Bill Moyers, at the conclusion of "The Arming of the Earth," an episode in his 1984 Public Broadcasting System series, "A Walk through the 20th Century with Bill Moyers."

BIBLIOGRAPHY

MANUSCRIPT SOURCES

Air Force Historical Research Agency of the United States Air Force, Air University, Maxwell Air Force Base, Ala.
  Air Corps Tactical School Files
  Army Air Forces Planning and Operational Records
Franklin D. Roosevelt Library, Hyde Park, N.Y.
  Map Room Files
  President's Secretary Files
  Papers of Harry Hopkins
George C. Marshall Research Library, Lexington, Va.
  Papers of George C. Marshall
Hoover Institution on War, Revolution and Peace, Stanford University, Stanford, Calif.
  Papers of Frederick L. Anderson
Library of Congress, Manuscript Division, Washington, D.C.
  Papers of Henry H. Arnold
  Papers of Ira C. Eaker
  Papers of Curtis E. LeMay
  Papers of Carl A. Spaatz
  Papers of Nathan F. Twining
  Papers of Hoyt S. Vandenberg
National Archives, Suitland, Md., and Washington, D.C.
  Record Group 107, Office of the Secretary of War
  Record Group 165, War Department General and Special Staffs
  Record Group 218, United States Joint Chiefs of Staff
  Record Group 225, Joint Army and Navy Boards and Committees
  Record Group 243, United States Strategic Bombing Survey
  Record Group 319, Army Staff
  Record Group 332, United States Theaters of War, World War II
  Record Group 334, Interservice Agencies
  Record Group 338, United States Army Commands
Office of Air Force History, Bolling Air Force Base, Washington, D.C.

United States Air Force Oral History Interviews: Ira C. Eaker, Curtis E. LeMay, and Carl A. Spaatz
United States Army Military History Institute, Carlisle Barracks, Pa.
   Army War College Curriculum Archives
   Letters of Robert E. O'Donnell
   Papers of Ira C. Eaker
   Papers of Quintin S. Lander
   Papers of Elmer T. Lian
   Papers of Crawford F. Sams
   Papers of Edmund J. Winslett
   Senior Officer Oral History Program
United States Military Academy Archives and Special Collections, West Point, N.Y.
   Collected Letters of Earle C. Cheek
   Department of Civil and Military Engineering Files
   Papers of General of the Army Omar N. Bradley
   Papers of George A. Lincoln
Sterling Memorial Library, Yale University, New Haven, Conn.
   Diary of Henry L. Stimson (microfilm copies used)

INTERVIEWS BY AUTHOR

Burns, James McGregor. Former enlisted Army historian in World War II. West Point, N.Y., 11 April 1986.
Franks, Lt. Gen. Frederick. Commander of U.S. Army VII Corps in Operation DESERT STORM, Fort Leavenworth, Kans., 30 May 1991.
Kestenbaum, Martin. World War II veteran and president of the New Jersey chapter of the Eighth Air Force Historical Society. West Point, N.Y., 23 May 1992.
Roland, Charles P. Military historian and World War II infantry officer. West Point, N.Y., 30 January 1986.
Spiller, Roger. Military historian. Fort Leavenworth, Kans., 28 February 1991.

BOOKS AND DOCUMENTS

Acheson, Dean. The Korean War. New York: W. W. Norton, 1971.
Anderton, David A. B-29 Superfortress at War. New York: Charles Scribner's Sons, 1978.
Ardery, Philip. Bomber Pilot. Lexington: University Press of Kentucky, 1978.
Arnold, H. H. Global Mission. New York: Harper, 1949.
Arnold, H. H., and Ira C. Eaker. Winged Warfare. New York: Harper, 1941.
Batchelder, Robert C. The Irreversible Decision, 1939–1950. Boston: Houghton Mifflin, 1962.
Beck, Earl R. Under the Bombs: The German Home Front, 1942–1945. Lexington: University Press of Kentucky, 1986.
Bekker, Cajus. The Luftwaffe War Diaries. Translated by Frank Ziegler. New York: Ballantine, 1969.
Bendiner, Elmer. The Fall of Fortresses. New York: G. P. Putnam's Sons, 1980.

Bergander, Gotz. *Dresden im Luftkrieg*. Cologne: Bohlan Verlag, 1977.

Best, Geoffrey. *Humanity in Warfare*. New York: Columbia University Press, 1980.

Bidinian, Larry J. *The Combined Allied Bombing Offensive against the German Civilian, 1942–1945*. Lawrence, Kans.: Coronado Press, 1976.

Blair, Clay. *The Forgotten War: America in Korea, 1950–1953*. New York: Doubleday, 1989.

Bowman, Martin W. *Castles in the Air*. Wellingborough, Eng.: Patrick Stephens, 1984.

Brittain, Vera. *Seeds of Chaos*. London: New Vision Publishing, 1944.

Brodie, Bernard. *Strategy in the Missile Age*. Princeton, N.J.: Princeton University Press, 1965.

Brodie, Bernard, and Fawn M. Brodie. *From Crossbow to H-Bomb*. Bloomington: Indiana University Press, 1973.

Caidin, Martin. *Black Thursday*. New York: Bantam, 1981.

Cannon, M. Hamlin. *Flying Training at West Point*. Colorado Springs: U.S. Air Force Academy, 1970.

Cantril, Hadley, and Mildred Strunk, eds. *Public Opinion, 1935–1946*. Princeton, N.J.: Princeton University Press, 1951.

Chomsky, Noam. *American Power and the New Mandarins*. New York: Pantheon, 1969.

Clark, Ronald W. *Tizard*. Cambridge, Mass.: MIT Press, 1965.

Clodfelter, Mark. *The Limits of Airpower: The American Bombing of North Vietnam*. New York: Free Press, 1989.

Coffey, Thomas M. *Hap: The Story of the U.S. Air Force and the Man Who Built It*. New York: Viking, 1982.

———. *Iron Eagle*. New York: Crown, 1986.

Collins, John M. *Grand Strategy: Principles and Practices*. Annapolis, Md.: Naval Institute Press, 1973.

Copp, DeWitt S. *A Few Great Captains*. Garden City, N.Y.: Doubleday, 1980.

———. *Forged in Fire*. Garden City, N.Y.: Doubleday, 1982.

Corn, Joseph J. *The Winged Gospel: America's Romance with Aviation, 1900–1950*. New York: Oxford, 1983.

Cortesi, Lawrence. *Target: Tokyo*. New York: Kensington, 1983.

Craven, Wesley Frank, and James Lea Cate, eds. *The Army Air Forces in World War II*. 7 vols. Chicago: University of Chicago Press, 1948–1953.

Current, Richard N. *Secretary Stimson: A Study in Statecraft*. Hamden, Conn.: Archon Books, 1970.

Dallek, Robert. *Franklin Roosevelt and American Foreign Policy, 1932–1945*. New York: Oxford, 1979.

Dean, Lt. Col. David J. *Airpower in Small Wars: The British Air Control Experience*. Maxwell AFB, Ala.: Air University Press, 1985.

Doolittle, Gen. James H., with Carol Glines. *I Could Never Be So Lucky Again*. New York: Bantam, 1991.

Doughty, Maj. Robert A. *The Evolution of U.S. Army Tactical Doctrine, 1946–1976*. Fort Leavenworth, Kans.: Combat Studies Institute, 1979.

Douhet, Giulio. *The Command of the Air*. Translated by Dino Ferrari. 1942. Reprint. New York: Arno Press, 1972.

Dower, John. *War without Mercy*. New York: Pantheon, 1986.

Drew, Col. Dennis M. *ROLLING THUNDER 1965: Anatomy of a Failure*. Maxwell AFB, Ala.: Air University Press, 1986.

Dugan, James, and Carroll Stewart. *Ploesti*. New York: Ballantine, 1962.

Dyson, Freeman. *Weapons and Hope*. New York: Harper and Row, 1984.

Earle, Edward Mead, ed. *Makers of Modern Strategy*. Princeton, N.J.: Princeton University Press, 1941.

Eschmann, Karl J. *Linebacker: The Untold Story of the Air Raids over North Vietnam*. New York: Ivy Books, 1989.

Fili, William J. *Passage to Valhalla*. Media, Pa.: Filcon Publishers, 1991.

Foster, Henry A. *The Making of Modern Iraq: A Product of World Forces*. Norman: University of Oklahoma Press, 1935.

Fredette, Raymond H. *The Sky on Fire: The First Battle of Britain, 1917–1918*. New York: Harcourt Brace Jovanovich, 1976.

Freeman, Roger. *The Mighty Eighth; Units, Men, and Machines: A History of the U.S. 8th Army Air Force*. New York: Orion Books, 1989.

———. *The U.S. Strategic Bomber*. London: McDonald and Jane's, 1975.

Frisbee, John L., ed. *Makers of the United States Air Force*. Washington, D.C.: Office of Air Force History, 1987.

Fuller, Maj. Gen. J. F. C. *Generalship: Its Diseases and Their Cure*. 1963. Reprint. Fort Leavenworth, Kans.: Combat Studies Institute, 1987.

Fussell, Paul. *Wartime: Understanding and Behavior in the Second World War*. New York: Oxford, 1989.

Futrell, Robert Frank. *Ideas, Concepts, Doctrine: A History of Basic Thinking in the United States Air Force, 1907–1964*. Maxwell AFB, Ala.: Air University Aerospace Studies Institute, 1971.

———. *The United States Air Force in Korea, 1950–1953*. New York: Duell, Sloan and Pearce, 1961.

Galland, Adolf. *The First and the Last*. Translated by Mervyn Savill. 1957. Reprint. New York: Ballantine, 1973.

Gaston, James C. *Planning the American Air War: Four Men and Nine Days in 1941*. Washington, D.C.: National Defense University Press, 1982.

Geffen, Lt. Col. William, ed. *Command and Commanders in Modern Warfare*. Colorado Springs: U.S. Air Force Academy, 1969.

Giovannitti, Len, and Fred Freed. *The Decision to Drop the Bomb*. New York: Coward-McCann, 1965.

Glantz, David M., ed. *Historical Precedents*. Fort Leavenworth, Kans.: U.S. Army Command and General Staff College, 1981.

Glubb, Sir John Bagot. *War in the Desert*. New York: W. W. Norton, 1961.

Goss, Hilton P. *Civilian Morale under Aerial Bombardment, 1914–1939*. Maxwell AFB, Ala.: Air University Press, 1948.

Gow, Ian. *Okinawa, 1945*. Garden City, N.Y.: Doubleday, 1985.

Greenfield, Kent Roberts. *American Strategy in World War II: A Reconsideration*. 1963. Reprint. Westport, Conn.: Greenwood Press, 1979.

Greer, Thomas H. *The Development of Air Doctrine in the Army Air Arm, 1917–1941*. Maxwell AFB, Ala.: Air University Research Studies Institute, 1955.

Grinker, Roy R., and John P. Spiegel. *Men under Stress*. Philadelphia: Blakiston, 1945.

Haines, William Wister. *Command Decisions*. New York: Dodd, Mead, 1974.

Hansell, Haywood S., Jr. *The Air Plan That Defeated Hitler*. Atlanta: Higgins-MacArthur, 1972.

————. *The Strategic Air War against Germany and Japan*. Washington, D.C.: Government Printing Office, 1986.

————. *Strategic Air War against Japan*. Maxwell AFB, Ala.: Airpower Research Institute, 1980.

Harper, Stephen. *Miracle of Deliverance: The Case for the Bombing of Hiroshima and Nagasaki*. London: Sidgwick and Jackson, 1985.

Harrison, Gordon A. *Cross-Channel Attack*. Washington, D.C.: Office of the Chief of Military History, 1951.

Hastings, Donald W., et al. *Psychiatric Experiences in the Eighth Air Force*. New York: Josiah Macy, Jr., Foundation, 1944.

Hastings, Max. *Bomber Command*. New York: Dial, 1979.

Havens, Thomas R. *Valley of Darkness*. New York: W. W. Norton, 1978.

Hayes, Grace Person. *The History of the Joint Chiefs of Staff in World War II: The War against Japan*. Annapolis, Md.: Naval Institute Press, 1982.

Henshall, Philip. *Hitler's Rocket Sites*. New York: St. Martin's, 1985.

Herken, Gregg. *The Winning Weapon*. New York: Alfred A. Knopf, 1980.

Higham, Robin. *Air Power: A Concise History*. New York: St. Martin's, 1972.

Holley, I. B., Jr. *Ideas and Weapons*. Hamden, Conn.: Archon Books, 1971.

Howard, Michael. *The Causes of War and Other Essays*. Cambridge, Mass.: Harvard University Press, 1984.

————. *Studies in War and Peace*. New York: Viking, 1971.

Hull, Cordell. *The Memoirs of Cordell Hull*. 2 vols. New York: Macmillan, 1948.

Hurley, Alfred F. *Billy Mitchell, Crusader for Air Power*. Bloomington: Indiana University Press, 1975.

Impact: The Army Air Forces' Confidential Picture History of World War II. 8 books. 1943–1945 periodicals. Reprint. Harrisburg, Pa.: Historical Times, 1982.

Infield, Glenn. *Big Week*. Los Angeles: Pinnacle, 1974.

Irving, David. *The Destruction of Dresden*. New York: Ballantine, 1965.

Kaplan, Fred. *The Wizards of Armageddon*. New York: Simon and Schuster, 1983.

Kaplan, Philip, and Rex Alan Smith. *One Last Look*. New York: Abbeville Press, 1983.

Kennett, Lee. *A History of Strategic Bombing*. New York: Charles Scribner's Sons, 1982.

Kerr, E. Bartlett. *Flames over Tokyo: The U.S. Army Air Forces' Incendiary Campaign against Japan, 1944–1945*. New York: Donald I. Fine, 1991.

Kreis, John F. *Air Warfare and Air Base Air Defense*. Washington, D.C.: Office of Air Force History, 1988.

Leahy, William D. *I Was There*. New York: McGraw-Hill, 1950.

LeMay, Curtis, with MacKinley Kantor. *Mission with LeMay*. Garden City, N.Y.: Doubleday, 1965.

Lilienthal, David E. *The Journals of David E. Lilienthal*. Vol. 2, *The Atomic Energy Years, 1945–1950*. New York: Harper and Row, 1964.

Loewenheim, Francis L. et al., eds. *Roosevelt and Churchill: Their Secret Wartime Correspondence*. New York: E. P. Dutton, 1975.

MacArthur, Douglas. *Reminiscences*. New York: McGraw-Hill, 1964.

MacDonald, Charles B. *Company Commander*. New York: Bantam, 1978.
———. *The Mighty Endeavor*. New York: William Morrow, 1986.
Macdonald, Dwight. *Memoirs of a Revolutionist*. New York: Farrar, Straus, and Cudahy, 1957.
Maclear, Michael. *The Ten Thousand Day War: Vietnam, 1945–1975*. New York: Avon Books, 1981.
McKee, Alexander. *Dresden 1945: The Devil's Tinderbox*. New York: Dutton, 1984.
Manchester, William. *The Glory and the Dream*. New York: Bantam, 1975.
Mann, Carl. *Lightning in the Sky*. New York: Robert H. McBride, 1943.
Marshall, George C., H. H. Arnold, and Ernest J. King. *The War Reports*. New York: J. B. Lippincott, 1947.
Marshall, S. L. A. *Men against Fire: The Problem of Battle Command in Future War*. 1947. Reprint. Gloucester, Mass.: Peter Smith, 1978.
Maurer, Maurer, ed. *The U.S. Air Service in World War I*. 4 vols. Washington, D.C.: Office of Air Force History, 1978.
May, Ernest R. *Lessons of the Past*. New York: Oxford, 1973.
Mets, David R. *Master of Airpower*. Novato, Calif.: Presidio Press, 1988.
Middlebrook, Martin. *The Battle of Hamburg*. New York: Charles Scribner's Sons, 1980.
Mierzejewski, Alfred C. *The Collapse of the German War Economy, 1944–1945: Allied Air Power and the German National Railway*. Chapel Hill: University of North Carolina Press, 1988.
Momyer, Gen. William M. *Air Power in Three Wars*. Washington, D.C.: Government Printing Office, 1978.
Moran, Lord. *The Anatomy of Courage*. 1945. Reprint. Garden City Park, N.Y.: Avery Publishing, 1987.
Morgenthau, Henry. *The Presidential Diaries of Henry Morgenthau, 1938–1945*. 7 vols. (Microfilm edition.) Frederick, Md.: University Publications of America, 1981.
Morison, Samuel Eliot. *The Two-Ocean War*. New York: Ballantine Books, 1972.
Morrison, Wilbur H. *Fortress without a Roof*. New York: St. Martin's, 1982.
———. *Hellbirds: The Story of the B-29's in Combat*. New York: Duell, Sloan and Pearce, 1960.
———. *Point of No Return*. New York: Times Books, 1979.
Muirhead, John. *Those Who Fall*. New York: Random House, 1986.
Murray, Williamson. *Strategy for Defeat: The Luftwaffe, 1933–1945*. Maxwell AFB, Ala.: Air University Press, 1983.
Nalty, Bernard, and Carl Berger. *The Men Who Bombed the Reich*. New York: E. P. Dutton, 1978.
Newby, Leroy W. *Target Ploesti: View from a Bombsight*. Novato, Calif.: Presidio Press, 1983.
Odishaw, Hugh. *Radar Bombing in the Eighth Air Force*. Cambridge, Mass.: Overseas Office, Radiation Laboratory, Massachusetts Institute of Technology, 1946.
The Official World War II Guide to the Army Air Forces. 1944. Reprint. New York: Bonanza Books, 1988.
Olsen, Jack. *Aphrodite: Desperate Mission*. New York: Pyramid, 1972.
Overy, R. J. *The Air War, 1939–1945*. New York: Stein and Day, 1981.
Paret, Peter, ed. *Makers of Modern Strategy, from Machiavelli to the Nuclear Age*. Prince-

ton, N.J.: Princeton University Press, 1986.

Parton, James. *"Air Force Spoken Here"*: *General Ira Eaker and the Command of the Air.* Bethesda, Md.: Adler & Adler, 1986.

Pearton, Maurice. *Diplomacy, War and Technology since 1830.* Lawrence: University Press of Kansas, 1984.

Pogue, Forrest. *George C. Marshall.* 4 vols. New York: Viking, 1963–1987.

Polenberg, Richard. *War and Society: The United States, 1941–1945.* New York: J. B. Lippincott, 1972.

Reed, Col. William B., ed. *Condensed Analysis of the Ninth Air Force in the European Theater of Operations.* 1946. Reprint. Washington, D.C.: Office of Air Force History, 1984.

Retaliation: Japanese Attacks and Allied Countermeasures on the Pacific Coast in World War II. Corvallis: Oregon State University Press, 1975.

Reynolds, Quentin. *The Amazing Mr. Doolittle.* New York: Appleton-Century-Crofts, 1953.

Ridgway, Matthew B. *The Korean War.* New York: Popular Library, 1967.

Rostow, W. W. *Pre-Invasion Bombing Strategy.* Austin: University of Texas Press, 1981.

Sallagar, F. M. *The Road to Total War.* New York: Van Nostrand Reinhold, 1975.

Saundby, Air Marshal Sir Robert. *Air Bombardment.* New York: Harper, 1961.

Schaffer, Ronald. *Wings of Judgment: American Bombing in World War II.* New York: Oxford, 1985.

Schaller, Michael. *The U.S. Crusade in China, 1938–1945.* New York: Columbia University Press, 1979.

Schlight, John. *The War in South Vietnam: The Years of the Offensive, 1965–1968.* Washington, D.C.: Office of Air Force History, 1988.

Seversky, Maj. Alexander P. de. *Victory through Airpower.* Garden City, N.Y.: Garden City Publishing, 1942.

Sherman, Maj. William C. *Air Warfare.* New York: Ronald Press, 1926.

Sherry, Michael S. *Preparing for the Next War.* New Haven, Conn.: Yale University Press, 1977.

———. *The Rise of American Airpower: The Creation of Armageddon.* New Haven, Conn.: Yale University Press, 1987.

Shiner, John F. *Foulois and the U.S. Army Air Corps, 1931–1935.* Washington, D.C.: Office of Air Force History, 1983.

Shrader, Lt. Col. Charles R. *Amicicide: The Problem of Friendly Fire in Modern War.* Fort Leavenworth, Kans.: Combat Studies Institute, 1982.

Smith, Maj. Gen. Dale O. *Screaming Eagle: Memoirs of a B-17 Group Commander.* New York: Dell, 1990.

Snow, Donald M., and Dennis M. Drew. *Introduction to Strategy.* Maxwell AFB, Ala.: Air Command and Staff College, 1982.

Southworth, Herbert R. *Guernica! Guernica! A Study of Journalism, Diplomacy, Propaganda, and History.* Berkeley: University of California Press, 1977.

Spector, Ronald H. *Eagle against the Sun.* New York: Vintage, 1985.

Speer, Albert. *Inside the Third Reich.* New York: Avon, 1971.

Stewart, James T., ed. *Airpower: The Decisive Force in Korea.* New York: D. Van Nostrand, 1957.

Stiles, Bert. *Serenade to the Big Bird*. New York: Bantam, 1984.

Stimson, Henry L., and McGeorge Bundy. *On Active Service in Peace and War*. New York: Harper, 1948.

Stouffer, Samuel A. et al. *The American Soldier*. 2 vols. Princeton, N.J.: Princeton University Press, 1949.

Summers, Harry G., Jr. *On Strategy: The Vietnam War in Context*. Carlisle, Pa.: U.S. Army War College, 1982.

Terkel, Studs. *"The Good War": An Oral History of World War Two*. New York: Ballantine, 1985.

Terraine, John. *A Time for Courage*. New York: Macmillan, 1985.

Thomas, Gordon, and Max Morgan Witts. *Enola Gay*. New York: Pocket Books, 1978.

Thomas, Lowell, and Edward Jablonski. *Doolittle, A Biography*. New York: Da Capo, 1976.

Thorne, Christopher. *Allies of a Kind: The United States, Britain, and the War against Japan*. New York: Oxford, 1978.

Toland, John. *The Rising Sun*. New York: Bantam, 1971.

U.S. Department of the Air Force. *White Paper: Air Force Performance in Desert Storm*. (Draft.) Washington, D.C.: Government Printing Office, April 1991.

U.S. Department of the Army. *Field Manual 27–2, Your Conduct in Combat under the Law of War*. Washington, D.C.: Government Printing Office, 1984.

———. *Training Circular 27-10-1, Selected Problems in the Law of War*. Washington, D.C.: Government Printing Office, 1979.

U.S. Department of State. *Foreign Relations of the United States: The Conferences at Washington and Quebec, 1943*. Washington, D.C.: Government Printing Office, 1970.

———. *Foreign Relations of the United States, Diplomatic Papers, 1939*. 5 vols. Washington, D.C.: Government Printing Office, 1955–1957.

———. *Foreign Relations of the United States, 1950: Asia and the Pacific*. 7 vols. Washington, D.C.: Government Printing Office, 1977–1980.

U.S. Department of War. *Training Regulations No. 440–15, Air Corps: Employment of the Air Forces of the Army*. Washington, D.C.: Government Printing Office, 1935.

———. Bureau of Public Relations. *The Background of Our War*. New York: Farrar and Rinehart, 1942.

United States Strategic Bombing Survey. Pacific Reports. New York: Garland, 1976.

———. *Summary Reports*. 1945–1946. Reprint. Maxwell AFB, Ala.: Air University Press, 1987.

Walzer, Michael. *Just and Unjust Wars*. New York: Basic Books, 1977.

Watts, Barry D. *The Foundations of U.S. Air Doctrine*. Maxwell AFB, Ala.: Air University Press, 1984.

Weigley, Russell F. *The American Way of War*. Bloomington: Indiana University Press, 1977.

———. *Eisenhower's Lieutenants*. Bloomington: Indiana University Press, 1981.

Werrell, Kenneth P. *The Evolution of the Cruise Missile*. Maxwell AFB, Ala.: Air University Press, 1985.

———. *"Who Fears?" The 301st in War and Peace, 1942–1979*. Dallas: Taylor Publishing, 1991.

Wittner, Lawrence S. *Rebels against War: The American Peace Movement, 1941–1960*.

New York: Columbia University Press, 1969.

Wolff, Leon. *Low Level Mission*. New York: Berkley, 1958.

Wolk, Herman S. *Planning and Organizing the Postwar Air Force, 1943–1947*. Washington, D.C.: Office of Air Force History, 1984.

DISSERTATIONS

Brower, Charles F. IV. "The Joint Chiefs of Staff and National Policy: American Strategy and the War with Japan, 1943–1945." Ph.D. dissertation, University of Pennsylvania, 1987.

Mountcastle, John W. "Trial by Fire: U.S. Incendiary Weapons, 1918–1945." Ph.D. dissertation, Duke University, 1979.

Smith, Melden E., Jr. "The Bombing of Dresden Reconsidered: A Study in Wartime Decision Making." Ph.D. dissertation, Boston University, 1971.

ARTICLES

Amory, Cleveland. "The Man Even Hollywood Likes." *Parade* (21 October 1984): 7–12.

Bernstein, Barton J. "America's Biological Warfare Program in the Second World War." *Journal of Strategic Studies* 11 (September 1988): 292–317.

————. "The Perils and Politics of Surrender: Ending the War with Japan and Avoiding the Third Atomic Bomb." *Pacific Historical Review* 46 (February 1977): 1–27.

————. "Why We Didn't Use Poison Gas in World War II." *American Heritage* 36 (August–September 1985): 40–45.

"City Bombing Backed by Cousins and Eliot." *New York Times*, 31 March 1944, p. 3.

Davis, Richard G. "Bombing Strategy Shifts, 1944–45." *Air Power History* 36 (Winter 1989): 33–45.

Doerner, William R. "In the Dead of Night." *Time* 127 (28 April 1986): 28–31.

Dougherty, Kevin A. "R&D Strategy in WWII." *Army Research, Development, and Acquisition Bulletin* (March–April 1990): 44.

Dugan, Gen. Michael. "First Lessons of Victory." *U.S. News and World Report* 110 (18 March 1991): 32–36.

Feist, Joe Michael. "Bats Away." *American Heritage* 33 (April–May 1982): 93–94.

"Flak versus Heavy Bombers." *Coast Artillery Journal* 89 (March–April 1946): 24–25.

Ford, John C. "The Morality of Obliteration Bombing." *Theological Studies* 5 (September 1944): 261–309.

"Franco Exhibits Himself." *New Republic* 94 (30 March 1938): 205.

Gellman, Barton. "70% of U.S. Bombs Missed Their Targets, Figures Show." *Kansas City Star*, 16 March 1991, sec. A, p. 15.

Gleason, Robert L. "Psychological Operations and Air Power." *Air University Review* 22 (March–April 1971): 35–41.

Gregory, Lt. Col. Jesse O. "Headaches of Strategic Bombing." *Coast Artillery Journal* 89 (March–April 1946): 26–28.

Hassler, Alfred. "Slaughter of the Innocent." *Fellowship* (February 1944): 58–62.

Hopkins, George E. "Bombing and the American Conscience during World War II."

Historian 28 (May 1966): 451–473.

Horner, Lt. Gen. Charles A. "The Air Campaign." *Military Review* 71 (September 1991): 16–27.

Irvine, Dallas, D. "The Misuse of Air Power." *Infantry Journal* 44 (May–June 1937): 255–256.

Keegan, John. "We Wanted Beady-eyed Guys Just Absolutely Holding the Course." *Smithsonian* 14 (August 1983): 34–43.

Kohn, Richard H. "The Scholarship on World War II: Its Present Condition and Future Possibilities." *Journal of Military History* 55 (July 1991): 365–393.

Kurata, Yasuo. "Americans Are Insensitive to Casualties Because Their Country Hasn't Been Bombed." *Kansas City Star*, 5 May 1991, sec. K, p. 2.

"Letters to the Times." *New York Times*, 9 March 1944, p. 16.

"Massacre by Bombing." *Politics* 1 (April 1944): 67–68.

Mathews, Tom. "The Secret History of the War." *Newsweek* 117 (18 March 1991): 28–39.

"Obliteration Raids on German Cities Protested in U.S." *New York Times*, 6 March 1944, p. 1.

Reed, Fred. "NATO Is in the Business of Projecting Uncertainty." *El Paso Times*, 1 October 1989, p. 8B.

Sawin, Capt. H. C., and Capt. Mac Harlan. "The Rules of Land Warfare." *Coast Artillery Journal* 87 (November–December 1944): 30–33.

Schaffer, Ronald. "American Military Ethics in World War II: The Bombing of German Civilians." *Journal of American History* 67 (September 1980): 318–334.

Schwarzkopf, Gen. H. Norman. "Central Command Briefing." *Military Review* 71 (September 1991): 96–108.

Sherry, Michael S. "The Slide to Total Air War." *New Republic* 137 (16 December 1981); 20–25.

Smith, Perry M. "Douhet and Mitchell: Some Reappraisals." *Air University Review* 18 (September–October 1967): 97–101.

Summers, Col. Harry. "Conventional Forces, Not Nuclear Bombs, Are Now 'Strategic.'" *Kansas City Star*, 26 April 1991, sec. C, p. 7.

Taylor, Joe Gray. "They Taught Tactics." *Aerospace Historian* 13 (Summer 1966): 67–72.

Villa, Brian L. "The U.S. Army, Unconditional Surrender, and the Potsdam Proclamation." *Journal of American History* 63 (June 1976): 66–92.

Wallace, Irving. "Significa." *Parade* (31 July 1983): 19.

Werrell, Kenneth P. "The Strategic Bombing of Germany in World War II: Costs and Accomplishments." *Journal of American History* 73 (December 1986): 702–713.

Wilson, P. W. "Are Laws of War Scraps of Paper?" *New York Times*, 3 October 1937, sec. 4E, p. 1.

Wolk, Herman S. "The B-29, the A-Bomb, and the Japanese Surrender." *Air Force* (February 1975): 55–61.

Yavenditti, Michael J. "The American People and the Use of Atomic Bombs on Japan: The 1940s." *Historian* 36 (February 1974): 224–247.

INDEX

199

Printed in the United States
96526LV00005B/88-126/A